"WELCOME TO YOUR NEWBORN'S WORLD

It is the place where understanding the mix of learning, love and attention leads to having smarter babies; where adult fascination with growth, change, and development, combined with pure parental instincts, provides limitless joy.

Here's where the art and science of Infant Stimulation begins. You present your baby with experiences that foster learning and growth, *not by force-feeding knowledge* but rather through interactive, loving relationships that never fail to form when you practice stimulation that *pleases* your baby.

Infant Stimulation is a form of play that challenges your baby's mind and satisfies his or her newly discovered preferences earlier than we ever thought possible."

HOW TO
HAVE A
SMARTER
BABY

DR. SUSAN LUDINGTON-HOE

WITH

SUSAN K. GOLANT

BANTAM BOOKS
TORONTO · NEW YORK · LONDON · SYDNEY · AUCKLAND

HOW TO HAVE A SMARTER BABY

*A Bantam Book / published by arrangement with
Rawson Associates*

PRINTING HISTORY
Rawson edition published September 1985
Bantam edition / June 1987

*Bantam Books are published by Bantam Books, Inc. Its trade-
mark, consisting of the words "Bantam Books" and the por-
trayal of a rooster, is Registered in U.S. Patent and Trademark
Office and in other countries. Marca Registrada. Bantam
Books, Inc., 666 Fifth Avenue, New York, New York 10103.*

Contents

Book II
The Infant Stimulation Program: What You Can Do to Stimulate Your Baby's Development

---

Appendixes

Acknowledgments

An infant is molded by his environment and experience. The Infant Stimulation Program exists because of countless nurses, health professionals, and parents who listened, tried the toys, tools, and techniques, and reported back that the babies with whom they used Infant Stimulation really responded positively. Their enthusiasm and dedication resulted in the formation of the Infant Stimulation Education Association. And the attention spans of the babies they worked with were longer, the babies smiled more, reached out more deftly, cooed sooner, gained weight faster, and were more contented.

I especially wish to thank two people. Ms. Susan Sverha, Director of Continuing Education in Nursing at Georgetown University, made Infant Stimulation known to the health profession, and her compassionate and constructive nature guided me in developing and disseminating this knowledge in a scholarly fashion. I am immensely grateful to Ellyn Cavanaugh-Duerr, who was instrumental in moving Infant Stimulation into the hands of parents. Her astute observations, creative inclinations, and driving spirit have moved our knowledge of the benefits of Infant Stimulation to babies and parents to pulsating levels.

This project could never have been fulfilled without the devotion and commitment demonstrated by my sisters, Dorothy Ludington and Mary Roach. They have been there through thick and thin, throughout the years. I also want to express gratitude to Mrs. Laura Hoe Harris, who spent hours on the first draft, and Mrs. Thyrza Hoe Pelling, who also was there when the going got tough. A special thanks to Ms. Nancy Allen, who revived the reasons for living when they had been suffocated by tragedy.

We would like to acknowledge Toymakers, Inc., for the use of Bright Baby* Products throughout this project.

—Susan Ludington-Hoe, Ph.D.
University of California, Los Angeles
1985

I would like to thank Barbara LaPan Rahm for first drawing my attention to pregnancy superstitions and Scott Berman and his parents, Sallee and Dr. Victor Berman, for sharing their knowledge that some of these beliefs may, in fact, be based on new scientific findings about fetal capabilities. Their astute referral to Dr. Ludington-Hoe sparked the beginning of an exciting and creative working relationship which has come to fruition in this book.

Our editors, Eleanor Rawson and Jane Shoenberg, proved invaluable in shaping the work for parents and in helping to inject just the right tone of loving acceptance. Our agent, Allison Byrne Clemente, couldn't have found a better publisher for our book.

I am also grateful to Dr. Micheline Sakharoff; Dr. Sheila Gross; Norma Kapp, M.S.W.; Dr. Bette Harrell; Dr. Clara Zilberstein; Dr. Robert Kirsch; Janice Mall; Dr. Dorothy Clark; Dorothy Dudovitz, M.S.W.; Dr. Nan Krakow; Dr. Bruce Phillips; Barbara Gown Elias, M.A.; Laura Atoian, M.A.; Carmen Tolivar, M.A.; Dr. Linda Golden; Laurel Friedberg; and Barbara Hall—friends, colleagues, teachers—who know of my dreams and are helping to see them come true.

Most of all I would like to thank my family: Arthur and Mary Kleinhandler, Henriette Kleinhandler, and Sam and Evelyn Golant, who offer their unconditional love and support; my husband and soulmate, Dr. Mitch Golant, whose vision and ever-present faith in me is a constant source of strength; and our daughters, Cherie and Aimee—our very own smarter babies—who provide the wellsprings of inspiration and love from which the work takes form. This book is for them and for the generations to come.

—Susan K. Golant, M.A.
Los Angeles
1985

*BRIGHT BABY™, BRAINY BEAR™, MR. MOUSE™, MIND MOBILE™, MIND MITTEN™, and TACTILE TILLIE™ are the exclusive trademarks of Toymakers, Inc., Los Angeles, California.

BOOK I
WHAT YOUR BABY THINKS AND FEELS ABOUT HIS WORLD AND YOU

I. THE INFANT STIMULATION REVOLUTION

1. What We Didn't Know

until Now

For most of the three and a half million babies born in 1984, there was a set of parents wanting desperately for *their* child to be the smartest, happiest, best emotionally and physically adjusted baby he or she possibly could be.

If those parents used Infant Stimulation, those goals are not only possible, they are realistically attainable. Infant Stimulation isn't some esoteric mystique dreamed up in an isolated laboratory. It is a direct, simple, satisfying approach to enjoying your child more fully.

To understand Infant Stimulation, it is important, first, to dispel the myths that babies only eat, sleep, and excrete; that they don't see well; can't hear at all; and in general don't know what's going on around them until they are three months old.

We must replace those myths with these eight revolutionary *proven* facts of life:

- Fetuses respond to their mother's heartbeat and voice while still in the womb.
- Up to six weeks before birth, fetuses actively use their senses of taste, touch, sight, hearing, and movement, as documented by changes in fetal brain-wave patterns

- In the first two hours after birth, *newborns maintain alertness longer than they will for the next two months*.
- Infant Stimulation can help babies repeat sounds and facial movements like tongue thrusts when only four days old, recognize a simple word at nine months, and construct complete sentences before eighteen months.
- Babies have a *biological* need to learn.
- Any stimulation provided during the first twelve months has more impact on the brain's growth than at any other time in baby's future life.
- *By six months of age, a full 50 percent of baby's brain growth has occurred.*
- By one year of age, 70 percent of brain development is completed. *Baby's mind grows faster in the first year of life than it ever will again.*

Since 1979 thousands of health professionals throughout the United States have attended my lectures and read my publications on Infant Stimulation. The hundreds of parents who attended my workshops have learned the easy, rewarding techniques that make their babies smarter and encourage bonding.

These professionals and parents alike have expressed their desire for me to write a book covering all the tools, toys, and techniques that make the Infant Stimulation Program so successful. They wanted a workable resource of proven ideas based on existing research and my own investigations with infants at every stage of their first six months of life.

What has emerged is a book designed to help you maximize your child's learning pleasure with a minimum of time expenditure: 15 minutes a day. That's a realistic amount of time for most busy parents, even in families where both parents work.

How to Have a Smarter Baby is the product of my fruitful collaboration with Susan Golant, a writer specializing in bio-psychosocial issues. We are delighted to share the results of our explorations into Infant Stimulation. In *How to Have a Smarter Baby* you will find:

- A complete step-by-step guide to expand your joys in ~~enting~~ and help you maximize your baby's learning ~~both during your pregnancy and in his or her~~ ~~s of life.

- A program of appropriate and rewarding techniques to simulate your baby's senses of hearing, sight, touch, taste, smell, and motion, in order to:

  - promote faster growth
  - coordinate muscle movements
  - increase concentration span from 10 seconds to as long as 45 minutes
  - start the process of raising baby's I.Q. as much as 15 points.

All with a simple 15-minute-a-day program.

The sample Stimulation Programs put new Infant Stimulation research at your fingertips. We have also included an illustrated chapter on how to make appropriate toys.

The Origins of Infant Stimulation

My interest in how and when newborns respond to their world was first aroused during my early education as a maternal-child health specialist.

As a staff nurse at the University of California Medical Center in San Francisco, in 1972, I was attracted by the sight of a new mother in the Premature Nursery gazing lovingly into the eyes of her month-old, two-pound son. She was holding him in the palm of her hand, stroking him gently as she cooed ever so softly about his enchanting beauty.

Every day this mother came into the premie nursery to carry out the same routine. She talked and stroked and sang to her tiny infant. And somehow, over the weeks and months, despite our fears and doubts, this small beloved person gained weight and thrived. By the time he reached five months, he was well enough to be released from the hospital.

This little premie's struggle for life and his eventual growth prompted a number of questions for me. Could he actually hear his mother's voice and feel her touch all through those long hours that she lingered over him? Was he aware of *her* presence, as distinguished from that of a nurse or hospital attendant? Could all her talking, holding, and stroking have made a difference in his growth? And why was it that this little baby grew and flourished when so many others like him did not?

These questions gave rise to other, more general queries about all newborns. How much and how well can they actually see at birth? Do they recognize certain sounds? Can they distinguish voices, faces, tastes, and odors? Do they prefer one toy over another? Does it make sense to consider them as *people* rather than as tiny, unsensing beings?

My desire to seek answers led to graduate studies specializing in child development. I received my bachelor's and master's degrees in Maternity Nursing at the University of California Medical Center in San Francisco, completing my doctorate in Maternal-Child Health and Child Development at Texas Woman's University in Denton, Texas. In 1979, I became a certified nurse-midwife at State University of New York, Downstate in Brooklyn, New York.

As a professor of maternal-child health, I taught maternity and neurological nursing and child development at the University of Illinois in Chicago; Baylor University in Dallas, Texas; the Imperial Medical Center of Iran; Georgetown University, Washington, D.C.; American University, Washington, D.C.; and the University of California at Los Angeles.

My fascination with infants led at last to my becoming director of the Infant Stimulation Education Association of America. In this capacity I have conducted five research studies throughout the United States, and have taken pleasure in teaching physicians, nurses, occupational therapists, play therapists, special education teachers, child-life specialists, childbirth educators, and early childhood education specialists about Infant Stimulation, as well as developing consumer products and pamphlets about Infant Stimulation.

Both Susan Golant and I sincerely hope that what began as a personal effort to meet the needs of the health professional community, and grew in response to parents' excitement, will now also prove to be helpful and enjoyable to all parents and children.

A Word about Terms

Although the designations *newborn, infant,* and *baby* often seem interchangeable, the terms can be loosely identified as birth to one month for newborns; one month until speech begins for infants; and babyhood extending for a year or

two, or until your child is a toddler. These are the designations we have followed throughout the book.

You will also find that we refer to babies in the masculine. Please rest assured that we have neither forgotten nor ignored your daughters. We made the choice of one gender for the purpose of clarity, expediency in expression, and in deference to conventional English usage. "He or she" can become cumbersome (especially when we talk about what baby can do himself or herself).

2. How Infant Stimulation
Builds Sensational Babies

Welcome to your newborn's world! It is the place where understanding the mix of learning, love, and attention leads to having smarter babies; where adult fascination with growth, change, and development, combined with pure parental instincts, provides limitless joy.

Here's where the art and science of Infant Stimulation begins. You present your baby with experiences that foster learning and growth, *not by force-feeding knowledge* but rather through an interactive, loving relationship that never fails to form when you practice stimulation that *pleases* your baby. Infant Stimulation is a form of play that challenges your baby's mind and satisfies his newly discovered preferences earlier than we ever thought possible. The scientific community has yet to discover any manner of promoting your infant's *total growth* that equals simply appealing to your baby's preferences.

The Elements of Growth

An individual's total growth is made up of the interrelationship of physical, mental, emotional, and social development. From my research and from my years of hands-on experience with parents and babies, it is clear that Infant Stimulation will impact on your child's *total* growth without stressing one area at the expense of the others.

8

Physical Growth

Physical growth is the easiest to measure accurately by scale and chart. It refers to your baby's height and weight. Comparative studies have shown that infants who are caressed and cuddled more than others actually gain weight faster. Parents who thoughtfully touch their infants, talk to them, help them exercise appropriately, and provide them with a variety of pleasing visual targets actually enhance their youngsters' ability to sit, crawl, walk, and develop.

Mental Growth

Infant Stimulation accelerates a baby's mental ability and increases a child's skills in finding ways to stimulate himself. Studies have shown that with continued and consistent stimulation over a two-year period, I.Q. can be boosted by 15 to 30 points, when I.Q. measures are taken at four to five years of age.[1] Did you know that:

- If you stimulate your baby's sense of sight, it actually helps him to concentrate longer?
- When you stimulate your baby's sense of smell, it helps his motor development?
- When you rock or move your baby rhythmically in space, you may be helping his memory to develop?
- When you appeal to one or two of your baby's senses at the same time, you improve his curiosity and attentiveness?

Emotional and Social Growth

I'm sure you recognize what a glorious feeling it is to have your every need satisfied on cue. And when such attention is bestowed on infants, their sense of security, love, and understanding is encouraged. Through Infant Stimulation you become familiar with your baby's cues, and your responsiveness encourages trust, warm attachments, and enhanced emotional growth.

Loving interactions with children form the firm basis of all human growth. They bond parent and child for life. During Infant Stimulation you present enjoyable situations to your baby and the response is gurgling and attentiveness. So you try it again, stimulating baby even more. You're *both* having such a good time that happy smiles just keep appearing. The babies I see in my practice are smiling from the day of birth!

Children who feel loved and secure are most likely to get along with others in their world. They are the sociable little ones who have learned the fundamentals of satisfying interaction with people and situations. And they are the ones who as adults are likely to make positive contributions to the society in which they live.

There are countless studies that document the effectiveness of the kind of physical, mental, and emotional growth stimulation I have mentioned. I would like to share two especially interesting studies with you. I've chosen these particular ones because of the dramatic results that they showed, one from a negative and the other from a positive point of view.

Dr. Warren Dennis, an American pediatrician interested in child development, examined children in an Iranian orphanage in 1960 and brought the following shocking facts to light:

- Sixty percent of the two-year-olds in that institution could not sit up unsupported (remember, normal age for this is six to seven months).
- Vocabularies were markedly underdeveloped; in fact, the youngsters were significantly limited in *every* area of development in *every* age group.

Dr. Dennis concluded that because these children had received only minimal amounts of touching, rocking, talking, and general nurturing attention, their growth and development had been severely stunted.[2]

Then, in 1967, a developmental anthropologist, Dr. Mary Ainsworth, observed that babies in Uganda were cuddled, carried, and rocked by family members some eighteen out of every twenty-four hours. Along with these overt expressions of warmth and caring, the Ugandan children were strapped to their mothers' bodies while the women worked in the fields, and thus were exposed to continuous movement, rhythmic talking, and singsong communications.

As a consequence of this constant attention, the Ugandan babies were able to:

- Sit unsupported before five months of age
- Crawl at five months of age
- Walk at seven months
- Complete toilet training by an amazing eleven months.[3]

The famous Swiss developmental psychologist, Dr. Jean Piaget, and other researchers in this field have stated conclusively that infants require sensory stimulation in order to grow and learn. From these studies we can plainly see that the first six months of life is a crucial time for parents to supply the stimulating events and objects necessary to keep infants' minds active.

Infants under six months of age cannot create their own thoughts about puppy dogs or ice cream cones. They need someone to provide information and materials for them to think about. This is *your* parental role. You will be able to fulfill it expertly by interacting with the six senses already very keenly developed in your newborn: sight, touch, taste, smell, hearing, and movement. The chapters that follow will give you a road map for helping your baby develop all these senses to the utmost.

Using Infant Stimulation Immediately after Birth

During the first two hours after your baby is born, he enjoys an unparalleled period of alert quietness that he will *not recapture for at least two months*.

You'll notice your baby's reaction right in the delivery room. If he is laid on mother's chest, he looks around for mom and dad with a searching, intent expression. He wants to learn to recognize their voices and their faces. *This is not a time for him to become attached to a warmer or crib. Rather, he should be attaching to you.*

That's his whole purpose. In fact, research has shown that newborns removed from their mothers and placed in cribs during these all-important first two hours behave differently from those left to bond and make the immediate connection between themselves and their parents. Newborns removed from their mothers at this time swat at their faces with their hands, trying to find their thumbs as a substitute for suckling activity that should naturally occur at mother's breast.

You will want to capitalize on this period after birth. In Chapter 23, I provide instructions on ways of structuring the birth experience to use this invaluable two-hour period effectively.

Following these first hours your baby goes into a twelve-hour state of disorganization. He sleeps fitfully and has fussy periods of wakefulness. Since baby tries to sleep during this period, mother should be sleeping and recuperating from the work of labor too.

After the First Twelve Hours

You may still be in the hospital or you may be at home with your baby when you begin to notice that your newborn develops a pattern of periods of *alert inactivity*. Usually these periods revolve around the feeding cycle.

Babies are often awake, alert, and quiet *45 minutes before feeding time and 10 to 15 minutes after* (unless they have succumbed to sleep during their feeding). It is possible to make fruitful use of these periods before and after feeding. Infant Stimulation itself will help you to lengthen your baby's periods of attentiveness. His alertness in turn will automatically encourage interaction with you and his environment. The more you play with him, the longer those periods of alertness will be.

There may be other times when you notice that your baby is alert and quiet, "telling" you he is receptive to interaction. So come up to him, face-to-face. Talk to him. Tell him how much you love him.

Remember, the key to a successful Infant Stimulation program is the *relationship* you develop with your baby, and not his "accomplishments." The *process* of loving play has more value than the final product. So make sure that you *approach each stimulating task as an opportunity for interaction with your child*. Your baby's early education occurs during these *playful interactions* with you and others in his life. *Play* is a child's *work* during childhood.

Since newborns cannot seek out their own stimulation, their parents must provide all interaction. As parents you need to learn to recognize when baby is ready and when he is not. He is less able to adjust to your patterns than you are to his, so be sensitive and responsive to his very individual rhythm.

Play when he is awake and "doing nothing," but don't overstimulate or demand too much when he lets you know that he has had enough by moving restlessly, crying, or acting drowsy. Your infant may easily be overstimulated and irritable if situations continue to be presented to him that he cannot control.

Skip a play session when *you* are feeling grouchy or out of sorts. Inadvertently, you communicate negative as well as positive feelings to your emotionally sensitive baby.

As baby grows, he will be able to stimulate himself with his own exploratory free play. He becomes an active partner in the learning process. You may tiptoe up to his crib and find him quietly studying his newly discovered hands or reaching for and manipulating fascinating and appropriate toys that you've left within reach. You'll want to allow baby some private time for his curiosity, active involvement, and imagination to flourish.

Remember, yours is the position of power. Use it wisely and reap the benefits of increased love and affection in your family. Interact in a positive, loving way and watch your child develop a zest for learning and loving that will stay with him forever.

II. WHAT YOU CAN DO
TO STIMULATE YOUR
BABY BEFORE BIRTH

3. The World within the Womb

Haven't we all grown up with the romantic notion that the womb is a quiet, warm, safe environment that nature provides for the unborn baby to develop in "peace"? We have an image of the baby—floating free in the dark amniotic sac—completely oblivious to the outside reality.

Well, this fantasy may be comforting, but it is not what fetal life is all about. Not even close!

How do we know?

In 1976 a conductor and instructor of the Tokyo Symphony was complaining to his friend, Dr. Hajime Murooka, an obstetrician at the University of Tokyo, that the children he was teaching weren't able to distinguish between right and wrong notes. "If only we could catch them soon enough to train their ears," the conductor lamented.

What would be soon enough? Age six? Three? At birth? Or maybe even *before* birth!

Dr. Murooka was fascinated by the idea of fetal perception. He proceeded to construct a study.

First, he inserted a tiny microphone into the dilated cervix of a woman just before she went into labor. For twenty-four hours he recorded all of the sounds coming through the womb. The recording was then analyzed on a computer to determine the predominant sound the fetus might be hearing. Without a doubt the rhythmic pounding of mother's heart and arteries was the loudest.

Dr. Murooka then played back the recorded heartbeat sound to newborn babies. They quieted down and soon fell asleep after they heard it. He realized, then, that the newborn must have had some previous exposure to this heartbeat sound in order to be consoled by it after birth.[1]

What a discovery! Although it was already known that the fetal brain could respond with electrical activity to sound, no one before then even suspected that the fetus was capable of *hearing* or actually had listening preferences. Suddenly, the scientific community realized that the fetus was an aware being in utero, with the ability to *recall* sounds heard in the womb.

Since then, many other scientists have duplicated Dr. Murooka's findings. Today, it is obvious that the mother's heartbeat is such a familiar and important reminder of life before birth that the newborn will actually seek it out by turning his head to be closer to the sound.[2]

Researchers have also investigated the sensory capabilities of premature babies in order to determine what fetuses can sense. They have found that premies born during the seventh month of pregnancy, or later, look at black and white patterns, listen to certain kinds of music, move in response to touch, and show displeasure with sour tastes and offensive odors.[3]

If the little premie can sense his environment once he's born, isn't it reasonable to expect that just prior to birth he was the same sensing, feeling being? The growing body of research in this field bears this out.

In fact, there is evidence to suggest that fetuses can hear, see, taste, feel, and experience movement throughout the last half of pregnancy,[4] and that these capabilities don't change dramatically at the moment of birth.

Fetal specialists' investigations include shining lights at, playing sounds to, and rubbing the pregnant abdomen in an attempt to measure fetal reactions. And the fetuses have responded! They move, and experience changes in heart rates and brain waves during these experiments.

As a result of these findings, along with my own education and observations, I can enthusiastically validate the Infant Stimulation Program we provide for your use even *before* your baby is born.

Floating in the Amniotic Sea

The world within the womb is noisy, stimulating, and extremely complex. The fetus needs this stimulation to help his nervous system develop.

During the first half of pregnancy your fetus is floating free within the amniotic sac (or bag of waters). In those early months there is four times as much fluid as there is fetus, so he or she is buoyed in a weightless state. As the fluid is constantly manufactured and reabsorbed (it is replaced entirely every eleven days), its movement causes a gentle, swirling action that provides some stimulation for your fetus's sense of touch.

But your fetus is not an idle floater. He's quite busy stimulating himself! In his gravity-free environment he rotates, moves arms and legs, turns and bends his body, head, and back, and all of this as early as only five weeks old. He gains practice using weak muscles with little effort. Muscle tone will develop in utero only after he has had the opportunity to carry out this gravity-free workout.[5]

And that's not all. As early as the twelfth week (third month) of pregnancy, your fetus swallows amniotic fluid regularly. He takes in only a very small amount each day. Some goes into his lungs but most goes into his digestive tract. This activity helps him to practice swallowing so that eventually, he will be able to coordinate his sucking and swallowing as he nurses. The bitter amniotic fluid may also stimulate the sensitivity of his forming taste buds.[6]

Finger sucking begins as early as eleven weeks. Your fetus must suck in order to develop his jaw and cheek muscles so that they in turn will be ready for the task of nursing at birth. He brings his hand to his mouth with good coordination, and since he opens his eyes at twenty-nine weeks (seven months, one week), it is possible that he can see his hand and his environment in the womb.

Trained observers have noticed that frequently, starting about the sixth month, fetuses make facial movements that resemble crying. This may help lung development and certainly helps strengthen facial muscles. We still don't know if sound accompanies this grimace, but if so, the fetal vocal cords would benefit from the practice.

Even though there is no exchange of gases, as there would

be with normal breathing, your fetus moves his chest walls as if he were breathing in and out. These faint fetal breathing movements begin at eleven weeks and are necessary for lung and diaphragm development.

Mother's natural movements include rotating, sitting, walking, bending, and lying down. As she does this, the amniotic sac rocks and rolls along with her. Even mother's breaths (normally 12 every minute when she is at rest) cause gentle waves within the sac. And when mom exercises, especially to music and rhythm, her activities provide movement and sound stimulation. As your fetus grows larger, coming into contact with the uterine wall stimulates his sense of touch.

Mother's Body

During the second half of your pregnancy, your fetus gains enough weight to "sink" to the bottom of the uterus. The walls offer resistance, so he pushes with his arms and legs in order to right his position. This, of course, is what mothers feel when the fetus seems to be poking them from inside out. (The muscle-strengthening activity doesn't stop at birth! If you hold a four-month-old on your lap with his feet resting on your knees, he'll kick as if pushing off from the side of a pool. He is making preparations for walking.)

The womb is a very noisy home for your fetus during the last four months of his stay. Since amniotic fluid, like water, conducts sounds, he is treated to a symphony of digestive gurglings (including hunger pangs), swallowing, heartbeat and blood circulation pulsations. He hears them at a loud 72 to 84 decibels. (Normal speech is 65 decibels.) His ears even pick up mother's intestinal grumblings at 60 decibels. Of course, he can't distinguish these sounds; for him, they all are heard as a low background noise.[7]

However, the sound he *does* distinguish is his mother's voice! It differs in pitch from all other sounds and comes through at approximately 84 decibels, despite the muffling caused by all the tissue and organs that separate mother's vocal cords from the fetal ear. (Later, we will show you how to make a prenatal tape of mother's and father's voices to improve communicating to the fetal ear. Consistent use of this tape may help in the bonding process.)

The Great Big World Out There

Toward the end of pregnancy the uterine and abdominal walls stretch, allowing both sounds and light to filter through from the world outside mother's body. Curiosity has prompted scientists to investigate what passes from the environment through the thinner walls that may have an impact on the unborn baby within. And their efforts have been rewarded! There's plenty that does penetrate.

Researchers have found that fetuses react excitedly to pure musical tones! Their heart rates rise a full 15 beats per minute for the first 2 minutes of a listening session.[8] And the music doesn't even have to be close to mother's abdomen for such a reaction. As early as 1927 the research team of H. S. Forbes and H. B. Forbes at the Department of Pediatrics/ Biology, University of Rochester, documented fetal responses to distant music. In their study, pregnant women who attended a symphony concert had to leave long before it was over because their fetuses were kicking so vigorously in time to the music that the mothers simply couldn't stand it![9]

In another investigation, mothers in their last six weeks of pregnancy were asked to play their favorite classical music to their fetus for 10 minutes a day at decibels just a little bit louder than normal speech. The researchers found that the fetuses *immediately* recognized the change in their environment. Their heart rates increased distinctly! I find it even more fascinating to note that fetuses do not respond in this way to monotonous, single notes—even when played very loudly and only three feet away. They seem to love harmonious music.[10]

Numerous studies have probed the negative effects of airport noise on fetuses. In one investigation, researchers found that women living under airport approaches gave birth to babies who were smaller, had lower birth weights, and tended to be premature more frequently than the norm.[11]

Although the noise and vibration created by planes seem to have a detrimental effect on fetal development, normal sounds within your home don't have this negative effect. When your microwave beeps, your dryer buzzes, your doorbell and phones ring, your fetus may hear them and move in response. Researchers have played such noises to fetuses and noted changes in brain waves, body movements, and heart rate.[12]

The thinner uterine and abdominal walls of advanced pregnancy may admit more intense light than in early pregnancy, which quite possibly stimulates the fetus's sense of sight. Even the changing patterns of darkness and light play a role in the development of your fetus's day/night cycling.

In 1980 a team of Israeli obstetricians, headed by Dr. Dan Peleg and Dr. Jack Goldman at Hasharon Hospital in Petah Tikva and the Sackler School of Medicine of Tel Aviv University, were trying to devise ways to arouse fetuses in order to measure their state of well-being in a short period of time. They concentrated bright lights on mothers' pregnant abdomens. Immediately the fetuses' heart rates jumped by 15 beats per minute! When the heart rates returned to normal, the doctors repeated the experiment and again the heart rates rose dramatically and simultaneously with the flash of light.

Even more exciting, those fetuses who responded consistently were healthy babies at birth. Fetuses whose responses were weak were found to have problems breathing and regulating their heart rates. They required further care and close observation.[13]

What does this extensive new research mean to you as an expectant parent? Simply that the sensory stimulation that is a natural part of your fetus's environment for the last two to three months of pregnancy, and the extra stimulation *you* can provide by following a program of prenatal Infant Stimulation, will affect your baby's behavior and influence his growth and development.

It does *not* mean that you should bombard your developing fetus with bright lights, loud noises, or other intrusive stimuli in order to get a response. You may wish to catch his "attention" by playing some soothing music, or you may wish to "teach" him, in a very loving way, to recognize your voice. However you choose to relate, know that you and your fetus will be developing bonds of attachment even before he is born!

We will tell you more about how to do this in Chapter 5.

4. Your Fetus's Developing
Nervous System

Consider the following facts about your fetus's developing senses and nervous system:

- MOVEMENT: The vestibule of the ear, the organ that senses movement, is formed by the seventeenth week, and the nerve responsible for transmitting the sense of movement is insulated by twenty-four weeks. (Although we commonly say pregnancy is nine months long, full term really lasts forty weeks or ten months.) Current information suggests that movement is the fetus's earliest functioning sense.
- TOUCH: The nerves that sense touch are formed by the twenty-fourth week of your pregnancy. The fetal brain responds to touch at twenty-six weeks.
- SIGHT: The optic nerve, which transmits light from the eye to the brain, is formed by the eighth week. The fetal brain first responds to light at twenty-seven weeks. The eye of a premie can maintain its gaze on patterned stimuli by thirty weeks—a full ten weeks before normal birth would occur.
- TASTE: The taste buds are formed by the twentieth week. In experimental situations thirty-four-week-old fetuses have been observed to swallow a sweetened amniotic fluid more often than distasteful amniotic fluid.
- HEARING: The nerve supply to the fetal ear is completed by the beginning of the twenty-eighth week. The ear canal is open by thirty-six weeks and fetal brain responses to sound are completely mature at thirty-five weeks.
- SMELL: The olfactory bulb and nerve, responsible for the sense of smell, are fully formed by seventeen weeks. And

surprisingly, activity in the area of the brain responsible for smell is present even before birth.

How can scientists pinpoint when fetal responses occur? They check the fetus's heart rate for quick or sudden increases. The fetal heartbeat will jump a minimum of 15 beats per minute within 5 seconds of a stimulating event! It remains fast for about 2 minutes and then returns to its resting rate.[1]

You should not worry about this sudden increase. It's perfectly natural—even desirable. It means that your fetus has become aware of the stimulation and is learning to accommodate to the new events in his environment. The excitement of this awareness causes his heart to speed up a bit, just as yours would under the same circumstances. Once the fetus has become accustomed to the stimulation, his heartbeat slows down, enabling him to respond to the next arousing event.

Your fetus also responds to stimulation by moving his arms and legs and twisting his body.[2] His heart rate must increase to accommodate his activity. Just as when you exercise, your heart beats faster in order to feed oxygen and energy to your muscles, so your fetus's heart rate responds in the same way. And if he keeps on moving, his heart rate remains high.

In a study conducted at the University of Illinois in 1982, fetal movements increased dramatically from a resting state of 12 movements every 5 minutes to 23 movements in the same time span every time medium- to high-pitched sounds were played to the fetus via stereo headphones placed on mother's abdomen. The fetuses continued these extra movements for thirty minutes after the sounds were played.[3]

Even during labor, with so much other stimulation going on, healthy fetuses will react to sound by moving.[4]

With all of these movement and heart-rate changes going on, it follows that your fetus's brain will also respond to the stimuli. Messages come into your fetus's brain from his developing senses and make synapses with other nerve cells within the brain (See Chapter 7). The electric activity can be measured on an electroencephalogram (EEG). Studies have charted changes in fetal EEG brain-wave patterns after the sixth month of pregnancy as a result of stimulation.[5]

The responses you are likely to observe in your fetus depend on whether or not he is awake. Through ultrasound technology researchers know that fetuses sleep and are aroused every 20 to 40 minutes. They may awaken themselves or may be awakened by sudden loud noises, as you might be.

Your fetus is most alert during the evening from eight o'clock until about midnight. When observed during this period through ultrasound, he has been found to be twice as active as during the rest of the day![6] No wonder mothers often complain that their fetuses seem to wake up as soon as they lie down for the night.

It is at this time, of course, when your fetus will be most responsive to Infant Stimulation.

All of this exciting research gives us invaluable information about a period in your baby's life that until recently has gone unnoticed. So enjoy the sensations and knowledge that come with realizing your fetus has the capability to sense and respond to his world within your womb.

5. Fetal Learning

A Rootin' Tootin' Tape

Tom and Judy Cornet, five months into their first pregnancy, approached me after one of my Infant Stimulation classes at the Natural Childbirth Institute in Culver City, California.

They wanted to bond to their baby even before he was born. They thought it exciting to apply the new information I had just shared about their fetus's sensory capabilities and the world within the womb.

"Why not make a prenatal tape?" I suggested. "All you have to do is record both your voices talking in a loving singsong voice to your fetus, naming him and identifying yourselves as mommy and daddy."

They followed my advice. First, they nicknamed their fetus. This is very important because it helped them (and will help you) recognize the fetus as a separate being. Since their name meant "horn" and they didn't know the sex of their unborn child, they chose "R.T.," an abbreviation for "Rootin' Tootin'."

Judy's tape went something like this:

"R.T., this is your mother speaking. I love you, R.T. R.T., this is your mother speaking. I can't wait for you to be born, R.T. I love you, R.T. R.T., this is your mother speaking. You're going to be such a welcome member of this family, R.T."

Then she added, "R.T., I'm going to read *Mother Goose* to you," and she proceeded with a verse from the age-old nursery rhymes.

Tom's tape was similar, but he injected some of his own wry humor.

"R.T., this is your daddy speaking. I love you, R.T. R.T., this is your daddy speaking. My name is Tom. I love you,

R.T. R.T., this is your daddy speaking. Are you being good to your mommy, R.T.? I love you, R.T. R.T., this is your daddy speaking. This pregnancy is costing me twenty-five hundred dollars and I *still* love you, R.T."

The Cornets each spoke 3 to 5 minutes. During the seventh month of Judy's pregnancy, they began playing the tape daily, placing stereo headphones on Judy's lower abdomen near R.T.'s ears.

Finally the big day arrived. R.T. was born. We videotaped his birth and subsequent reactions. Immediately following his delivery, we placed him on Judy's chest. He nuzzled into his mother's breast, as most newborns do.

Tom, positioned on his baby's left, repeated the phrases, "R.T. this is your daddy speaking. I love you, R.T. R.T., this is your daddy speaking. My name is Tom. I love you, R.T."

Imagine everyone's astonishment when, at the first sound of Tom's voice, little R.T. *lifted his head and turned to the left to find the source of the familiar intonations!* As long as Tom talked, R.T. maintained his gaze in his father's direction.

Then, during a pause, Tom moved to the other side of the delivery table and repeated the sentences again. R.T. lifted his little head once more and turned it 180 degrees to find Tom on his other side!

In fact, whenever Tom changed positions, uttering the same phrases, the baby turned his head. It was evident that amid all the noise in that major hospital delivery room, little R.T. was able to distinguish his father's voice and actually seek it out!

Later in this chapter I'll give you instructions for preparing your own personal prenatal tape. But for now, consider the wonderful new vistas that open for you and your family when you talk to your baby before he is born. Aside from the extra stimulation that this activity gives your baby's brain, you will be connecting with him in a positive and loving way. You may even be teaching him or *conditioning* him to recognize your voice.

Of Pavlov and Parental Love

Every time Ivan Pavlov, the nineteenth-century Russian scientist, fed his dogs, he rang a bell. Over time the dogs learned that the "ding-a-ling" meant "chow time," and they salivated in response. Then Pavlov altered the procedure. He rang the bell but hid the food. At first the dogs were fooled. They continued to drool, because they had been conditioned to expect food with that particular sound. Eventually, however, they got wise and the bell lost its power to produce a response.

Can your fetus be conditioned by and learn from his environment too? The surprising answer is *yes*. Evidence began mounting as early as 1932 to suggest that, indeed, fetuses are capable of *conditioned* learning long before they're born.[2]

Conditioned learning, or the learning of *a pattern of behavior* in response to a situation, is elementary learning. ("When X happens, I do Y.") It precedes the more complex cognitive learning, which is based on *conscious decision making* in face of the same situation. ("When X happens, I could do Y, but I could also do Z or even H.") The first traces of cognitive learning can appear in children as early as nine months of age.

In 1948 a research team at Cornell University used a combination of vibrator and wooden clapper to see if they could train fetuses to respond. First they laid the vibrator across mother's abdomens, causing a gentle vibration within the womb. The fetuses did nothing. Then they tried the clapper. When the two pieces of wood slammed together, the fetuses moved in a startled way at the loud, unexpected noise. Next the researchers combined the two devices: clapper and 5 seconds of vibration with 4 minutes of rest time. After sixteen such training sessions, the majority of the fetuses reacted to the vibration alone. From this the team concluded that fetuses can be conditioned.[3]

Although this particular study was conducted over thirty-six years ago, today there are many new explorations into fetal learning. Dr. F. Rene Van de Carr, an obstetrician in Hayward, California, telephoned me in 1982 to discuss his ongoing work in conditioning fetuses to their mothers' voice and touch.

Convinced that bonding begins during pregnancy, Dr. Van de Carr wanted to help his patients identify their fetuses as individuals who could sense the environment and mother's presence. He asked the women of they would be willing to try something new. Would they talk to their unborn babies?

Those who agreed to this unique approach tape-recorded their own voices, saying, "Ha, ha, ha, ha..." This stylized laugh was played to the fetus daily during the last two months of pregnancy. The obstetrician hoped that once born, the newborns would be able to recognize their mothers' voices.

But nothing prepared him for what actually *did* happen! After the delivery, Dr. Van de Carr had instructed his patients to call him if they noticed anything unusual. Well, several mothers reported that their *four-day-old newborns were making very distinct sounds*! In fact, the parents heard their babies say, "Haha... Haha... Haha..."

Amazed, the good doctor tried the same technique with his own pregnant wife. Sure enough, by one week of age, little baby Van de Carr was making those very same laughing sounds, even while being audio- and videotaped.[4]

"That's wonderful!" I said. "Think of the possibilities! If babies can be trained to repeat sounds while still in the womb, we can begin teaching language at an earlier age than we ever dreamed possible! Have you been sharing this information with your patients?"

"Yes," he replied. "But we've even gone one step further. Now we're teaching fetuses to associate mother's words with her actions."

Dr. Van de Carr explained that he now instructs mothers to say "pat," and gently pat their bellies, "stroke," and gently stroke, "rub," and rub in a circular fashion, and "squeeze," and squeeze the skin over their abdomens firmly but not roughly, twice a day during the last two months of pregnancy. He asks them to speak up so that their fetuses will hear.

The obstetrician had the opportunity to test out his theory when some of these same patients needed an ultrasound examination for other reasons. He asked them to repeat the "pat, stroke, rub, squeeze," *without touching their abdomens*, while he observed the fetal movements.

The fetuses moved in response to each of the four words! And when mothers *didn't* speak but only rubbed, patted, stroked, and squeezed, the fetuses repeated those same patterns.

Dr. Van de Carr is still actively engaged in this work. In 1984 he created a prenatal learning program called the Prenatal University, which to date has had over four hundred graduates. It incorporates his ideas on training the fetus and stimulating the fetal brain to learn through associations and conditioning (you'll find his address in Appendix 2).

Dr. Van de Carr's findings on prenatal learning will have to be verified by further scientific experimentation. Nevertheless, I believe that his private research is so exciting and so positive for mother/child bonding, that I have incorporated it into my practice.

Getting in "Touch" with Your Fetus

You might want to try Dr. Van de Carr's suggestion for getting in "touch" with your baby even before he is born by stroking your fetus. Here's how. From the thirteenth to twenty-seventh week of pregnancy, you should stroke your abdomen lightly from below up to the belly button. By the twenty-eighth week, however, ask your health care professional to outline your fetus's body on your abdomen so that you can stroke from his head to his toes. This enhances the development of his neuromuscular pathways.

Dr. Van de Carr suggests that you:

- *Stroke* your fetus and say, "Stroke, I'm stroking you."
- *Pat* your fetus and say, "Pat, I'm patting you."
- *Gently squeeze* your fetus and say, "Squeeze, I'm squeezing you."
- *Rub* your fetus in a gentle circular motion and say, "Rub, I'm rubbing you."

If you stroke after your fetus has kicked, you may be teaching him that his activity brings about some change in his environment. This is called initiative behavior and is important because he learns that he has some control in the world. Maybe he's even thinking, "When I kick, Mommy pats me and rubs me and talks to me. What power I have. This is marvelous!"

Some women may experience the sensation of contraction when they begin to rub their abdomens. If you feel any discomfort or contraction during this activity, *stop* immediately and consult your health professional.

The Cat in the Hat

Now, there are even ongoing studies examining whether or not fetuses can be conditioned to recognize stories. In 1980 Dr. Anthony DeCasper, at the Department of Psychology, University of North Carolina, Greensboro, reported on his study in which fetuses preferred to hear their mother reading to them instead of a strange female.

After the birth of the babies, he devised a "suckometer"—a nipple sensitive to the pattern and strength of sucking—to help determine if the newborns could recognize their mothers' voices. When the babies sucked in a burst of rapid sucks, the device triggered a tape recording of mother reading *The Cat in the Hat*. Other sucking patterns elicited an unfamiliar woman's voice reading the same story. The newborn chose mother's voice most often.[5]

Then, in 1982, Dr. DeCasper tried something different. He asked sixteen mothers to read *The Cat in the Hat* to their fetuses for five hours over the last six weeks of their pregnancies. Again, after the babies' births he used the suckometer. But this time, different sucking patterns produced mother reading other stories. The newborns, some only hours old, chose *The Cat in the Hat* most often![6]

The real and long-lasting effects of such prenatal conditioned learning on a baby's personality are still a matter of speculation and conjecture. However, fetal psychologists are actively exploring this very new and exciting field of fetal behavior and personality development.

Talking to Your Fetus

You might try for yourself a simple program that I've devised for parents who want to expose their baby to pleasing auditory *sensations* even before birth. *My program is based on the growing body of evidence that fetuses respond to sensory stimulation in the womb.*

The very first step of your baby's language acquisition is the recognition of intonation patterns. Therefore, it is important that *both* parents engage in this one-way conversation. While mother's voice is often more melodic and more appealing to the fetus, father's voice is heard more loudly since it's much lower in pitch and doesn't have to travel through all of those internal organs.[7] That may be why prenatally stimulated newborns distinguish and turn readily to Daddy's voice immediately after birth.

Making a Prenatal Tape

To start talking to your fetus:

1. If you don't know your baby's sex, or have not yet selected a name, make up a "pet" name and use it consistently throughout the pregnancy and in your tape.

2. Record 5 minutes of mommy's voice followed by 5 minutes of daddy's voice.

3. Each parent should begin his or her segment by calling the baby's name three times very slowly, phonetically, and in a singsong voice. Repeat the name and loving phrases often.

4. Identify yourself and say, "I love you, do you know that?" Ask many questions, since they raise your voice's pitch and may catch the fetus's attention. Repeat three times.

5. Tell a story. Recount the day's experiences. Read a nursery rhyme. Hum or sing a song.

6. Make *positive* suggestions for positive image building like, "You're going to be such a happy baby." "You're going to be such a smart baby." "You're going to be loving, kind, and generous."

7. Then play 5 minutes of your favorite classical music, introducing the piece by name. Try a lullaby.

8. Repeat the same tape throughout the last two months of pregnancy. Here's a sample script for a tape you can make with ease:

"Kim, this is your mommy. I love you, do you know that?" (Repeat three times.)

"Would you like to hear a song? I'm going to sing 'Twinkle, Twinkle' to you." (Sing the song.)

"Kim, this is your mommy. I love you, Kim. Do you know what I did today? I went to the supermarket. Do you know what I bought? I bought chicken and zucchini and bananas and potatoes. Soon you're going to be able to eat chicken and zucchini and bananas and potatoes too!

"Kim, this is your mommy. I love you, Kim, and I can't *wait* till I see you.

"Kim, you're going to be so bright. Kim, you're going to be so loving and kind. Kim, you're going to be so honest and good. I love you, Kim.

"And now here's your daddy."

Daddy goes through similar routine but closes with, "And now, would you like to listen to some music? This is from Vivaldi's 'Four Seasons.' We'll listen with you."

Playing Your Prenatal Tape

- Begin play as early as the twentieth week of pregnancy. Make sure to do it regularly during the last two months.
- Place two drops of water on the abdomen where the headphones will go. Water helps the sound conductance.
- Place each of the stereo headphone earpieces on either side of the pregnant abdomen at the bikini line.
- Play at a volume of 3 or less (a good guide to loudness—if it's comfortable for you, it'll be just fine for your fetus).
- Remember that your fetus is most alert and responsive from eight P.M. to midnight.

If you can tolerate the repetition, play your 15-minute tape four times during this evening period (at 8:00, 8:30, 9:00, and 9:30). Once is fine, but, of course, the more frequently you play the tape, the more likely you are to have results.

You can also record 3 minutes of the sound of your own laughter, as Dr. Van de Carr had suggested with his patients. Don't be surprised if you hear those sounds repeated during the first month of your baby's life!

If you're feeling really adventurous, you can tape yourself reading a story to your fetus, as Dr. Anthony DeCasper had mothers do in his experiments. Just make sure you choose a story that you'll enjoy hearing once a day for the last six weeks of pregnancy—and once baby is born.

6. Fetal Behavior and
Personality Development

It is important to recognize that your fetus is receptive and sensitive to environmental stimulation. His experiences in the womb may not only affect his behavior, but may also modify his entire personality for the rest of his life. You cannot wait until your baby is born to concern yourself with the influence of his environment upon his development.

Shake 'n' Bake

Anna C., seven months pregnant, came into the clinic, as she always did, with a confident stride and a broad smile. A picture of healthy pregnancy, she plopped into a chair and patted her growing belly.

As is my habit, I asked if she had been dreaming about her fetus. Usually, at the seventh month, women have pleasant dreams of babies-at-ease, doing nothing at all. I was taken aback by her reply!

"I don't need to dream about my baby! I already know what his personality is going to be like. When I go into the kitchen to cook, he starts to kick. As soon as I leave, he stops! Nothing else seems to get his attention *except* my husband's violin music. This baby is just in love with Gypsy violin! Really fast-paced . . . it gets his adrenaline moving.

"I *know* what my baby is going to be like! He's going to be a shaker and a baker!"

I'll never forget Mrs. C.'s confidence. She was certain that she could predict her unborn child's personality from his activity level while still in her womb.

Of course, the development of personality—the psychological makeup of a person, which renders him different from
everyone else—is extremely complex. Psychologists, in an
attempt to understand what makes people who they are,
theorize that personality is determined both by what is innate
and what we encounter during the rest of our lives.

Innate characteristics develop during fetal life. They result,
in part, from your fetus's complex world within the womb: his
sensory perceptions[1] and his responses to his own development, to the intrauterine environment, and to stimulation
coming from mother and beyond.

It is clear that Mrs. C. felt her baby already had some
inborn personality traits. But is that really possible? Can we
actually know what a baby will be like after he is born by
measuring his activity level as a fetus? In the following
fascinating studies, scientists have attempted to link individual responses (particularly movement and heart-rate changes)
to later personality traits. The correlations indicated in a
number of cases are nothing short of remarkable.

The Ups and Downs of Activity

As early as 1938, a research team measured the responses
of fetuses to the stress of loud noises. Fetuses that kicked
sharply or made strong punching movements when the loud
sound was played were characterized as "active." "Inactive"
fetuses squirmed slowly or moved only sluggishly.

After the babies were born and had reached six months of
age, the researchers retested the infants' mental and motor
abilities on a Gesell Test (a standard developmental test
constructed by Dr. Arnold Gesell at Yale University in the
1940's). As you might expect, the babies who had been
"active" fetuses were further along in their motor and mental
development than the "inactive" children. Other researchers
repeated this experiment and confirmed the results.[2]

In 1953 the research team of Dr. M. Fries and Dr. P. Woolf
at the Menninger Clinic in Topeka, Kansas, wanted to learn if
fetal activity had a *long-term* effect on development, and if
that, in turn, influenced children's relationships to others.
They found that active fetuses developed into active children
during their first few years of life. Parents reported more

stressful relationships with these highly active, more independent children.[3]

The ups and downs of active babies were all too familiar to Barbara M. Her firstborn, Jason, had just entered kindergarten and her second child, Michelle, was still a toddler. The birth of her third baby was only four weeks off when she came into my office looking worn out and overwhelmed.

"Susan," she asked, almost pleadingly, "is this going to be a *good* baby?"

Uncertain as to how she defined *good,* I asked, "Do you mean a healthy baby? Why, yes, from all indications—"

In her anxiety, she interrupted. "Well, no, not exactly. You know what I mean. Quiet, like Jason. I can take another Jason but I don't think I have the stamina for another Michelle.

"She's all over the place, all the time. Never sits still, gets into this, gets into that. Do you know, this morning she climbed out of her crib! She won't even stay put at bedtime, when I read to her.

"I should have known as much. Jason is cuddly and quiet and calm. He was just like that when I was pregnant with him. And Michelle was a devil on wheels—even then!

"Do you think this baby will be more like Jason because it's less active? I sure do hope so. . . ."

I could only confirm that there is a *possibility* that an active fetus might be born as an active baby, but I stressed that more than *just* prenatal activity would determine the type of person her new baby became. It was also possible that her third child would be different from *both* Jason and Michelle. Besides, there are some indicators other than activity that researchers have been considering in approaching fetal behavior and personality development.

Fetal Heart Rate as a Predictor of Personality

An interesting study conducted in 1984 by Dr. Clifford Olds, a research psychologist at Runwell Hospital, Wickford, England, looked into personality traits among fetal twins, using the fetal heart's response to music as a predictor of personality!

Dr. Olds played classical music to sets of unborn twins. If the fetal hearts responded identically, he identified the twins as identical. Conversely, fraternal twins (conceived of two different eggs) presented differing heart rates after the musical stimulation.

In some instances, fraternal twins reacted quite differently. One twin's heart rate rose while the other's dropped in response to the same music. Dr. Olds predicted that those fetal twins whose heart rates increased would turn out to be extroverted children.

At two years of age the toddlers were evaluated on a personality test. The majority of those whose fetal heart rates rose exhibited the qualities usually attributed to extroverts. So as to avoid any conscious influencing, the parents were not informed of Dr. Olds's predictions of personality during the initial testing.[4]

Dr. Olds did further testing. He monitored fetal heart rates while playing Gounod's *Faust* to the tummies of several other mothers. Some fetuses enjoyed the music. Their heart rates quickened in response. Others showed no change in heart rate. He concluded that a fetus may already have a preference for certain types of music. In addition, two years later, those mothers whose fetuses responded positively reported that their toddlers were "mellow."[5]

Personality development is indeed complex and should not be reduced to simple cause-and-effect formulas, as these studies might suggest. Such studies should, however, serve to show us that there is *some* relationship between fetal behavior and personality development. They do *not* say, however, that fetal behaviors create personality or that personality creates the fetal behaviors. There is much to learn in this complicated new field before we even can begin to approach some answers.

III. HOW YOUR BABY'S BRAIN DEVELOPS (AND HOW INFANT STIMULATION CAN AFFECT IT)

7. Giving Your Baby a Head Start

If you were able to peer into the womb during the fifth month of pregnancy, you probably would be struck by the *size* of your fetus's head. It would seem enormous in relation to the rest of the body. During pregnancy, your fetus's brain grows at a furious pace.

At birth your newborn's brain will already have reached 25 percent of its eventual adult size. But brain growth doesn't stop there. In fact, during his first year, your baby's brain will grow at an unprecedented rate. By the time you're lighting those first birthday candles, your one-year-old's brain will have reached 70 percent of its adult weight. In addition, 70 to 85 percent of all the previously set down brain cells will be completely developed.[1] Forty-five percent of your baby's brain growth takes place during his or her first year!

We refer to this crucial time in your child's development from conception to one year of age as the period of the *brain growth spurt*.[2]

- Did you know that during the brain growth spurt, brain cells are extremely sensitive to what goes on in their environment and are *dramatically* affected by both positive and (unfortunately) negative conditions?[3]
- Did you know there are simple things that you can do to influence your baby's brain development even *before* he or she is conceived?
- Did you know that a well-developed brain will help ensure that your baby's *whole body* grows properly, as well?[4]

These facts about brain development have been proved by many years of research. So, take advantage of your baby's brain growth spurt; it is your ideal opportunity to give your baby a head start.

Join me now for an exploration into why Infant Stimulation makes a difference in brain development and what you can accomplish, *very simply*, to stimulate this fascinating organ that makes your child human.

What Is the Brain?

Everyone knows what a brain is, right? It's that convoluted mass of gray tissue that does our thinking for us. It's the mind. The seat of intelligence. The source of universal, eternal mystery. Brains are pretty complicated organs!

Actually, the brain is composed mostly of nerve cells. Millions of them. These three-part nerve cells, called *neurons*, with the help of different chemical compounds, do the work of the brain (see illustration).

Here's how it works: If baby happens to smell a wedge of lemon, the message travels from his nose on up to the brain. There, it is received by the *dendrites*, the parts of the brain cell that pick up messages. In this case, the dendrites receiving the message are in the olfactory (smell) area of the brain.

The dendrites pass the message to the *cell body*. This second part of the brain cell decides what to do with the message. It can store it, share it with other brain cells, and/or react to it.

If it reacts, the cell body sends another message, via the *axon*, back to the muscles and nerves of baby's face, telling

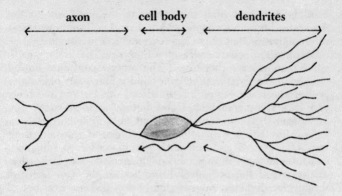

axon   cell body   dendrites

Brain cell (neuron)

the nose to get away from that sour-smelling lemon and telling the mouth to stay shut.

Fortunately for baby, the cell body can also store the information so that the next time he smells something that sour, he'll move away with conviction. He has *learned* an important sensory lesson.

Insulating the Wiring

Imagine the electrician's nightmare: a jangle of several million *live* uninsulated electrical wires lying across one another. You'd have nothing but short circuits if those millions of wires were not protected in some way. Well, neurons are very much the same. In fact, the messages they receive, store, and send are nothing but electrical impulses. So neurons need insulation. But instead of plastic and black electrical tape, brain cells are coated with a sheath of protein called *myelin*.[5]

This is important for you to know, because neurons don't come into being with their protective myelin sheaths in place. Time and *stimulation* help the coating to develop. *Myelination* (the process of insulating the nerve cells) begins in early pregnancy, with brain cells first. It proceeds from head to toe[6] and from the center of the body out to the fingers and toes. (In chapters 14 and 16, I will share with you some activities that encourage myelination in your baby.)

Myelination occurs more rapidly during the brain growth spurt than at any other time.[7] The process continues during childhood, and by the time your child is four years old, major body nerves are completely insulated. When you see four-year-olds tying their shoes and buttoning their coats, you know that they have myelinated out to their fingertips.

This insulation helps the nerve fibers to transmit their messages quickly and efficiently.[8] It allows for coordination, control, and rapid muscle movement. According to Dr. Arthur R. Jensen of the School of Education at the University of California, Berkeley, the *reaction time* of the nerves is one of the keys to intelligence.[9] That should not come as a surprise, because even non-scientists refer to dull people as slow and bright people as having quick minds. Stimulation speeds the myelination process and thus helps accelerate reaction time.

Taking Matters into Your Own Hands

We've all heard of gray matter and white matter in the brain. Which matter *matters* most for your smarter baby? Both do.

The white matter is simply the concentration of axons which transmits messages between the body and the conscious brain. The conscious brain—also known as gray matter, or the outer cortex region—covers the outside of the brain. Although less than two inches thick, this gray matter is like dense felt packed with cell bodies and dendrites lying on top of one another, and continuously communicating through connections called *synapses*.[10] During a synapse, electrical activity is passed from one nerve to another. Fetuses' first synapses have been documented as early as the seventieth day after conception.[11]

Specialists in fetal and infant brain development stress that the fetal stimulation of your baby's senses can affect the development of these synapses. In fact, the lack of these connections can cause nerve cells to die, especially in the eighth month of pregnancy.[12] Current studies speculate that sensory stimulation of the fetus in utero during the last half of pregnancy (which, of course, creates more synapses) may act as a preventative to brain cell death, although to date these theories are unproven.

The Right Brain and the Left Brain

You might have thought that your baby has only one brain. He does, but it is divided into two halves or hemispheres, each with its own distinct function.

The cortex (or gray matter) of the left hemisphere is mainly responsible for logic, reasoning, and cognitive or analytic skills, like language and math. The cortex of the right hemisphere is responsible for artistic development, music, non-language sounds, emotion, and intuitive thought.

Infant Stimulation enhances the development of *both* hemispheres of the brain because it provides specific techniques to challenge both the right and the left hemisphere.

For example, when you sing to your baby, the lyrics impact the left hemisphere while the melody affects the right. Naming baby's body parts while you stroke them has the same effect, as does having baby look at a bull's-eye design while he traces it with his finger.

Simple? Yes! Yet very significant, for such activities promote communication and cooperation between both hemispheres. A universal characteristic of genius is tremendous communication and interaction between the right and left hemispheres. *Any activity that stimulates both hemispheres simultaneously will promote intelligence.*

Your baby's brain and nervous system are wonderfully sophisticated; they direct all bodily functions, movements, and thoughts. But these systems don't suddenly spring into being whole and ready to go. From the moment of conception onward, they develop in stages. Let's look at these stages, both in prenatal life and during the first year, so that you can more fully understand the positive effect of Infant Stimulation on your baby's brain development.

8. How Your Fetus's
Brain Develops

The First Stage

By the fifth month of your pregnancy the number of brain cells that your baby will have is already set, fixed, and determined. Astounding as it seems, neurologists studying brain development have proven that immediately after conception, the mechanism for producing the number of brain cells kicks into action and does not stop until five months have passed. Then it ceases operation, never to create another brain cell again!

The Second Stage

How does the brain continue to grow if no new brain cells are added? Easy. From this point forward, the brain will grow by increasing the *size* and *complexity* of its already existing cells. *Sensory stimulation affects brain cell growth.*

As the cells get larger, they begin to migrate away from the center of the brain, which causes that organ to get larger. The axons grow very long. Dendrites develop, and after the eighteenth week, they branch out, forming an elaborate network of interconnections designed to pick up every electrical impulse produced by stimulation.[1] The more stimulation and sensory messages received, the greater the development of dendrites and the better individual cells can communicate. Fortunately, the brain accommodates to this need by producing more of these interconnecting filaments.

You might have thought that your fetus's brain is quiet until he is born. Not so. By the seventieth day after conception, as previously noted, his brain cells have begun communicating with each other, forming synapses, as a result of stimulation they receive within the uterus. Sometimes the fetus provides his own stimulation by swallowing, changing position, kicking, sucking, and touching his face. Sometimes stimulation occurs as a reaction to changes in mother's environment[2] (see chapters 3 to 5, on fetal development).

Stimulation of your fetus's senses is vitally important—even necessary—in order for the growing brain to continue its development.[3]

An Extra Boost

Around the eighth month of pregnancy your fetus's brain undergoes another big change. It doubles in weight. Now, the elaborate network of brain cells is actively forming synapses.

I am forever fascinated when I observe the changes in mothers' behavior that correspond to the fetus's heightened brain growth at this time. At the university medical centers where I've taught, women often come in for their eighth-month visit with their hands resting on their protuberant bellies. Every once in a while they pat and rub, sometimes talking to the fetus within. "Oh, I know you're there," they say sweetly. "It won't be long now." They may even rock back and forth, gently swaying the fetus.

In contrast, most women in their fourth through seventh months don't engage in this kind of activity. It almost seems as if, intuitively, mothers are adding to the stimulation that the fetus provides for himself—especially during this period of heightened brain growth.

The Size of Things

The gentle stimulation provided by many mothers during the eighth month could well be affecting their unborn baby's brain size and ultimate intelligence.

In 1976 a team of scientists headed by Dr. Robert Fisch, at the pediatric department, University of Minnesota, Minneapolis, investigated the factors associated with superior intelligence in seven-year-olds. They found that the best predictor of superior intelligence was a favorable parental social and educational background. The second best predictor was a large head size at one year of age.[4] Large head size (the measurement of the head's circumference in relation to established standards of what is considered "normal") is a direct reflection of the number of brain cells and the density of the dendrites.

The chart that follows shows how your baby's brain develops in utero and in the first three years after birth.

Brain Growth Time Chart

AGE	EVENT
10 to 18 weeks pregnant	Phase One of brain growth: the number of brain cells is established.
20 weeks pregnant (to two years old)	Phase Two of brain growth: the brain growth spurt. Cells increase in size. Dendrites develop.
20 weeks pregnant (to 4 years old)	Nerve fibers insulated at rapid rate. (Process slows after 4 years of age.)
8 months pregnant	Brain doubles in weight.
Birth	Infant's brain has reached 25 percent of adult weight.
6 months old	Infant's brain 50 percent of adult weight.
1 year old	Infant's brain 70 percent of adult weight. Majority of DNA (genetic material) in brain cells has been set down.

3 years old

Child's brain has reached over 90 percent of its maximum size.

The majority of brain growth occurs in the first year following birth.

9. Yes, Your Diet *Can*

Influence Baby's Brain Growth

Since no new brain cells are being added after the first five months from conception, the phenomenal growth of your baby's brain during the rest of pregnancy and in the first year occurs entirely through the elongation of axons and cell bodies and the branching of dendrites. As we've said, this is the only way that your child's brain will continue to grow and develop during his lifetime.

But your diet can play a major role in helping things along. *What you eat just before conception and during pregnancy and lactation actually can influence your baby's brain.* Good nutrition—both yours and baby's—and stimulation of your baby's senses *directly affect* the development of his brain cells.[1]

Bear in mind, however, that brain growth is extremely complex and occurs as a result of many interdependent factors. Nevertheless, there are some ways that you can help nudge nature along.

The Genetic Link

Of course, genetics are an essential element of your child's intelligence. There is a tendency for smart parents to have smart children. However, since a child's performance is not dependent on genes alone, but also on a stimulating environment and proper nutrition, there is an opportunity to make a positive contribution no matter what the genetic inheritance.

The question of how many of your child's eventual accomplishments are determined by his genes and how many by environment, or upbringing, remains part of the age-old nature versus nurture controversy. Despite extensive research into this issue, we can still only reasonably conclude that *both* play an integral part in your child's development.

Food for Thought

But we cannot overemphasize the importance of nutrition—both for pregnant mothers and babies—when it comes to having a smarter baby. It's important for mother to watch her diet even while she's *trying* to get pregnant. World War II data showed that babies conceived while their mothers were suffering from malnutrition had a much higher rate of poorly developed brains and bodies, and a 169 percent increase in brain and central nervous system *defects*, than babies conceived by mothers with adequate diets. Some of the babies in the study died.[2] Even giving malnourished mothers a high protein diet during the last half of pregnancy does not alter the damage done by malnourishment before conception and during the first half of pregnancy.[3]

During pregnancy, what mother eats directly influences her offspring's brain development! Mother's poor nutrition can be devastating to the fetal brain. Study after study has shown that when mother's nutrition is inadequate:

- the fetal brain gets less of its DNA or genetic predisposition
- the concentration of protein in brain cells is inadequate
- brain size and weight are lower than normal
- nerve cell insulation (myelination) is delayed
- dendrites form fewer branches than normal.[4]

All of this means that a fetus that has suffered malnutrition because of its mother's poor eating habits can be born with a serious disadvantage. Problems beget problems. Because of poor brain development, the child cannot respond normally to sensory stimulation in utero and once born. Thus, his or her physical growth and health will be impaired. Behavior becomes retarded.[5] In fact, scientific evidence suggests that malnutrition during the last half of pregnancy may contribute to baby's poor motor coordination, producing a clumsy child.[6]

Reasons for Good Nutrition during Pregnancy

Good nutrition at conception promotes proper inheritance of genes.

Good nutrition at conception prevents under-development and abnormal development of fetus's brain cells.

Good nutrition throughout pregnancy insures proper brain development.

Good nutrition helps fetus and baby respond to environment appropriately.

Infant Stimulation has a greater effect on well-nourished infants than on undernourished and underdeveloped infants.

Negative Effects of Malnutrition During Pregnancy

The brain may get less of its DNA.

The concentration of protein in brain cells is insufficient.

Brain weight is much lower than normal.

Myelination is delayed.

Brain size is smaller than normal because there are fewer brain cells.

There is less branching of dendrites than normal.

Babies cannot respond to sensory stimulation in a normal way.

Physical growth and health are impaired.

Behavior is retarded.

Motor activity and coordination are impaired.

Some Dietary Cautions

You may be surprised to learn that *your body needs only 300 extra calories a day during pregnancy, so don't load up on extra sugars and carbohydrates*. Aside from being empty calories, a heavy concentration of these foods (when taken at one time) can cause your red blood cells to clump together. This prevents the blood from transfusing through the tiny capillaries in your body, and may deprive your fetus of some nutrition and oxygen essential to growth.

While I'm on the subject of *don'ts* during pregnancy, I urge you to refrain from both drinking *and* smoking. That may be a tall order, but consider the potential risks, especially if your goal is a healthier and smarter baby.

Alcohol constricts mother's blood vessels, which ultimately decreases the amount of blood and nutrients available to the fetus through the placenta.

A recent landmark study at the Kaiser Permanente Hospital system in northern California conclusively showed the negative effects of alcohol consumption on newborn birth weight. The researchers documented the drinking habits of 35,000 pregnant women and the birth weights of their 28,000 babies. They found that when the mothers consumed only 1 ounce of alcohol per week during the first twelve weeks of the pregnancy, the babies' average weight at birth was dismally low—so low, in fact, that they were in the lowest 6 percent birth-weight range of *all* babies born in the United States.[7]

Even more alarming is the potential for fetal brain damage when pregnant mothers drink. The fetus absorbs the alcohol in mother's blood into his own body. *Actually, if you become intoxicated, so does your fetus!* But unlike mother's, the fetus's liver is not yet capable of filtering out the harmful substance. The alcohol remains, circulating in the fetus's bloodstream, where it has a special affinity for brain tissue.

The tragic by-products of alcohol consumption in pregnant women include:

- premature labor
- babies' mental retardation
- a variety of neurological defects in babies

These negative effects are permanent.[8] The Surgeon General of the United States has recommended that women totally abstain from drinking alcohol during pregnancy.

The outlook on smoking is also bleak. Cigarette smoke, too, causes the blood vessels of the placenta to constrict, which decreases the flow of nutrients to the fetus. Typically, babies of smoking mothers are smaller than normal. In fact, your fetus is *so* sensitive to smoke that as soon as you've taken that first drag, his heart rate will increase in order to compensate for the eventual decrease in oxygen and nutrition.

All of the results aren't in yet on coffee and tea drinking, however. The effects of caffeine on pregnancy and unborn babies are still under active investigation. Great controversy surrounds the various conclusions about whether or not coffee and tea are harmless. In this matter, it would be best for you to consult with and follow the advice of your own health professional.

While the negative effects of malnutrition are alarming, there are some simple things that you can do to avoid its damage. *You need extra protein before you conceive and when you're pregnant.*

The brain is composed mainly of protein. For your fetus's optimal brain development, I suggest that in the weeks before conception and throughout pregnancy you eat 80 to 106 grams of protein daily.[9] That's as much protein as you'd find in about two 7-ounce cans of solid pack white tuna or in eight to ten 8-ounce glasses of low fat, protein-fortified milk.

You can safely begin this extra protein weeks before you plan to conceive. Remember, however, before undertaking any dramatic dietary change, especially one that involves a high-protein intake, you should confer with your health care professional. *This diet is not recommended for women with kidney, heart, blood pressure, or toxemia problems.*

Normally, we eat about 43 grams of protein a day, so 80 to 106 grams can seem like a large increase. And it may be a real challenge to pack in those extra grams of protein without overloading your system with excess animal fat.

Dr. Victor Berman is an obstetrician, and his wife, Sallee, is a certified nurse-midwife. They are co-founders of the National Childbirth Institute in Culver City, California, the first free-standing birth center in the United States. They recommend a protein shake that can be prepared and consumed once a day (along with a well-balanced diet)—a painless, nutritionally sound and delicious way to insure a high protein intake. Since 1973, 3,000 of their patients have sipped this concoction, and the Bermans find that it has been beneficial in helping to relieve complications due to insufficient protein.

Make sure to drink plenty of liquids when you embark on

your high-protein diet (eight 8-ounce glasses of water, milk, or juice daily). That will speed your kidneys' processing of the protein.

The Bermans' Protein Shake

20 grams of protein supplied by milk-egg protein powder (available in health food stores)
8 oz. low fat or skim milk
1 raw egg

½ cup fresh, frozen, or canned fruit (without syrup). Choose from such fruits as bananas, strawberries, blueberries, peaches, papaya, pineapple.

Combine ingredients and whirl in blender. Drink once a day. I recommend that you take it as an afternoon snack.

A Well-balanced Diet

A well-balanced diet is of great importance before conception and during pregnancy. You should eat adequate amounts of the six basic food groups as recommended by the Maternal Child Health Branch of the California Department of Health Services in the following chart:

Daily Food Guide for Pregnant Women and Those Planning to Be Pregnant

FOOD GROUP	EXAMPLES	NUMBER OF SERVINGS
Protein foods	beef, chicken, fish, eggs, beans, nuts, dried peas, tofu	four 2-oz. servings
Milk and milk products	milk (low, nonfat), buttermilk, low fat cottage cheese, ice cream, yogurt, custard	four 8-oz. glasses of milk or equal amounts of other foods (see menus)
Breads and cereals	whole-grain breads, oatmeal	four servings

FOOD GROUP	EXAMPLES	NUMBER OF SERVINGS
	and cracked wheat cereals, rice (brown and white), potatoes, whole-wheat noodles, tortillas	
Vitamin C-rich vegetables and fruits	peppers, tomatoes, cabbage, cauli-flower, cantaloupe, papaya, citrus fruits and juices, strawberries	one ¾-cup serving
Dark green and leafy vegetables (rich in calcium)	asparagus, brussels sprouts, broccoli, romaine, spinach, beet or collard greens	one 1-cup serv-ing (raw) or one ¾-cup serving (cooked)
Other fruits and vegetables	your choice	one ½-serving

It's easy to incorporate these foods into your daily diet. The following suggestions are based on recommendations of the Maternal Child Health Branch of the California Department of Health Services. (For your own free brochure, see Appendix 3.)

Here are five days of sample menus to get you started:

The Smarter-Baby High-Protein Diet for Pregnant Mothers

DAY ONE

Breakfast:
½ medium cantaloupe
1 egg (cooked any way you like it)
2 slices whole-wheat toast)
1 cup low fat milk

Lunch:
4 oz. tuna salad (preferably from tuna packed in water) prepared with ½ cup celery on 1 slice whole-wheat toast
1 cup low fat milk

Afternoon Snack:
Bermans' Protein Shake

Dinner:
4 to 6 oz. broiled chicken (preferably with skin removed)
1 cup mashed potatoes or 1 baked potato with skin
¾ cup steamed broccoli
1 cup low fat milk

Evening Snack:
1 small banana
1 cup low fat milk

DAY TWO

Breakfast:
Breakfast pizza (a toasted, split whole-wheat English muffin, topped with a small sliced tomato and 3 oz.—about 2 slices—Muenster, jack, or cheddar cheese melted under the broiler)
4 oz. orange, pineapple, or grapefruit juice

Lunch:
1 cup raw spinach/mushroom salad topped with a grated hard-boiled egg and ½ cup toasted sunflower seeds
4 whole-wheat or cracked-wheat crackers
1 cup low fat milk

Afternoon Snack:
Bermans' Protein Shake

Dinner:
6 oz. meat loaf
½ cup brown rice
½ cup cooked green peas
1 cup low fat milk

Evening Snack:
1 cup pudding or custard made with low fat milk

Breakfast:
½ grapefruit sweetened with ½ teaspoon honey or sugar
1 cup cooked oatmeal made with ¾ cup low fat milk, topped
  with ½ cup raisins

Lunch:
Chef's salad composed of 1 cup romaine, 2 oz. ham, chicken,
  garbanzo, or kidney beans, and scallion garnish
1 small bagel
8 oz. frozen low fat yogurt dessert

Afternoon Snack:
Bermans' Protein Shake

Dinner:
6 oz. broiled or baked red snapper or other fish fillet
½ cup cooked spinach or whole-wheat noodles or macaroni
½ cup steamed carrots
1 cup low fat milk

Evening Snack:
8 oz. ice milk or ice cream

DAY FOUR

Breakfast:
½ papaya stuffed with 1⅓ cup cottage cheese
2 slices whole-wheat toast

Lunch:
1½ cups split pea, bean and barley, or lentil soup
1 slice rye bread
1 cup low fat milk
1 small apple or peach, in season

Afternoon Snack:
Bermans' Protein Shake

Dinner:
Lasagne casserole made with ½ cup cooked lasagne noodles;
  4 oz. combined ricotta, mozzarella, and Parmesan cheeses;
  4 oz. sauteed (in small amount of fat or in nonstick pan) and
  drained ground beef; your favorite marinara sauce
Endive and tomato salad

Evening Snack:
½ cup unsalted dry roasted, or raw peanuts

DAY FIVE

Breakfast:
1 cup plain low fat yogurt sweetened with ½ teaspoon honey
   or sugar
¾ cup sliced strawberries
1 whole-wheat waffle (Roman Meal is good, or make your own
   from a mix)

Lunch:
¼ cup peanut or cashew butter and 1 small sliced apple, or
   banana, or ¼ cup raisins on 2 slices whole-wheat bread
1 cup low fat milk

Afternoon Snack:
Bermans' Protein Shake

Dinner:
8 oz. lamb, pork, or veal chop (allowing for bone), broiled,
   baked, or sauteed in small amount of fat
1 medium baked potato
¾ cup steamed asparagus
1 cup low fat milk

Evening Snack:
2 large oatmeal-raisin cookies
1 cup low fat milk

As a pregnant mother who maintains high levels of protein
and carries out a well-balanced diet, you protect your baby
from the dangers of malnourishment.

Once your baby is born, you are best advised to follow the
guidelines set by your pediatric professional for the feeding of
your infant. Their recommendations will certainly fulfill your
baby's dietary needs.

Stimulation

Good nutrition combined with Infant Stimulation can give
your child bigger and better brain cells both before and after
birth. And we now know that these brain cells *are responsive*
to stimulation even while your baby is still in the womb.

10. The Smarter-Baby Guide to Maximizing Brain Power

From my many years of fascinating research and my extensive experience with parents and their babies, I have formulated ten principles which are the very foundation of my Infant Stimulation Program. These basic principles are based on current research in the fields of brain development and psychology. Use them as you interact with and enjoy your child. I am certain they will contribute to your sense of confidence as a parent and to your successful, loving interactions with your baby.

The Ten Principles of Infant Stimulation

1. Your child's environment has the *strongest* impact on his brain during the growth spurt period.

There is a reciprocity between your baby's brain development and his environment. Stimulation or experience during the growth spurt is necessary for maturation of the brain,[1] and maturation of the brain is necessary for baby to process new stimulation or experience. *Use this period of the first year wisely. That's when your baby's brain is growing the fastest that it ever will.*

The more appropriate stimulation you provide during this time, the greater the brain development. The greater the brain development, the more stimulation baby can enjoy. It's as simple as that!

John G. illustrated this point with his new baby, Evelyn. Soon after Evelyn came home from the hospital, John held her on his lap in an easy chair in his living room. It was seven

P.M.—John's normal time to read the newspaper. He established a loving ritual of reading the text to his newborn daughter every evening.

As they spent time together in this simple, affectionate way, John found that Evelyn cooed and gurgled every time he turned the page. He liked the fact that his baby was "talking" when he made those rustling movements, so he read more and longer with her.

When Evelyn was two months old, John reported that she was reaching out to turn the pages herself. John's interaction with his infant had impacted on her visual and auditory senses and had helped to trigger language and motor responses. Their evening play was helping Evelyn to mature so that she could do more of what she wanted to do.

Infant Stimulation has a more profound effect on brain development if it is given during the brain growth spurt period—the months before birth, and the first year of life. That is when babies are said to have *a biological need to learn*.[2]

2. Interaction is more valuable than observation.

John was interacting with Evelyn—not just allowing her to observe him. He held her on his lap and read to her. He was developing a *relationship* with his daughter. With that relationship came *learning*. That is the second principle of Infant Stimulation: *Babies learn more from interaction than from observation*.

This stands to reason, and again, can be easily demonstrated from examples in your own life. Suppose you've always wanted to play tennis. For years you've watched the championship matches on television. You follow Navratilova's backstroke and forehand. You observe her powerful serves and how she smashes the ball overhead. Do you suppose that this is enough to make you a good tennis player?

Of course not! You must get on the court, feel the racket in your hand, sense the speed and the spin of the ball, gauge the distance to your opponent, and learn how to stroke the ball. By watching, you may learn the rules but you won't know how to play. Hands-on experience is what it takes.

Your infant is not very different from you in this respect. He learns from interaction with people and tasks better than from observation alone. In fact, there is a marvelous study involving puppies that illustrates exactly this point.

Two puppies from the same litter were taken at birth and placed in a kitchen. One was put in a large cage, where he was able to move about and watch his surroundings. The other was allowed to roam the kitchen freely. The free pup was taught to sit, shake hands, roll over, beg, and lie down on command. He could even retrieve a ball. All of his education took place within the visual field of his brother, who remained in the cage and watched but was not involved in any interaction.

When the caged pup was a year old he was freed and given the same commands as his brother. He not only did not respond, but he ran right back into the cage, where he felt most secure. So, the commands were tried while he stayed in his cage. The researchers spent two months commanding him to sit, roll over, lie down, but he would do nothing. They concluded that puppies don't learn from observation alone. They need to interact.

If the findings of this study can be applied to people, what would this mean to you and your baby? Simply that: *The* best *way for your child to learn is when you hold him and play with him.* Don't just leave him in his crib or in a playpen with toys.

This issue was brought home to me when I visited Ed and Rochelle R. The couple had invited me for dinner and to observe their three-month-old, Katie. While the infant slept, Rochelle expressed her concerns.

"I had an upsetting incident with my neighbor last week," Rochelle said. "She said that I spend much too much time with Katie. 'Give her time alone to play by herself,' she told me. And she boasted about how her one-year-old, Jessica, plays alone in her crib *for hours*! Am I spending too much time with Katie, Dr. Ludington? I do want to do what's right for her, but I'm not sure...."

My response was immediate, loud, and visceral! "It's far better to play with Katie directly than to leave her alone in her crib for hours! How can she learn if you don't interact with her? You make her toys come alive. A stuffed animal lying next to her does nothing compared to one that you hold. You make it move and give it a voice. Until Katie has the capability for imagination, she will not be able to create that kind of play for herself. And the only way for her to develop her imagination is from *you*, her parents, talking and singing and playing with her."

This parental activity is of the utmost importance. Jessica, at twelve months, might indeed be capable of entertaining herself, but little three-month-old Katie *needs* her mother to engage her in play. Of course, while I'm not suggesting that Rochelle spend every waking minute stimulating her infant, she should establish a balance and rhythm with her child that makes *maximum* use of the time she is available to interact, play, and teach. A child's passive observation simply won't promote learning.

3. Curiosity: Stimulation begets stimulation.

Have you ever enjoyed an ice cream cone and wanted another?

Did you want to go back after the last time you visited Hawaii or Paris?

If so, then you're no different from the rest of us. Once you've had pleasing stimulation, you want some more.

Little Katie R. demonstrated this principle that very same evening. When she awoke after our dinner, Ed placed her in a wind-up swing. The R.'s had ingeniously tied a soft stuffed black-and-white mouse to a support leg of the apparatus. Rochelle showed Katie how to hit the mouse every time the swing came up to it. After a little while the baby started making deliberate, aggressive movements to bat the mouse whenever she approached it. The more stimulation she got, the more she wanted. And this stimulation, which she initiated herself, was very pleasing to her.

Katie's reaching behavior is not unusual. Researchers are finding that infants have reaching behaviors at younger ages than we ever thought possible.[3] We've never given babies the opportunities to reach because we assumed that they were incapable of that kind of activity.

Katie, by her batting action, was demonstrating the value of *active stimulation*. Her interactions with her mother had taught her how to stimulate herself. Passive stimulation occurs when someone else does the stimulating. This is common when your baby is first born. The eventual goal of your Infant Stimulation Program is to provoke your child's curiosity so that she seeks out interesting stimuli herself.

So, as Katie gets older, she will learn about contingencies. She will be able to understand the idea that the action of the mouse is dependent on her batting it, or that the mobile will move if she kicks it and will not move if she doesn't. Everyone likes to have *some* control over the environment, and *contingency play* gives your infant this satisfaction.

With repetition, loving praise, and maturation, your baby will gain a sense of accomplishment in learning to do things for himself. With your involvement and guidance, you will help him to become actively involved in his own stimulation. Although eventually he will be playing by himself, your role as early teacher and guide is tremendously valuable in helping him to develop a sense of curiosity about the world around him.

And you *do* want your baby to be curious. A curious person asks the question, "What if . . . ?" He wants to know more, to dig for new insights and information. A curious person is very bright. The more he knows, the more he wants to know. He is always looking for *new* knowledge.

4. Baby's attentiveness is vital to successful stimulation.

Imagine yourself at the airport. There are myriad things going on around you. Planes roar overhead. Jostling travelers struggle with their luggage, greet relatives, or flop down on a bench for a snooze. The snack bar beckons. Your senses are assaulted by what seems like a thousand stimuli. But you're not paying attention to any of these. Instead, you are directing your full energy to listening to the loudspeaker announcements. You want to be certain that you won't miss your plane. Are they making that last call?

You certainly are alert and awake but you are attending to only one stimulus—the voice on the P.A. system. You discover your flight is still in the final boarding stages. You rush on, find your place, stow your carry-on bag, drop into your seat, and buckle your safety belt just in time to hear the engines wind up. Whew! You're exhausted but finally airborne. When the film comes on, you realize it's one you've already seen. Tired from all of the stimulation your senses have received, and lulled by the repetitiveness of the movie, you drift into sleep.

These different states of attentiveness that you might go through during a stressful day at the airport, while somewhat more dramatic than your everyday routine, serve to illustrate some of the sleep/wake states your infant goes through (see chapters 17 to 19).

There will be times when your baby will not pay attention

to the stimulation you are presenting. If he is crying, either because he needs "shut-out" time (from overstimulation) or because he's in distress, he will not be attentive to you. If he is alert and moving about, his own movements will be very distracting to him—and they are your signal to stop stimulation. If he is drowsy—either from repetition, overstimulation, or sheer exhaustion—he will fall asleep just as you did. Again, your opportunities for stimulating interaction are very limited. In order for your baby to benefit from the enriched environment you will be presenting to him, he needs to be *attentive. Your baby will learn the most when he is paying attention to you.*

Just as you tuned out all of the other input to your brain when you listened for the announcement of your flight, so will your baby tune out the other incoming messages when you present him with appropriate stimuli that catch and hold his attention.

But you must match the appropriate stimulation to your baby's state. He shouldn't be crying, squirming and kicking, or sleepy when you stimulate him. Only when he is alert and still will he be able to achieve attentiveness.

During baby's first months you'll know he's paying attention by physical changes and his very *subtle movements:*

- His head turns toward you or the stimulus.
- His facial expression changes—he may even smile.
- His pupils dilate and his eyes seem to widen. His eyes won't waver from the object of their attention. Your newborn maintains his gaze at a stimulus for from 4 to 10 seconds.
- His fingers and toes stretch forward as if to touch the stimulus.
- His heart rates drops by 6 to 8 beats per minute.
- His breathing becomes slower and more even. He takes 4 to 6 fewer breaths per minute as he pays attention.
- His abdomen relaxes.
- If your baby is on a pacifier, his sucking rate will decrease as well.

This last point is important for you to know. During early nursing experiences, when you and your newborn are learning how to nurse, you shouldn't distract him by talking to him at feeding time. Your voice is far more interesting and distracting to him than the breast, until he's about two weeks old and fully understands what breast feeding is all about. (Of course, there are some little ones who are like barracudas at the breast! They know exactly what it's there for and allow nothing to distract them, even from the beginning!) If your baby is going to attend to something at feeding time, let him concentrate on the task at hand.

Baby devotes all of his energies to paying attention to what you've presented. It's a very calm state; he is really concentrating. You may see your newborn pay attention in very short bursts, lasting for only 4 seconds. With repeated practice and maturation, his attention span will grow to 2 minutes or more.[4]

It's important to remember, though, that not everything an infant sees, hears, and touches necessarily acts as an effective stimulus. The effect of any stimulation is more pronounced if the infant is paying attention *and if the stimulus is age-appropriate*. You will find many suggestions for age-appropriate stimuli throughout the pages of this book, and suggestions on how to use them in the How-to section beginning with Chapter 22.

The longer your baby pays attention to a stimulus, the better the stimulation is for his development. As your infant reaches out for an exciting new toy in his line of sight, new messages about the size, color, shape, sound, feel, and even smell and taste of the object are constantly sent to his brain.

When your infant is attentive, he makes an effort to understand what is happening in his world and to come to grips with it. Then, and only then, is your child ready to learn.

Your newborn "tells" you that he is paying attention when:

- His breathing rate becomes slower and more even.
- His sucking rate slows down.
- His pupils dilate and his eyes widen.
- His abdomen relaxes.
- His head turns toward you or the stimulation.
- His eyes gaze on the stimulation for the length of his attention span (4 to 10 seconds at birth).

- His fingers and toes fan toward you or the stimulation.

Watch for these signs of overstimulation and respect them:

- Your baby may cry and not be consoled by further stimulation.
- His arms and legs flail and his body squirms.
- He splays his fingers and toes and thrusts his tongue or droops his chin.
- His eyes become very wide and he stares fixedly with either a wrinkled brow or a pained expression.
- He becomes drowsy.

---

5. Emphasize repetition rather than habituation.

There is a fine line between useful repetition and habituation. Repetition, in some forms, gives us excellent memories of our childhood. As adults we often look back on repetitious events with nostalgic affection. "Remember how, when we were kids, we used to make popcorn every Friday night before we settled down in front of the TV?" Most of our memories are of repetitious interactions.

You will want to initiate repetitious interactive events with your baby which foster a sense of security and enjoyment. In the first six months, holding your infant in your arms while you rock and sing to him can be wonderful for both of you. Some parents repeat a loving phrase or sing a lullaby at bedtime to soothe their babies. Done over a period of time, this enhances closeness and security.

Claire B., a sensitive, loving mother, developed the habit of tucking her baby son Nathaniel into bed every night with a kiss and the words, "If you need me, I'll be here."

When Nathaniel was three he reached out one night as his mother kissed him good night, hugged her around the neck, and said, "Mommy, if you need me, I'll be here." Those reassuring bedtime words, repeated nightly for three years, were the greatest offering of love that this child could give back to his mother.

Repetition is especially useful when it comes to *learning*.

How else could we master the alphabet, learn to read books or musical scales, understand foreign languages, or memorize the Gettysburg Address? Practice, practice, and more practice.

Think of a piano piece that you might have played as a student. The first hundred attempts were probably hard work, as your fingers stretched to reach the cords and your mind absorbed the pattern, timing, and flow of the music. It seemed as if you'd never get it right.

But then one day, you did get it right. Finally, it was under your control. You could close the book and play from memory. And once you learned the piece, you moved on to a new challenge—a more difficult piece.

When you get *habituated* to something through repetition, it no longer excites your intellect. You need not pay attention to it because it is no longer challenging.

When you use repetition to teach your baby a shape, for instance, you must be sensitive to that fine line that separates repetition from habituation. He must have the repetition in order to learn, but once he habituates to something, he may become bored and tune out. Watch his signs of attention to see that he maintains his interest in the stimulation you are presenting. Once he has habituated, his responses will diminish or may even stop. That is the time for you to stop stimulating. Your activity is no longer useful to him.

Babies learn through repetition. You should repeat a stimulus until habituation occurs; then stop. Stop for the moment, not forever, and allow your baby to store the information he has received. Try the stimulus again. If he is not interested—either because he is tired, has had enough, or is bored with the toy—put the stimulus away and use it again, at a later time. Try a different toy or shape.

6. Your baby's position makes a difference in how much he learns.

Position can mean two things. On the one hand, it refers to the position your child's crib occupies in his room. If you leave his crib in the same place for months on end, he will habituate to the room's having a certain orientation and perspective. Looking through the bars, he will see the windows in a certain way and the closet on the opposite wall as being always the same. He may never be able to see the door through which you enter his room, or his changing table.

When you move the crib to a different position in his room

once a month, he will be afforded a new perspective on his world. He will have more information to learn. And you will help him to avoid developing a crick in his neck (or a flattened head) from always lying on the same side. You can even change his orientation in bed, alternating placing him at the head or foot of the crib at regular intervals.

Once your baby has reached eight or nine months, however, this change in routine might be disconcerting for him. At this point, babies like their routine to be established. They derive a feeling of security from a consistent environment. So, it will be time to stop moving his crib around the room.

Positioning also means where and how your baby is positioned in space when you are actively carrying out Infant Stimulation. Research has shown that people are more apt to daydream when reclining as opposed to being more alert when sitting up,[5] *so make sure that your baby is in the upright position on your lap when you offer stimulation. Straight up is even better than at a 30-degree angle.*

Mother is holding baby in the correct position for stimulation: upright, with arms, legs, and feet flexed.

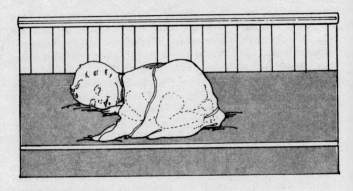

Put your newborn to sleep in the fetal position.

During stimulation sessions that require attentiveness in the *first month of life*, your newborn should be wrapped snugly—but not tightly—in a receiving blanket, with his arms bent at the elbows and legs bent at the knees and hips, as illustrated in the drawing. This flexed or "fetal" position is favored by newborns. It may help to speed the insulation of baby's nerve cells with a myelin sheath, and myelination, as you learned in Chapter 7, may eventually enhance your baby's motor coordination and development.[6] Besides, your new baby is comforted by the touch of his own skin against skin and by the brief, gentle reminder of the secure confinement he experienced in the womb.

Baby should be contained in this fashion, especially during stimulation games, because his arm and leg movements are very distracting to him at that time. Of course, if you are assessing your newborn's interest in a stimulating toy, you may want to leave his hands free to watch his fingers fan toward the item or to reach for it. In general, however, your newborn's arm and leg movements send sensory messages to his brain that compete for his attention. You'll notice that in the illustration, mother also supports baby's feet in a flexed position, with toes pointing up gently.

When you put your new baby down to sleep on his tummy, you will notice that he naturally tucks his legs up under his body and draws his arms close. When on his back, during diapering, your newborn will also pull his knees in toward his abdomen. Simply draw the receiving blanket around his flexed body once you've finished and he will be wrapped snugly in the position I suggest. If baby kicks to stretch his legs, that's fine too.

As baby grows and develops, his body begins to unfurl. By the second and third month, you'll find him scooting around his crib and eventually rolling over. After the first four weeks of life, you'll want to allow his body more freedom of movement.

When your baby is horizontal (lying in his crib, on the floor, or on your bed) his position is also important. Babies need "tummy time." Here's why: Your infant's motor development proceeds from the head on down. This is accomplished when he lies on his abdomen. The developmental progression of baby gaining head control, lifting his head, raising his shoulders, twisting his torso, rolling over, sitting up, crawling, standing, and finally walking, begins with baby on his abdomen. *Make sure that your baby has at least 15 minutes of "tummy time" play every day.*

Putting baby down for a nap on his tummy is a good way to incorporate this position easily. If you leave stimulating pillows, fabric swatches, sheets, a comforter, crib bumpers, stuffed animals (we'll be talking about all of these in great detail in Chapter 11 and in Book II) within baby's view, he'll be motivated to look around and eventually lift his head and reach out for the toy once he awakens.

You can also carry out some of the games in the Infant Stimulation Program we'll be suggesting in Book II with baby on his tummy. The best way to play with your infant while he's in this position is to spread a blanket out on the floor, lay him on it, then get right down on the floor with him. When you are eye to eye with each other, you can show him a mobile or other fascinating object. You may place toys directly in front of him, making sure that they are within his reach. This kind of play also encourages your baby to lift his head and reach in front of him for his toys. And you have the opportunity to make eye contact with him.

Of course, there are times when your baby will be on his back, especially when you are changing his diaper. This is an excellent opportunity for him to bat and kick at a low-hanging black-and-white mobile that is sure to catch his attention. Very often parents use this position to exercise their infant's arms and legs. They play patty cake to gently open and close the arms and "bicycle" to get those little legs moving up and down. These activities promote muscle development.

When you're playing with your newborn on his back, remember not to leave him in that position for sleep. As we have noted, it is better for him to sleep in the flexed position, wrapped in a receiving blanket on his tummy or side. Once he awakens he may try lifting his head, beginning the all-important motor development progression.

During stimulation play, avoid bright lights and harsh, unshaded lamps. For the first two months of life, infants see better in dim lighting, because their eyes can't yet accommodate to brightness or glare. You'll often see babies blinking and squinting when first brought into the sunlight, so be sure to shade your infant's eyes while outdoors. Indoors, and especially in the nursery, use soft light—well-shaded lamps with 25- to 40-watt bulbs. This increases visual alertness so much that your baby will spend 70 percent of the time in alertness under dimly lit conditions compared to going into total shutdown in harsh light.[7]

Your Baby's Position Makes a Difference

- Until 8 or 9 months of age, change the position of your baby's crib in his room once a month.
- Alternate where he sleeps in his bed.
- Hold him upright when stimulating.
- Wrap him in receiving blanket with arms and legs bent in a fetal position.
- Incorporate 15 minutes a day of tummy time play.
- Use back time for exercise and "batting practice."
- Put your baby to sleep on his tummy or side. Alternate positions until you are aware of his preference.
- Avoid bright lights.

7. Understanding baby's lateralization patterns will help him develop.

For the first three months of life your baby's right side is more sensitive than his left. This is true regardless of his eventual right- or left-handedness.

Although scientists do not yet know *why* this occurs, they have documented that newborns will turn to the right more often than they will turn to the left.[8] The right side of the body sends messages to the brain faster than the left and is initially quite sensitive to touch, soft sounds, and visual objects. In fact, your newborn will turn away from objects presented on his left faster than he will from those presented on his right. *To catch your baby's attention, always begin your interaction with him by presenting stimulation on his right side first.*

Begin your stimulating experiences on the right with your baby. You gain his attention by whispering softly into his right ear, stroking the right side of his body with different textures, and showing visual patterns on the right side first. The rationale for this stems from this early right-sided dominance.

Of course, just because your infant's right side is more sensitive, you should not neglect his left side. In fact, because of this difference in sensitivity, he may be unaware that his left side exists. So make sure that whatever you do on the right side you repeat on the left. In that way, your baby's body will develop *bilateralism* or sensitivity on *both* sides.

8. Provide warmth: Babies sense how you feel.

One of the most important bits of advice I give all couples embarking on parenting is: *Babies are emotionally sensitive at birth*.

Though scientific documentation is still lacking, anyone who has spent time with babies will readily admit that infants are sensitive to your moods and feelings. They can sense when you want to play and when you don't. *Don't ever try to deceive your infant*. He will be confused by your double message. And you do want to give as much attention to him as you'd like to receive. So, if you're not really ready to play with your infant, if your heart isn't in it, then wait until you feel more available. You'll do your baby a greater disservice by playing with him when you don't want to than by not playing with him at all for a while.

There are some activities that help provide warmth and foster his feelings of security in your love.

- Position your baby so that he's not precariously situated or held out on the edge of your knee.
- Hold your baby firmly and cuddle him close to your body when you start to play, so he can feel your body warmth and smell your scent.
- Open your heart to your child. Give yourself permission to love your baby. Recognize the feeling of intense warmth and enjoy the privilege of loving your child.

A loving approach is the main ingredient of quality time together.

9. Homeostasis: Use Infant Stimulation to arouse and quiesce.

Homeostasis is a physiological term used to describe a state in which all systems are in balance. You are at ease with yourself. You are not exerting more energy than necessary and you are not experiencing dulled senses. You are in equilibrium.

Your baby also enjoys the state of homeostasis. That is why I advise you to avoid overstimulating him to the point where he is agitated or fatigued, or under-stimulating him so that he is bored. As you play with your baby and interact with his changing moods, you will develop a sensitivity to his states. With trial and error you will discover when he is ready and when he has had enough. Depending on the feedback you get from your newborn, you will find that there are certain things that either cause arousal or drowsiness.

Certain forms of Infant Stimulation can be used to catch your baby's attention. For example, most babies will become *alert* when they hear classical music like violin concertos. And other forms of stimulation, such as rocking, can be used to *quiet* your active baby back into a state of inactivity. *Use the appropriate form of Infant Stimulation that suits your baby's state*.

Many parents use Infant Stimulation techniques to help put their infants to sleep. Babies like monotonous, repetitive movements when they are being lulled. That's why parents walk and pat their babies or gently rock them in rocking chairs or cribs equipped with springs (available at some department stores, such as Montgomery Ward and J. C.

Penney). Often, babies fall asleep in moving cars—I've heard tales of parents taking their babies out for a drive at three A.M. just so that *they* could get some rest. One mother even set her baby up in an infant seat on the running clothes dryer because the vibration and the hum seemed to do the trick. As I said—trial and error will teach you much about your baby's states.

10. Practice the three R's of Infant Stimulation: rhythm, reciprocity, and reinforcement.

The three R's of Infant Stimulation should form the core of your at-home program. They are principles that take into account your baby's learning patterns and emphasize the importance of your relationship with him.

Rhythm

Dr. T. Berry Brazelton, the famous pediatrician at Harvard University, has described a newborn's rhythm of interaction, which occurs in several stages.

INITIATION STAGE: Some event arouses your infant. It could be some external stimulus, like a loud noise, or it could be you calling his name softly. Once he has heard his name, he orients himself toward the stimulus. He turns his eyes, face, head, and eventually his body toward what has caught his attention in an attempt to get closer to it.

ATTENTIVENESS: His eyes widen, his abdomen relaxes, and his fingers and toes stretch toward the stimulation. But as he pays attention, he reaches his limit or capacity for concentration. He will then start to move his arms and legs or squirm about.

ACCELERATION: Body movements speed up. He is no longer paying attention to the stimulus.

PEAK OF EXCITEMENT: Your baby's own movements add so much sensory input that he is entirely distracted from what he was attending to.

WITHDRAWAL: He now has no choice but to withdraw. He may do so by crying, shutting his eyes, or turning his head away.

RECOVERY: It takes your infant 10 to 20 second to recover from the excited state to a quiet, attentive state where he can pay attention once more.[9]

It is important for you to remember that babies don't always go through the rhythm stages in a predictable time sequence. Sometimes the stages are run through so quickly that you won't even notice how your infant moved from a quiet, attentive state to one of withdrawal. Some babies even skip a stage from time to time. Others may stay in one stage for long periods of time. Every baby has his own rhythm.

By six to eight weeks of age, most babies have established their own rhythm. Your baby's rhythm flows like a wave. Once you recognize it, you can act in accordance with it. That leads us to the second of the three R's of Infant Stimulation.

Reciprocity

Carol J. was playing with her infant son, David. Holding David in her left arm in a rocking chair, she called his name softly. "David, this is your mother. How are you, David?" David responded by diverting his gaze to her face and perceptibly turning his head in her direction.

"Oh, David. I see you. You look so lovely," Carol continued. "Are you paying attention to me? Can you see my eyes?"

David's face brightened. Carol recognized his attentive state. She began to add stimulation by stroking his legs, rocking him gently and singing.

Then she noticed that David started to kick.

"I saw that kick," she said. "I know what that's all about. It's time to stop touching, stop rocking, and just talk to you. Oh, dear. This isn't going to work. You've still got too much going on. Yes, I can see it coming. Oh, there it is. There it is. You're crying."

Carol became silent and placed her hand around David's back so that she engulfed him. She held him firmly in place that way until his crying subsided.

Carol was being sensitive to her son's rhythm and was reacting to it. Just as when your baby is hungry, you feed him, so when he's ready to play, you play with him, and when he's ready to rest, you let him. Ideally, you will become so adept at recognizing your baby's signs that he won't have to retreat into the withdrawal stage and cry. You can slowly remove the stimulation, carefully taking one stimulus away at a time. Carol might have stopped touching first, then rocking, and then speaking. Babies like gradual changes or progressions. Abrupt movements frighten them. *You are more adaptable than your baby, so be sensitive to his stages and be reciprocal to them.*

Reinforcement

There are those who believe that praise makes people lazy. I am not among them! From my experience and from research, it is clear that a word of encouragement produces more positive behavior. You can remember that from your school days. One A would motivate you to try for more. And at work, a pat on the back from the boss is almost as valuable as a raise to get you to work harder.

Apply this principle to your Infant Stimulation Program and be liberal with your praise to your baby. You will want to praise (and therefore reinforce) baby's attempts as well as his successes and any activity that you would like him to continue. For example, if your infant makes a gurgle or a coo, you might say, "Oh, my goodness! I heard that. What a wonderful sound. What are you trying to say to me? Can you say that again?" When your baby gets so much positive attention for gurgling, he'll want to try that again. And in this way, you'll encourage him to vocalize and eventually talk early.

There are many reinforcers of behavior. I've found the most potent to be:

- *A Look:* Eye-to-eye and face-to-face.
- *A Word:* Warm praise. The more you use words, the more your baby will "talk" back, acknowledging your words.
- *A Touch:* You only touch people you really care about. Touch is a very strong communicator of feelings.

It is important for you to reinforce (by positive recognition) any attempt that your baby makes to initiate and maintain social interchange.

Make sure that you *smile* at your baby. It is the most rewarding look that he can receive. And babies understand smiles. Just as you wait for his smile, he waits for yours. Remember, you are your baby's reason for living. That's how much your reinforcement and encouragement mean to him.

When we embark on the How-tos of my Infant Stimulation Program, keep the principles of this chapter in mind and refer back to them often. They are the essence of Infant Stimulation.

IV. THE WORLD
THROUGH YOUR
BABY'S SENSES

11. What Does My Baby See?

When your newborn looks at his world:

- He sees clearly within 13 inches from his face.
- He identifies mother by the time he is four days old.
- He can follow appealing objects with his eyes when they are held 10 to 13 inches from his face.
- He can move his eyes from one object to another when they are held 10 to 13 inches from his face.
- He can see and distinguish all colors.
- He looks at the edge of figures for contrast between the shape and background.
- He can discriminate among shapes and choose one of his preference.
- He perceives depth and three-dimensional objects.

Actually, your newborn child sees quite well at the moment of birth. Although his eye cells are not yet capable of adjusting to varying distances, he can see a 3-inch-tall object without fuzziness when it is held 10 to 13 inches from his eyes (about the distance from mother's breast to her face).

In a scientific experiment conducted to determine exactly what images were focused on newborns' retinas, it was discovered that infants actually could see sixteen stripes in a 1-inch square without fuzziness.[1]

In fact, newborns in their first six weeks of life love to look at stripes. Try sitting your newborn on your lap and showing him an 8 × 11 inch piece of white cardboard with five 8-inch-long, 1-inch-wide black stripes running horizontally across it. When his eyes are open, it will be easy for him to see, if you hold it 10 to 13 inches from his eyes. You'll be amazed at how his face brightens as he looks at it. He will try to lift his head and move his eyes directly to the stripes.

Your infant's vision improves rapidly; all parts of his visual system—muscles, lens, retina—quickly become finely tuned. At two months his eyes have matured to the point where they can function together. He is able to see things at the end of his nose. You can hold visual toys 20 inches from his eyes and he'll see them clearly. By three months he will be seeing objects within a distance of 10 feet, indicating that he now has near and far vision.

Fixation

Not only can your baby see clearly at birth, but he can fixate or maintain his gaze intently on an object. His eyes will seem to widen and his pupils will dilate when he does so.

At first, baby's fixation or attention span varies from 4 to 10 seconds. When his interest wanes, he closes his eyes or shifts his gaze aimlessly.

The repeated sight of *appropriate* objects, however, will help increase your baby's attention span. Many parents have reported that their new-born's attention span increased from 10 seconds to 60 to 90 seconds *after only one week of looking at black-and-white checkerboards for about 3 minutes a day!*

Because of this, fixation helps learning! If your baby fixates on one object, the information about that object gets through to the cortex—the deepest part of the brain—which means that there is an intact pathway for stimulating the brain's growth.

Tracking

Babies are said to be "tracking" when they try to follow appealing objects with their eyes. The more appealing the object, the more intense and prolonged the tracking. In the first two months of life tracking is difficult, but not impossible. When you use high-contrast designs, like black-and-white bull's-eyes that move slowly across your baby's visual field, he will be able to track with more ease because of his interest in the stimulator.

Tracking helps your baby to learn where an object is in space and how it differs from its background so that he can reach for it. He discovers that objects have permanence by seeing that they move, yet remain the same.

Scanning

Show your child several different objects (like a pink ball, a white rattle, and a black dot 3 inches in a diameter, drawn on a white background). Watch closely as he lets you know which one he prefers by choosing that one to fixate on. Before making the choice, you'll notice that he moves his eyes from one to the other in a series of little jumps. He is "scanning" his choices.

When your baby scans, he learns how to see and compare *entire* objects. This ability eventually helps him to distinguish all the objects in his environment.

Some babies scan by moving their heads, others by moving their eyes only. Once baby picks an item, he fixates on it. He has chosen.

You may find that your baby is slow to see. It takes many babies a bit of time to realize there's something to look at. Try to leave the object that you want your newborn to focus on within his view for at least 30 seconds—long enough for his eyes to follow and come upon it.

As your infant searches out objects, his eyes may appear sensitive to bright light. Bright sunlight forces him to squint and blink. Actually, for the first three months of life he sees better when facing away from a window and in a slightly darkened room.

What Your Infant Enjoys Looking At

How do we know what newborns and infants like to look at? Certainly they can't express their preferences in words. They have, however, indicated preferences very strongly! In scientific experiments their *choices* have told the story.

It's as Simple as Black and White

While studying the scientific literature about newborns' vision, I was fascinated to learn that researchers have used black-and-white geometric shapes in many investigations of what newborns *like* to look at. I never would have guessed that the combination could be even slightly appealing to infants.

Would you have believed that newborns really *prefer* to look at black and white, rather than at bright colors or pastels? Research repeatedly has shown this to be true.

In the early 1960's, Dr. Robert Fantz, a developmental psychologist at Case Western Reserve University in Cleveland, Ohio, who believed that babies under two years of age could see well, designed a "peep box" that surrounded a baby sitting in an infant seat. He placed two objects directly in the baby's view: a patterned black-and-white checkerboard and a plain gray card. Undetected, Dr. Fantz watched the baby through a little peephole and was able to determine that babies preferred the checkerboard to the non-patterned surface. Their eyes traveled consistently to the checkerboard.[2]

Once this was known, other studies followed in rapid succession. Dr. T.G.R. Bower, the behavioral scientist at the University of Edinburgh well known for his studies in infant development, showed infants several different black-and-white shapes, as well as plain white, red, and yellow cards. Again, babies chose to look at the black-and-white items.[3]

Dr. Phillip Salapatek, a child psychologist at the University of Minnesota, Minneapolis, designed an elaborate electronic tracking device to follow an infant's gaze. He learned that infants move their eyes to the edge of a black triangle on a white background rather than looking at the center of the blackness or whiteness. It was then understood that babies' eyes seek the border because it is there that the contrast between black and white is the greatest.[4]

You may ask, "If this is so, then why does my baby look at a bright red ball of yarn or pretty pastel print crib sheets?" Of course, he can see the ball of yarn or sheets, and if there is nothing *else* for him to look at, he will look at whatever you show him. But things change dramatically when babies are offered choices! *Colors that provide the most contrast are the most appealing to babies. Black and white, of course, afford the greatest contrast.*

What's so terrific about contrast? It has to do with the development of your newborn's eyes. The rods and the cones—structures of the retina that perceive color—have not matured enough for him to perceive the values and intensities of red, blue, pink, yellow, purple, and green. Black and white are the easiest for him to perceive and his interest in these starkly contrasting colors continues until he is six to nine months old.

Mobile-izing the Resources

At the same time that I was investigating what infants like to look at, I was teaching a parent education class at Kaiser Permanente Hospital in San Francisco. I decided to check out local toy stores for the availability of appropriate black-and-white playthings and room decorations for infants. As you might have guessed, I found absolutely nothing worthy of recommendation to the parents in my classes. Bears, bunnies, and butterflies seemed to be the toy makers' total repertoire, and in pastel or calico print, at that!

After consulting Dr. Barry Chehrazi, now a neurosurgeon at the University of California at Davis, I devised a mobile for newborns that incorporated all the features researchers had shown were important for visual stimulation: black and white for contrast; checkerboard for pattern; cross for geometric shape; and a simple motor to control the mobile's movement.

I used this mobile in a study to determine how fast newborns could learn to manipulate their environment. As you can see from the sketch, I attached a string from the mobile to the infant's toe. The baby's kick tugged the string which, in turn, activated the motor, producing a one-quarter turn of the mobile. During 20 minutes of this kind of activity, the babies' kicking rates increased an *astounding 200 percent*.

The newborns in my study were learning what power they had to affect their environment. Their actions actually made a difference! This sense of power can affect ego development and contribute to a child's sense of self-worth and well-being, apart from the tracking and fixation practice such a device affords.

In truth, babies love this *contingency play*. At the age of three days, the newborns in my study were already smiling because they understood that they were not helpless, hopeless creatures. Dr. Lewis Lipsett of Brown University suggests that babies engage in this sort of activity simply because they derive pleasure from it. This fascinating study in stimulating and pleasing newborns was later *repeated* by other scientists and reported on Walter Cronkite's "From Cradle to Crib," a 1973 television special.[5]

After completing modifications on my original motorized mobile, I was ready to introduce my newly developed model (sans motor and kick-activated switch) to the parents in my classes. Not surprisingly, the strange new device caused a stir of amusement and disbelief in my classroom.

"Come now," said Mrs. P., who happened to have brought her two-week-old son Nelson to class. "No way would Nelson

Dr. Ludington-Hoe's experiment in pleasing babies. As the newborn kicked, the motorized mobile turned.

be able to distinguish those colors and shapes, let alone *create* the action to stimulate the mobile's movement."

Then one of the fathers, Mr. A., added what he knew to be an incontrovertible fact: "Babies can't see anything until they're two months old!"

"Actually," I said, "newborn vision studies were only started seven or eight years ago and they challenge our former beliefs about what babies can and cannot see. But if you're willing to let Nelson participate, Mrs. P., we can have an on-site demonstration here and now."

Nelson was propped comfortably on his mother's lap. I asked her to sit him upright and as he opened his eyes, I brought the mobile within approximately 10 inches of his nose. His face brightened and his eyes widened noticeably as they stayed riveted to the mobile. When I moved it very slowly from his right side to his left, his head and his eyes followed. This baby was fascinated by the stimulus I had shown him! Then I knew, beyond a doubt, that this, along with other simple, yet well-conceived toys and activities,

The black-and-white mobile for home use incorporates geometric designs and high-contrast colors.

could have a dynamic, positive effect on stimulating infant growth and development.

When my Infant Stimulation Program was featured on the "Today Show" in 1983, I experienced tremendous gratification in having my work recognized and validated. For the taping, I showed two different mobiles to babies: the standard multicolored butterfly variety, and the black-and-white geometric solids that I had designed. Not only did all but one baby choose to look at the toy that incorporated the checkerboard pattern, three-dimensional shapes and high contrast black and white, but many also reached for it and even tried batting at it.

The new parents in my class and on the "Today Show," as well as parents and professionals in all subsequent child development classes and seminars I have given around the world, discovered a new world to share with their infants when I made them aware of newborn preferences and capabilities. Now I would like you to share that excitement too.

Visual Stimulators to Make or Buy

Your mere presence provides many stimulators. Others are simple and fun to find or create. You will want to remember these suggestions when you buy toys for your newborn. Teddy bears, for instance, while the perennial favorites of toddlers, are not the best visual stimulators for infants. A black-and-white panda bear would be much more appropriate. A panda puppet is even better: When you animate the puppet and add your own voice, it comes alive with sound and movement for your infant and has a design that incorporates high contrast. What could be easier or more delightful?

If you check out toy stores, the way I did, you will see that most toys offered for sale do not appeal to newborn preferences. If the instructions direct you to place a mobile on the edge of a crib rail, it will be much too far away for your infant to see very well. How can he reach for or kick it if it is so high above him?

Choose or make a mobile like the one pictured. (It's available from Bright Baby Toys. For the address, see the Resource Guide in Chapter 33. Or, if you're adept at crocheting or knitting, you can devise your own.) Your baby's mobile should have both two- and three-dimensional geometric shapes to encourage your child to look at it and grab hold of it as well. (In fact, three-week-old newborns prefer three-dimensional shapes such as cylinders, pyramids, and cubes.) Be certain that the toy can be hung *safely* (avoid any long cord in which the baby could become entangled) within your child's reach and that the key elements are facedown, so that they are in full view.

Parents often ask me if they should decorate the nursery in black-and-white checkerboard fabric and wallpaper. Heavens, no! Too much of a good thing is not necessarily better! Even though these elements are stimulating for your infant, they will probably drive *you* to distraction if you look at them for long periods of time. Besides, your infant's preferences are changing so quickly during those crucial first six months that what he finds stimulating the first week would be a bore by his second or certainly his third month. You don't want to redecorate every two weeks!

Instead, consider making liberal use of posters and cardboard flash cards. Newborns find these patterns appealing:

- black-and-white stripes (3 by 2 inches)
- a 4-square black-and-white checkerboard (each square measuring 3 by 3 inches)
- a 3-inch white dot on a black background.

These are easy to draw (using a ruler, compass, and non-toxic black marker) on paper plates or white 8 × 11 pieces of cardboard.

Deborah Brateman, the former head nurse of the Neonatal Intensive Care Nursery at Walter Reed Hospital in Washington, D.C., reported to me that the flash cards incorporating the black-and-white patterns I suggest increase the amount of time babies spend looking at their environment from an average of 4 to 5 minutes to up to 45 minutes after being fed. (In subsequent chapters I'll explain just how to use them.)

Swatches of black-and-white checkerboard, houndstooth, and polka-dot cloth hung on the side of the crib at baby's eye level also make fine stimulators. Best of all, these are not permanent fixtures, so mixing, matching, and changing combinations are limitless.

Sally Brown, an enterprising staff nurse, after hearing my lecture on Infant Stimulation, put the appealing two-dimensional

Baby is fascinated by his "crib checks"—stimulating sheet, crib bumper, and Pillow Pal™.

shapes together in a black and white poster and placed it in the Intensive Care Nursery of Fairfax Hospital in Falls Church, Virginia, in 1981. From this we learned that even premature babies stared at black-and-white bull's-eyes, checkerboards, and stripes.[6] Mothers have been so enthusiastic about their newborn's response to the poster that we've been flooded with thousands of requests for it!

Why not make a black-and-white checkerboard or gingham sheet and crib bumper? They are sure to engage your infant's mind and senses, with very little effort on your part. During the first two months of life, simply make the crib up with these "crib checks" *every other day* (on alternating days he should have a rest with a plain sheet). On black-and-white days, he can spend his waking (and sleeping) hours on the sheet or next to the bumper whenever you lay him down.

Of all the geometric designs and shapes, babies seem most captivated by circles. It is much easier for the newborn eye to make a series of jumps around a circle's edge than to navigate around corners. Add to that the importance of dark and light contrast, and you can understand the appeal for an infant of a mother's dark nipple on a lighter breast. (Even for non-Caucasian women, the skin pigment of the nipple darkens appreciably during pregnancy, helping to provide contrast.) Mother's nipple is the first circle that your newborn will gaze upon as he nurses after birth.

The *Eyes* Have It

Many people are astounded by infants' preference for eyes. But that's perfectly natural. Not only do eyes offer light/dark contrast, but they move in every direction and even enlarge and reduce as the pupil widens and closes. At a very young age your infant will seek out your eyes. Help him practice by initiating eye-to-eye contact in the very first weeks of life.

About *Faces*

What do you think your baby would *most* like to look at? Even more than the patterns I've been discussing? The pattern he finds interesting, above *all* others, is—a human face. *Yours!* And when it's animated in song or talking, he thinks it's just the greatest. Of course, you can't station yourself by your infant's crib all day long in order to provide him with your face, but you can hang a simple black-and-white drawing of your features on a paper plate on the crib rail (see illustration). If daddy has a mustache or beard, make sure to include them in the drawing.

Don't draw the face with unhappy or misplaced features, as infants know the difference between proper and scrambled

Make simple but accurate drawings of mother's and father's faces on paper plates to hang in baby's crib.

countenances. They look longer and more intently at happy, "normal" drawings.

By the time your newborn is one month old, he'll be able to appreciate your smiling faces on an 8 × 10 black-and-white glossy photo. (At six months he'll love to look at a color picture of you.)

Complexity and Your Baby's Changing Visual Preferences

Increasing complexity of design is the key to your baby's changing preferences. Try a little experiment. Stare at your blank white ceiling. How long did it hold your attention? If there happen to be cracks in the plaster or fancily carved moldings, I imagine you had a little more to look at than plain white flatness. Nevertheless, every time I try this experiment with my nursing students or the parents attending Infant Stimulation classes, I find that 15 seconds is the maximum time people can tolerate this bland stimulation before turning away in boredom.

Now, I'd like you to try a different experiment. Look at a picture on the wall of your home that you find particularly pleasing. Note the time you start and stop examining the artwork. Assume it will be longer than the seconds you spent staring at the blank ceiling. Later in the day, come back to look at the same picture. Again, note your starting and stopping times. Do this two more times that same day.

I'll be willing to bet that the more often you look at the picture, the shorter each looking session becomes. Why? Because no new elements are added. It does not change or increase in complexity, so eventually you learn everything that you can learn about it and are ready to move on to a new challenge.

Your baby's mind works the same way yours does. When he repeatedly sees an object that interests him, his fascination will eventually fade unless something different catches his attention. *With infants, one of the best ways to increase interest is to increase complexity.*

We know that in the first six months of life infants love to look at stripes, checkerboards, bull's-eyes, and squares. But the size and complexity of these designs will have to change with time in order to keep your baby's attention.

As your newborn matures, the size of the checkerboard squares that you make for him to look at, for instance, should get smaller. They should change from 3 by 3 inches at birth to 2 by 2 inches at six to eight weeks of age. Instead of 4 squares to look at, your two-month-old should have 6 to 8 squares or elements that contrast light with dark—better suited to his growth, development, and interest.

This point was reinforced by an experience I had at Fairfax Hospital in Falls Church, Virginia. I was asked to consult with the nursing staff about a baby who had been quite sick at birth and who had remained in the hospital until he was three months old.

The staff of the nursery was proud that they had been working with black-and-white shapes. The nurses found them very popular with the newborns under their care, but they were very concerned with little Baby B., as they called him. Although he was much healthier than at birth, he was not alert and would not gaze at the stimulation the nurses were presenting to him.

The head nurse asked me if I could find a way to help. I picked Baby B. up out of his crib and I held him in an upright position on my lap. As soon as he opened his eyes, I placed the 2- by 2-inch black-and-white checkerboard that the nurses had been using in front of the infant. He gazed at it for 1½ seconds before closing his eyes. When he opened them again, the checkerboard was still in place, so he closed his eyes and turned his head to the right. Then he turned back, saw that nothing had changed, closed his eyes and turned his head to the right.

"It appears," I said to the head nurse, "that this baby doesn't like black-and-white checkerboards. Do you have anything else? Circles, bull's-eyes, faces maybe?"

"No, we don't," she replied. "But we do have some black-and-white houndstooth check cloth. It's very complicated, though, one-half-inch by one-half-inch."

She brought it over from another baby and we tried it on Baby B. The difference in response was remarkable. He opened his eyes, tilted his head back as if to look. His face brightened up as he began to gaze intently at the houndstooth design. He tracked it to the right and left, up and down. In fact, he followed it for a full 40 seconds before closing his eyes. We realized that Baby B. had been bored with the simple checkerboard.

Then we tried something else: a sample of fabric with tiny cartoon characters on a blue background. Baby B. wouldn't look at that at all. So we brought back the houndstooth cloth. He alerted to it as if it were new and looked at it for an additional 12 seconds.

This experience brings up a second aspect of complexity. While you want to make sure that the pattern you are showing is complex enough for your infant's capabilities and interest level, take care *not to show him something that's too complex or busy for him to understand*. When there are too many elements for your infant to concentrate on, he becomes overloaded. You can determine this because he will simply stop concentrating. He will either cry, move about, fall asleep, or just ignore it.

The issue here is not only one of balance (that is, not too much complexity or too little) but also one of increments. Your infant will need to start with simple designs and work up to more complicated ones in order to get the full benefit from his Infant Stimulation Program. So, as your infant's capabilities and preferences mature you'll want to add more and more complex stimuli. At the same time, you will be removing those that no longer seem of interest.

The Resource Guide in Chapter 33 lists a wealth of toys and tools that appeal to your baby's sense of sight. In Book II we will tell you exactly how to incorporate visual toys of gradually increasing complexity in a step-by-step program that is both pleasing and appropriately challenging to your baby.

12. What Does My Baby Taste?

Babies need to spend many hours a day satisfying their strong sucking reflex. In the first six months of life, infants who are able to satisfy their needs with unlimited sucking may be less likely to become thumb suckers in later years. So help your child find and suck on his fingers. Even hold his hand, so that while sucking, his fingers won't fall out of his mouth. Pacifiers help satisfy this important need, and contrary to popular belief, will not cause your child to have crooked permanent teeth.

Sucking may have additional significance. When babies put their fingers into their mouths, they produce saliva. The normal newborn's saliva contains nerve growth factor, a substance that helps heal wounded tissues, and in experimental mice, helps nerves grow. It is interesting that the human newborn swallows some of his saliva and that the nerve growth factor can then be digested and circulated through the blood to the nerves and the rapidly developing brain. Although the effect of the nerve growth factor on human nerve development has not yet been established, it is possible that it works in humans just as it does in mice. The effect of nerve growth factor on the body's central nerves (spinal column and brain) is still unknown.

Baby Tastes Everything

You may be surprised to learn that your baby has preferences in foods. Actually, his sense of taste is as keenly developed as yours. Since he can differentiate between sweet, sour, and bitter, there is an interesting physiological explanation for infants' tolerance of bitter-tasting food, such as breast milk and pablum.

"Bitter receptors" are located at the back of the tongue. When a baby is breast- or bottle-fed, the milk bypasses the sweet receptors at the tip of the tongue, shooting up to the palate and down onto the bitter receptors at the rear. Since only those receptors are stimulated, your baby will be quite content with bitter-tasting pablum or baby cereal. Some stimulation is better than none.

All of this is fine and good until, one day, your baby discovers something sweet—usually when spoon feeding starts. Food is placed on the tip of the tongue where the sweet receptors are located and then passed over the bitter and sour receptors farther back. The look first of surprise, then perplexity, and finally pleasure on your baby's face when you offer something other than breast milk or cereal, is a tip that, given the opportunity to differentiate between tastes, babies will prefer sweetness.[1]

Even though babies like sweet tastes, in the first six months of life they really do not require too many. Actually, the most satisfying taste to a newborn is breast milk. It provides all the nutrition and taste stimulation an infant needs for normal growth, including a substance called *taurine*, which promotes brain and nerve development. If your infant is taking a commercially-prepared formula rather than breast milk, make sure that it, too, contains taurine. Some do not.

The Exquisite Pleasures of Breast-feeding

One of nature's major contributions toward cementing mother/child bonds is breast-feeding. Nursing can and should be a time of great warmth and closeness. During feeding, an infant's senses are stimulated by a multitude of pleasures: he smells and tastes your milk, smells your body odor, feels your arm around him, touches your breast, looks into your face, your eyes, at your nipple, and often is being gently rocked in the rocking chair while experiencing these exquisite pleasures.

In fact, the nurturance that occurs during breast-feeding is so powerful that this activity has been correlated with later intellectual attainment. In one study that compared 1,291 breast-fed babies with 1,133 bottle-fed babies, the former scored significantly higher on picture intelligence and reading tests at eight years of age.[2]

But, whether breast-feeding or bottle-feeding more closely suits your baby's needs, be certain that *feeding time is always one of great warmth and nurturance*.

Never feed your baby in a hasty "I really am late for my appointment" manner. *Never, ever* prop your baby's bottle for him to manage alone. To do either would be robbing him of far too many sources of pleasure and stimulation.

Other Tastes?

If you feel a variety of tastes—other than breast milk or formula—would be in order, simply dab a cotton-tipped swab into a sweet juice, such as cherry or apple, and place it on the tip of your baby's tongue. Some experts would argue that if there is no *need* for variety, it is unwise to stretch for an early introduction of sweets. Some don't have strong feelings in this area, one way or another. I leave the choice of sweet to you.

But the experts do agree on salt. Babies don't need it! In recent years we have found an alarming rise in high blood pressure problems in young children that can be attributed to salt intake at an early age. Even though you might feel salt makes food more interesting, it should be avoided in your baby's food. It won't be missed and might well be harmful!

13. What Does My Baby Hear?

Your Newborn Can:

AT BIRTH   Discriminate loudness, pitch, and tone
                Pick up whispers
                Tune out monotonous sounds
                Localize sound by turning head to right or left
12 HOURS   Differentiate speech from non-speech sounds
                Coordinate subtle arm movements to speech
1 WEEK   Recognize his own name
                Recognize mother's and father's voices

Listen to a woman's voice as she approaches a baby. Do you notice a rise in *pitch* of an octave or two when she starts talking? This is one very effective way in which women unconsciously make themselves more desirable to baby—a lesson daddies should remember too.

Now, try to remember when you did something wonderful as a child and you heard your mother's pleased *tone* as she smiled and said, "Susan!"

It was a joy to hear your name.

Next, think back to the time you found that your mother's lipstick was great for coloring your sister's face. You heard the same word, "Susan!" from the same mother, but somehow the tone wasn't quite the same. Yet you got the message each time.

Tone and Pitch

In his first two months of life, your baby is extremely sensitive to both vocal tone and pitch. He prefers happy and soprano sounds to those that are angry and bass.[1] Monotone is boring to adults *and* babies alike. Monotone can be avoided if you E-X-A-G-G-E-R-A-T-E your words and ask lots of questions.

When phrasing questions, your voice automatically goes up in pitch, and a question elicits a response. Eventually your baby will meet this expectation and make gurgling sounds each time you ask questions. This is the beginning of communication.

Isn't it true for all of us that statements control, while questions encourage participation? So it is with your newborn. Keeping these two thoughts (exaggeration and questioning) in mind, you will notice your baby will not only be a happier listener but will be able to imitate sounds beginning around six weeks rather than the usual four to five months of age. He's had more exposure to the sounds and really wants to imitate them.

Loudness

Rock and roll bands play at a *loudness* of 110 to 115 decibels, and you know how ear-splitting *that* can be! Normal human speech is carried on at a loudness of 60 to 65 decibels. Your newborn can hear you whispering at just 30 to 35 decibels. Studies have shown that a baby's brain responds to such very soft sounds that there's never a need to shout at a baby. In fact, shrill, loud, and high-pitched sounds can startle and irritate your baby, so maintain a moderate sound range to keep him comfortable.

Localization

Babies are so interested in what they hear that they try to find the source of the stimulation. As your child gains control of his head movements, he will become increasingly proficient at locating where the sound comes from, a process called localization.

A. *Newborn awakens from sleep.*

B. *At three to four months, baby's head turns 45 degrees.*

C. *From four to seven months, baby can localize sounds to his side.*

As baby gets older, he gains control of his head and neck muscles and turns to locate sound.

The drawing here illustrates this point. It charts a baby's head movement in various directions as baby tries to find the bell. Speak to your baby face to face in the first month of life. Each month thereafter, you may occasionally move farther and farther away, even out of sight, temporarily, to help train head movements and sound localizations.[2] But for *most* of your communication, it is important to remain face to face. Watching you as you talk, your baby will become aware of the movements and facial expressions that accompany your speech and, in a subtle manner, convey meaning.

In fact, it has been found that babies will move their arms ever so slightly at a rate matching the speed and emphasis in the speech they are hearing. These movements seem to play an important role, indicating an infant's understanding of a verbal and non-verbal message.[3] They help babies internalize the rhythm, cadence, and intensity of speech, and may lead to earlier comprehension, much as tracing letters with fingers helps a child learn the ABC's.

Talking to Your Baby

In his first six months of life, your baby learns to differentiate language sounds from non-speech sounds (which include music, heartbeats, bells, and rattles).

Researchers have investigated whether or not it promotes language development for parents to talk to babies. One such study was begun in 1969. The investigators wanted to measure the impact that mothers' talking to their babies has on their infants' development. They evaluated several components of maternal speech, such as how much time was spent in conversation with baby, how many questions did mother ask, how many explaining or teaching statements did she make.

After observing the interactions, the researchers were able to divide the mothers into two groups: high talkers and low talkers. In the group of mothers who spent a lot of time talking (high talkers) to their infants and asking a lot of questions such as, "Are you wet again?" "Do you want to eat now?" the babies were making sounds or vocalizing to the mothers in response to mothers' speech as early as three months of age.

Twelve years later, the research team re-evaluated the children in the initial study and reported its findings. Those who were in the high talkers group showed improved mental performance! It is possible to take exception to these results, since many factors could have taken place during the twelve-year interval, but it is a fascinating study, nonetheless.[4]

One reason why the high-talker babies might have begun verbalizing earlier may be linked to some astonishing new findings, confirming that infants are born with the ability to identify and reproduce 47 different *phonemes* (sounds that help establish meaning in words).[5] If you, early on, expose your child to these sounds with your talking, he'll retain the ability to reproduce them. If you don't he will forget them as he matures.

The Right Ear Is the *Right Ear*

As you start talking to your newborn, remember that for the first three months of life his right ear is slightly more sensitive than his left. As we noted earlier, the right ear quickly sends messages (and especially speech sounds) to the left side of the brain,[6] the side that controls thinking, analyzing, and reasoning ability.

Start speaking to your baby by whispering in his *right* ear. It will catch his attention, even when there are loud sounds all around him. And *what* you say is as important as the tone and pitch you use.

Set the Stage with a *Setting Event*

Set the stage for interactions with your baby by starting each communication you whisper in his ear with *the same two or three loving phrases*—what I like to call a "setting event." *Repeat the setting event every time you interact with your baby.*

For example, if your baby's name is Mary, you might start your play time interactions with:

"Mary, this is your daddy speaking.

"I love you, Mary.

"You're such a good baby."

It is important for your newborn to become accustomed to these initial phrases so that she or he can learn to expect the pleasing play that will follow. The auditory setting event is especially valuable since your child learns to identify you, his mother and father, in the first week of life.[7]

Within two weeks of your repeating these words, your baby will associate them with the fact that his mother or father is going to talk to him. Frequent use of your baby's *name* will speed his recognition of his name and prepare him for the interaction to come. Studies show that when a baby recognizes his name, he will pay closer attention and often responds by turning his head and vocalizing.[8]

Gerry Page, Director of Perinatal Nursing at St. Joseph's Hospital in Marshfield, Wisconsin, took my advice for using a setting event with mothers and fathers of premature newborns, after attending one of my Infant Stimulation conferences in 1983. He taught parents to use a setting event each time they visited and held their premies. He also found that parents' prerecorded setting events worked wonderfully for the nursing staff, who used the tapes to calm the babies and help them to anticipate interactions in their parents' absence.

The mothers and fathers at St. Joseph's said, "Our baby recognizes us in no time at all! Every time we talk to him, he moves his head and alerts to our voices." The program was reported by the *New York Times* and the Gannett News Service. It was so successful that the American Hospital Association sent a bulletin to all of its member hospitals, telling them how easy and effective a program it is to use.

In the first few weeks of your baby's life, it is important to use the same words every time you begin speaking to him. This enables him to expect consistent types of interactions, which helps him to establish a sense of trust in his world.

Baby Talk

The first words your baby will imitate are simple *real* words. They are known as baby talk words, such as *to, go, ma, my, me, do, pa*, and *no*—one-consonant, one-vowel words. Use baby talk words when you talk with your child, especially names of common or familiar objects. The most familiar objects to your baby are—you guessed it—his parents. That's why his first words are often "mama" and "dada."

When your infant makes a sound—any sound—respond with more and different sounds. For example, if he says "Ugh," your response can be, "Oh, I heard that! What are you trying to say to me? Can you say maaaamaaa?"

Talking to Your Baby

- **Set the stage with repeated loving phrases (setting event).**
- **Whisper in his right ear.**
- **Call his name frequently.**
- **Talk face to face initially, making eye contact.**
  - *Use:*
  - ° **Simplified vocabulary**
  - ° **High pitched melodic voice**
  - ° **Exaggerated intonation**
  - ° **Phonetic pronunciation**
  - ° **Short, simple sentences**

° **Lots of questions**
° **Many one-syllable, one-consonant words**
• **Steadily increase time spent talking with baby.**
• **Respond to vocalizations that baby makes.**

After this initial response, show your baby an object like a ball and say slowly and phonetically, "Can you see the ball? Ball. Ball. Mama is holding the ball. Dotty, you can see the ball, can't you?" Don't worry about repeating yourself. Babies under two months of age may not locate and look intently at the ball until you have repeated the sentence several times or more.

Many fathers enjoy talking to their babies as they read a newspaper. Sitting with the newborn in your lap, slowly and with great expression and exaggeration read the headlines aloud, turning the pages frequently. As early as six weeks after starting this practice, most fathers note that every time they read a headline, the baby will coo and gurgle.

If Music Be the Food of Love...

Of all the non-speech sounds, music is by far the most powerful. It has been shown to stimulate the brain's right side (fostering creativity) and actually help babies gain more weight and cry less. The latest research has found that it even helps babies develop motor coordination![9]

Babies seem to have a very positive response to classical music in particular. They find it enormously soothing, whereas rock music may be very agitating (it causes some babies to flail about and cry). I often recommend what I call the "Baby B's": Bach, Beethoven, and Brahms. Violins concertos are especially appealing because of the treble sound of the violins.

You will know if your newborn enjoys the music because he'll quiet down, open his eyes, turn toward the source of the sound, flex his fingers, and cuddle into you. Some babies even move in time to the music, kicking their arms and legs. They stop when the melody is turned off! They truly have got *rhythm*.

Bach's *Preludes* and Brahms's *Lullaby* have proven so effective in calming babies that they are now being played in the nurseries at Children's Hospital of Los Angeles and a major hospital in the San Fernando Valley, to help regularize babies when heartbeats become unstable.

Ever wonder why lullabies have remained popular for newborns in every culture? It is because the music has rushes and pauses, varies from loud to soft and from high-to low-pitched sounds. Singing to your baby combines two pleasures: your voice and music. Hum a lullaby that you will enjoy humming over and over again, not necessarily on key or in tune, but just whenever you feel so inclined, which I hope will be often.

Dr. Leon Thurman, instructor of Vocal Music Education at McPhail Center for the Arts at the University of Minnesota, Minneapolis, and Ann Langness, Chair of Child Voice Education at the Richards Institute of Music Education, have developed a prepackaged set of taped songs for fetuses and newborns. These *Heartsongs* have been designed to both calm and arouse babies and even to encourage them to move in time to the music. (See the list of tapes and programs available to parents in Appendix 2.)

Getting to the *Heart* of the Matter

Dr. Lee Salk, the well-known pediatrician, discovered that the heartbeat is a powerful stimulus. While vacationing in Europe, he noticed that all of the paintings of the Madonna and Child he saw depicted the Holy Child on the Virgin Mary's *left* side.

When he returned to the States, he observed the Madonna and Child scene repeated by the majority of women in his waiting room. They, too, snuggled their babies on their left side. He decided to investigate the phenomenon, and after numerous studies, concluded that the reason mothers intuitively placed their babies on the left side of their chest was because the infants are soothed and quieted by their mothers' familiar heartbeat sound.[10]

We now know that babies respond to the heartbeat sound because it is a familiar reminder of their life inside the womb (See Chapter 3). This sound puts many babies to sleep, perhaps because it is so reassuring. Although recordings of heartbeat sounds are available on records and tapes and in toys, it is advisable to tape-record your own heartbeat sound, as this is the rhythm your baby became accustomed to throughout pregnancy and each time you snuggled him on your chest during infancy.

It is easy to make such a recording. Take a tape recorder on your next prenatal or post-partum visit to your maternity health practitioner. Ask to use the doptone, or dopler, a device which amplifies the fetal heartbeat so that everyone in the room can hear it. But this time, instead of placing it on your abdomen, have the practitioner place it over *your* heart. Simply record your own amplified heartbeat.

What Your Baby Likes to Hear

Your voice
His name
Questions
Simple words of familiar items
Baby talk
Humming
Lullabies
Bach, Beethoven, and Brahms
Rattles
Crumpling paper
Bells
Laughter
Heartbeat
Imitations of his own sounds

14. The Power of Touch

I always have been fascinated by the power of touch and its predominance in early parent-child relationships. The first thing most parents want to do after the birth of their baby is to cuddle the new infant in their arms. For my doctoral dissertation at Texas Women's University in Denton, Texas, I constructed a study to determine if touch actually had some effect on growth and development.

We saw to it that 120 babies were given about an hour and forty minutes of *extra* skin-to-skin stroking over the first three days of life. I was delighted to learn that the extra touch helped those babies gain weight faster and perform motor movements earlier than expected.[1]

I was so attracted by the power of touch that I continued my investigations further in post-doctoral research at Baylor University. I was especially curious about why babies who were stroked more lost less of their birth weight than those who were not stroked. A simple measure of the infants' blood sugar level showed that stroked babies had more of a derivative of sugar called *glycogen*, a chemical that plays an important role in providing baby with energy and allowing him to gain weight.

How complex we human beings are! It's a miracle that stimulating your baby's sense of touch with gentle, rhythmic stroking definitely can enhance his digestive functioning and growth.[2]

Baby Feels Everything

As with the other senses we have discussed, your newborn's sense of touch is so keen that he feels everything you feel and can differentiate between warmth/coolness, softness/firmness, rough/smooth, flat/ridged, sticky/slippery, and even wind and pressure.

Your Newborn Baby Is Capable of Feeling Everything

- Wind
- Pressure
- Warmth
- Coolness
- Softness
- Firmness
- Flatness
- Ridges
- Roughness
- Smoothness
- Stickiness
- Slipperiness

Special Sensitivities

Five parts of baby's body are especially sensitive to touch: his face, palms, backbone, genital area, and the soles of his feet. At these locations the nerve receptors that receive touch information (the haptic nerves) are particularly prominent.

Until your baby is about three months old, the right side of his body is more sensitive to pressure than the left side. Although this extra sensitivity has been well documented, it's still a mystery why this is so. There is much that science has to learn about the workings of the human being.

It is wise, however, to be sure to touch *both* sides of your newborn's body so that he becomes aware of his left side as well as his right (See Chapter 10.)

Your Baby's Most Sensitive Areas

- Face
- Palms
- Soles of feet
- Backbone
- Genital area
- The right side of his body

The best touch stimulus, by far, is skin-to-skin contact. Baby's skin should come in contact with his mother's and father's bare chests as soon as he is born, conveying warmth while caressing. Letting your baby lie against your skin for hours is very soothing. The closeness afforded by skin-to-skin contact is essential for his sense of security.

As your baby is snuggled on your chest, how can you help but stroke him? Rhythmic, repetitive stroking is very comforting and reassuring. Stroking toward the back of the head, from the forehead to the nape of the neck, is particularly effective in calming your baby. Body stroking, from the head toward the toes and from the center of the body out to the fingertips, can relax babies and possibly enhance nerve growth. It stimulates the pathway of neuromuscular development, nerve cell insulation, and eventually, coordination. Because the direction of stroking is significant, stroke from head to toe and from the center to the extremities (the pattern normal development takes).

As you stroke your baby, try to be aware of the amount of pressure you use. Very light touch is annoying, as well as tickling. Infants seem to prefer a firm but gentle touch, especially around the face. You may use petroleum jelly to help your hand glide over your baby's body. Within a few weeks he will become quite accustomed to the stroking and will visibly relax beneath your hands. This gentle massage can alleviate the tension that normally accumulates during an infant's day and is usually expressed during the fussy time that occurs from four to six P.M.

Fabrics Make Great Stimulators

- Corduroy . . . ridges
- Fake fur . . . piles
- Velvet . . . softness
- Vinyl . . . firmness
- Wool . . . roughness
- Satin . . . smoothness
- Nylon . . . slipperiness

Pass these textures over your baby's body one at a time, first on the right side, then on the left. Name the sensation as you use it. For example, you might say, "Michael, this is soft. Can you feel the soft? How does it feel? Do you like soft? Soft is on your right side and now it is on your left. Soft is on your nose, on your chest . . . it's in your hand and on your knee," etc.

These different fabrics can be sewn together to make a Tactile Tillie™, a toy with a multitude of textures. (We'll tell you where to buy one in the Resource Guide in Chapter 33, or you can put together your own touch stimulator from scraps of fabric you may have around the house. Directions are in Appendix 4.) Bend your touch toy to present each fabric to baby individually. You may gently stroke him with the toy, head to toe and center to side, naming the body parts and sensations as you do.

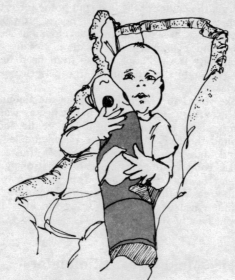

Baby loves his Tactile Tillie™.

Since baby's skin is so sensitive, he has a preference for cool water. (That's why children can play happily for hours in a cool wading pool but find hot tub baths extremely uncomfortable.) While bathing your baby, it is important to keep the water warm so that he doesn't get chilled, but you can help him experience coolness by filling a rubber glove with cool water and gently passing it over his body and placing it on his chest. You may try the same technique with warm water but remember that the glove should *never* be too heavy or too hot.

Your Baby Loves to Feel

- Skin-to-skin contact
- Rhythmic, repetitive stroking
- Firm but gentle touch
- Fabrics with different textures
- Tactile Tillie™
- Warm and cool water in a rubber glove

15. Baby's Sense of Smell

Have you ever heard it said that the birth of a couple's first child signals the beginning of the end of their *former* sex life? If you have, and wondered why, the answer may come as a surprise.

Smell! That's right! A newborn's sense of smell is so keenly developed at the time of birth, and especially attuned to the odor of mother's breast milk, that whenever milk is secreted from the breast, baby smells it. Many mothers have said that the odor seems to waft through the air, over bodies of water, through walls and straight to baby's nose. It actually awakens them from sleep. As sexual arousal triggers milk secretion from the breast, the odor finds its way to baby (who, naturally, would like to partake), a crying announcement of feeding desire issues forth, and there you have it—or rather *don't* have it. Sex goes on hold!

Not only can your baby distinguish his mother's breast milk from all others,[1] but he is also very aware of the scent of mother's lingerie. Actually, the body odor that permeates the fiber of the fabric is as unique as fingerprints. Within one month of birth, your baby can recognize your clothing by smell. Dr. Marshall Klaus, a pediatrician at Case Western Reserve University in Cleveland, Ohio, has done extensive research on bonding. He firmly believes that exposure to mother's and father's body odor is an important "marker" for babies, helping them to know to whom they belong.

When you must separate from your baby, even for an evening out—with a baby-sitter left in charge—leave a piece of mother's or father's clothing that has been worn for a day or two without washing near the baby. It can be a comforting security blanket.

Your newborn is capable of distinguishing between odors he likes and dislikes. If you pass the sweet odor of ripe banana beneath your baby's nose when he is only twelve hours old, he will appear very pleased and may even smile. If you were to pass an unpleasant odor (and please *never* do this!), such as ammonia, he would noticeably frown with disgust. Knowing your infant can differentiate between odors and can show a preference, you might consider having your baby in the kitchen while you cook. You'll enjoy the company and it's a fine opportunity to introduce fragrant whiffs, such as nutmeg or vanilla. Just be sure to keep baby safely away from stove, hot water faucet, and dangerous kitchen utensils or appliances.

When you use perfume, let your baby smell it. Always concentrate on sweet smells so that baby learns to associate you with pleasing sensory experiences. Conversely, try to avoid using noxious or annoying cleaning compound odors around your infant. Make every effort to avoid cigarette, pipe, or cigar smoke (which not only is unpleasant, but toxic to baby).

Smell is not only a source of pleasant sensations for your baby, it has also been found to be important for motor growth. It promotes both autonomic (involuntary) and skeletal movements: your baby's nose and facial muscles move in a rudimentary—but controlled—way when he sniffs.[2]

Odors Pleasing to Baby

- **Breast milk**
- **Parents' lingerie or scarves**
- **Perfumes and flowers**
- **Vanilla, cinnamon, nutmeg and chocolate**

Unpleasant Odors

- **Cleaning solvents**
- **Ammonia and bleach**
- **Cigar, cigarette, or pipe smoke**
- **Citric acid (like orange or lemon juice)**

16. Baby's Sixth Sense:

Movement

Movement, or vestibular stimulation, interestingly derives from the vestibule of the ear, the organ in the middle ear that perceives changes in position or states of balance. When movement occurs, the vestibule is responsible for transmitting the message to the brain. Your baby can accomplish movement stimulation either by himself or with activities you enjoy together.

Directing His Own Movements

When your baby directs his own movements, we refer to his vestibular competency—those movements that comprise what a baby is able to do. He can reach out toward things as well as protect himself with defensive movements such as pulling back, covering his face, and crying.[1] In so doing, he provides his own stimulation. But although newborns have these capabilities, you will not observe this kind of behavior unless you give your baby a chance to do it. How can he reach out for a panda bear if you never offer him one?

Newborns can move in time to speech when twelve hours old,[2] can imitate facial movements like fluttering eyelashes and tongue thrusts within the first week of life,[3] can reach for a little ball when they are ten days old.[4] Remember to position yourself or the object you are showing 10 to 13 inches from baby's eyes in order for him to see it clearly.

When you provide your newborn with opportunities to imitate and reach, stay with it, even if he doesn't seem to respond immediately. In the first six months of life it takes all infants time to organnize any of their responses and direct their muscle movements. This is called response latency. Your baby can take from 10 seconds up to 2 minutes to react to a given stimulus. So stay with it. Have patience and offer baby repeated opportunities.

Your Newborn Is Capable of Directing Some of His Own Movements

BIRTH	Moves head and eyes to inspect his surroundings
12 HOURS	Makes subtle arm movements in time to speech
LESS THAN 1 WEEK	Can grasp object but releases it after reaching for it. Can imitate tongue thrusting, fluttering eyelashes, mouth opening and closing
10 DAYS	Reaches for an object if presented while baby is held upright with arms free

Movements You Accomplish

Although your baby stimulates himself by his own actions, you, too, can stimulate his vestibular sense by moving him around in space.

Because your fetus's brain reacts to movement by the fifth month of pregnancy, I always recommend that pregnant women *rock* in a rocking chair. This stimulation of your fetus's sense of movement positively affects neuromuscular development and coordination ability. It may also help your fetus gain weight. Rock fairly slowly at the rate of 20 rocks per minute. You'll find the activity will be soothing to you and your fetus.

At birth your newborn can sense changes in his position. He quickly develops preferences. Some babies prefer lying on their backs, others on their stomachs, and *all* babies prefer being picked up to being put down—they are social beings who prefer to be held. Without experience with several types of movement, your baby cannot learn how to control his own motor coordination.[5]

Linear and Rotary Movements

Babies need exposure to two types of movement. The first—linear movement—occurs along straight lines: forward and backward, side to side, up and down and diagonally. When you pick up your baby, rock him in a rocking chair, or wheel him in a stroller, you are providing linear movement.

Baby skateboards or Cookie Monster Crawl-Alongs™ Muppets, Inc. are fun to use too. Simply lay baby tummy down on the board and gently propel him forward and backward. Eventually he will be able to use his own arms and legs to achieve the movements.

The second type of movement is rotary, which refers to circular movement. Gently waltzing your baby around the room is an efficient yet effortless way to provide rotary movement. If you use a Snugli®—a sling-type baby carrier suspended from your shoulders which hangs in front of you—when you do your marketing, you will stimulate your baby's vestibular sense while allowing him to listen to your heartbeat and feel the warmth of your body next to his. To add to this threefold pleasure and stimulation, you can even sing or hum!

Remember, any movement that allows the head to move separately from the body before one year of age may contribute to bruised brain tissue. So, by all means, avoid shaking your baby over your head or using jumpers that suspend from doorways. These dangerous movements throw the head forward, backward, up and down too sharply. The baby's brain is smaller than his skull and the brain can bruise as it falls forward and backward with such strong bouncing.

Even though the temptation to toss baby playfully in the air and catch him coming down looks like great fun for everyone, the "tossee" *can suffer serious consequences.*

Movement Stimulation Your Baby Needs

LINEAR MOVEMENT—ALONG A STRAIGHT LINE

TYPE OF MOVEMENT:	HOW TO DO:
Forward to backward	Rock in a rocking chair
Side to side	Rock in a cradle
Up and down	Picking up baby
Diagonally	Stroller
	Car travel
	Baby skateboard or Cookie Monster Crawl-Along™ Muppets, Inc.

ROTARY MOVEMENT—IN A CIRCLE

Holding baby as you turn gentle circles	Sling-type baby carrier like Snugli®

Avoid

Shaking baby	Suspended jumpers

Taken all together, your newborn's already well-developed senses offer you a wealth of opportunities for stimulation. In a caring, loving, unpressured environment, you and your baby can be working and playing toward maximizing his potential growth and *senses* of appreciation.

V. USING INFANT STIMULATION

17. Knowing When to Use Infant Stimulation

I watched Cheryl W. as she snuggled her son Jamie only two hours after his birth in an alternative birth center. Her movements and manner, her serene smile and gentle caress, all conveyed unqualified love as she rocked in a chair with her wide awake infant nuzzling into her breast. She stroked his head, tenderly touching his nose and his fingers every once in a while.

"Aren't you the Infant Stim Lady?" Cheryl asked warmly as I approached. "Sarah S. in your parent education class has told me all about it. I want to do it too." Then she paused, as if uncertain about how to proceed. "But when is the best time to do it? How do I know if Jamie is ready? Tell me, Dr. Ludington, when should I get started?"

"You already have," I told her.

Mrs. W., like countless parents who get in touch with me, was thrilled at the prospect of enrolling in an infant stimulation program. She couldn't wait to begin.

It's never too late to start an infant stimulation program. We humans are capable of incredible catch-up growth. So, whether the child is three months or 3 minutes old, the most important principle to remember is: *Infant Stimulation can be started as soon as your baby is ready.*

Sounds simple enough. "Of course, how obvious. But how will I *know* when he's ready?" you might be thinking to yourself.

I will help you to identify those times best suited for you to introduce Infant Stimulation to your baby, for, just as little Jamie couldn't tell Mrs. W. *in words* that he was ready to play, there were many signs and clues that signaled his readiness.

Identifying States of Activity in the Newborn

If you were to stand at the nursery window of your local hospital's maternity ward for an hour or so, watching what newborns actually do, you would be treated to a variety of performances. Some babies would be crying. Others would be moving around. Another group would be lying still, gazing at the ceiling. Some would be sleeping peacefully. Each baby probably would engage in several different activities while you were watching.

In 1964 Dr. Peter Wolff of the Menninger Clinic in Topeka, Kansas, made the same observation. In one study he watched newborns, noting that they moved from one state to another. He isolated six distinct states of activity in the newborn[1]:

- Alert Inactivity
- Drowsiness
- Light Sleep
- Deep Sleep
- Crying
- Alert Activity

When you tune in to the cues your baby is giving you during each of these six states, you can learn to recognize the best time to use your Infant Stimulation Program. Let's consider each of these states individually.

18. The Best Times to Use

Infant Stimulation

Matt P. is holding eight-week-old Beth on his lap. Beth is wide awake but quiet. She is not moving or fussing. Mr. P. calls his daughter's name in a high-pitched, singsong voice. "Be-thy, Be-thy, Be-thy..." She turns her head to find the source of the familiar sounds. Her eyes widen as if to study her daddy's beloved face. She is calm and relaxed. She is paying attention. This is the very best time for Mr. P. to carry on a program of Infant Stimulation.

When your baby is in the state of alert inactivity, he is not only awake, but he is also attentive (See Chapter 10). He is capable of paying attention to your voice, to visual items, and to his environment in general because he is not distracted by his own movements or cry. He is still, so he is able to concentrate on the stimulation available to him. *When your baby is awake and quiet, he can really explore his environment. This is the best time for Infant Stimulation.*

Your newborn's attention span increases dramatically with repetition and maturation. Because his attention span is so fleeting at first (only 4 to 10 seconds), you might think that he is not interested in what you show him. Just keep in mind that his attention span is still developing.

Once something catches your baby's attention, he'll want to come into closer contact with it. Typically, he will turn his eyes and head toward the source of the stimulation, just as Beth did when she wanted to experience her father as fully as possible. And when you sit down on a comfortable chair, hold your newborn on your lap, and watch his reaction as you call his name in a singsong voice, you, too, will feel the awe of the wonderful new relationship that is already developing.

Whenever I visit mothers in the maternity ward or birthing

center on the first day after delivery, I enjoy pointing out the almost imperceptible movements their baby's fingers and toes make. When your infant lightly fans his fingers and toes toward you, it's as if he were stretching them to take you in. This is a great sign of attentiveness. He is telling you, "I love that. I'd love to touch that wonderful thing that just happened to me." *This is the essence of an Infant Stimulation program: the feeling of love, warmth and attachment that grows as you interact with your infant in positive, stimulating ways.*

So, the period of alert inactivity is the *best* for making that all-important connection with your newborn. You know that your baby is ready for interaction with you because he is awake and quiet.

Just remember to watch your baby carefully. When he maintains his gaze or fixates on an object, make sure that his face has a relaxed expression. If his eyes get *very* wide and he has a wrinkled brow or a pained look, he may be in a state of hyperalertness or overstimulation. Then he really would not be paying attention to anything. His eyes may be open but staring off into space. This hyperalert state should tell you that baby needs a break. Allow him some shut-out time. Let him rest or look at a plain white wall. In the next chapter we'll cover all you need to know about when *not* to use Infant Stimulation.

19. The Wrong Times to Use
Infant Stimulation

When Baby Is Drowsy or Sleepy

Jim M. was playing with his month-old son Sean. Enjoying the activity immensely, Jim was coaxing responses from his little boy. He tickled his tiny toes and said, "Seany, now don't fall asleep on me. Come on... let's look at this doggy." He didn't take the cue from Sean's drifting eyes that the baby was about to fall asleep.

If you see that your baby is nodding off, don't try to play with him. Let him sleep. After all, when you're about to take a snooze you're not much in the mood for a tennis match. So respect your baby's needs. He's a person too.

And for babies, sleep is a very important *need*. The normal newborn sleeps twenty to twenty-two hours a day for the first month of his life! By the time he reaches six months of age, he will be sleeping much less—only sixteen hours a day. So don't bombard him with information and activity when he's not capable of enjoying them.

Drowsiness Is an Excellent "Time-Out" Signal

Whatever you do, don't get carried away by your own needs for success and continue to play when your child wants to sleep. After all, Infant Stimulation is a form of *interaction* with another human being, meaning there are *two* people involved.

Of course, should you need to arouse your infant for some reason, your voice and gentle touch are the best ways to go about it.

Light Sleep

During one class session Nancy and Arthur J. called me over to observe their sleeping infant. Heather's fine brown eyelashes fluttered as she slept. She pursed her lips and moved her tongue rhythmically, as if she were still nursing. Her face twitched periodically. Sometimes it seemed to Nancy and Art that Heather was even smiling in her sleep.

I assured these parents that Heather's activity was absolutely normal. She was experiencing the "light sleep state" during which rapid eye movement (REM) and active dreaming occur.

Actually, both adults and children experience four phases of sleep, but to simplify matters, I've grouped these into two major categories: light sleep and deep sleep.

Deep Sleep

Most of the brain activity that signals learning occurs during the deep sleep state, contradictory as that may seem. If, for example, you show your infant a picture of a cat and repeat the word *cat* shortly before he falls into a deep sleep (being careful, of course, not to impose on him when he's drowsy), the message "cat" tends to be laid down in his brain.

Why? Because the learning centers of the brain are very active during deep sleep. The information that you've shared has a chance to be processed without other competing messages intruding.

The trick, then, is to figure out how to get your baby to fall into a deep sleep. Most parents believe that infants need quiet in order to sleep best, so they tuck baby away in his room with the lights off and the door closed. Ironically, *darkness and quiet are not conducive to deep sleep for newborns!*

Remember, your baby has just spent nine months in a

womb that provided an abundance of stimulation. For at least the last two months there he became accustomed to sounds, movement, light, and activity. Thus, contrary to popular belief, your newborn will feel more secure and drift off into deeper sleep in the midst of the hubbub of your daily activities than if he were isolated in a darkened, soundproofed nursery. That's why babies fall asleep so deeply in the stroller when they're taken out for a shopping trip. They're used to commotion going on around them. They seem to welcome it. Small wonder parents always shake their heads in amazement that their little one has gone "out like a light" in the unlikeliest places.

At about six months of age, however, all of that activity does become distracting to your child. At this time baby becomes fascinated by the pulse of life surrounding him. He'd much rather be a participant, exhausted or not, than contemplate the alternative—sleep. (This is the beginning of a lifetime pattern!) For this reason you'll probably want to put your six-month-old to bed in a quieter place. He may continue to sleep in the middle of the hubbub of your kitchen, but most likely only because he's overwhelmed by exhaustion.

Although your newborn may be deeply asleep, his brain still responds to sound, touch, and movement. In experimental situations with newborns in the deep sleep state, Dr. Arthur Parmelee, Jr., professor of the Pediatrics Department at UCLA, and Dr. Kathryn Barnard of the Child Development Institute at the University of Washington, validated the occurrence of brain-wave changes.[1]

You may use the stimuli of sound, touch, and movement to help your baby go to sleep. If you hold him in your arms (touch) while rocking in a chair (movement) singing a favorite lullaby (sound), you will be providing these three kinds of stimulation in a very loving way.

But be careful not to overdo. There really is no reason to continue the stimulation during sleep. After all, you want the benefits of deep uninterrupted sleep, not only for your baby but for yourself as well. So it doesn't matter if you continue holding, rocking, and singing for a short time after he has fallen off to sleep. Just remember to stop and put him to bed once you've sensed that he is in the deep sleep state.

When Baby Is Crying

Linda and Allen R. are typical of many parents who become confused, sometimes even frantic, when their infant cries during "playtime." Linda and Al came to the clinic about three weeks after they had brought their daughter Samantha home from the hospital.

During that time they had played with her regularly, but when she started to cry during play, they became frantic. Reasoning that Samantha must somehow be unhappy or uncomfortable with the stimulation, they would turn on the musical mobile, wind up the swinging cradle, check her diaper, turn up some Vivaldi on the stereo, pat her back, offer a breast or a pacifier! "We tried *everything*," they lamented.

What they were doing, in effect, was adding stimulation to what may well have been an already overstimulated baby.

You can use a direct, simple way to check out the cries of an overstimulated baby while quieting him at the same time.

First, stop *all* stimulation (music, patting, and the like) for 30 to 60 seconds. Next:

- Present your face only. (You should be 10 to 13 inches from his face.)
- Talk in a low voice. (There is some controversy here. We are not yet certain if infants can hear your soft voice over their cry. The sound is so different from the cry, it may catch baby's attention during a breathing pause. It can't hurt to try!)
- Touch gently. Put your hand on his head, leg, or tummy and leave it there.
- Move your hand. Rub or pat your baby very softly.
- Embrace your baby. Pick him up and cuddle him.
- If his crying persists, add motion by walking, rocking, and swaying in a gentle rhythmic fashion.

This sequential approach is often consoling enough to turn off the cry, and avoids overloading an already overstimulated baby.

If baby's cries are *not* the result of overstimulation, they could be an indication of distress. Understandably, parents often become upset and feel helpless when they can't figure out exactly what is causing their infant to squawl.

In 1976 Drs. Jeffrey Helms and Donald Turner at Mitchell College, New London, Connecticut, developed a system to help you identify the meaning of your baby's different cries. These guidelines can help you ease the tension that arises from not knowing what's wrong when you hear your baby cry.

What to Do When Baby Cries

IF THE CRY IS...	AND YOUR BABY IS...	HE MAY...	TRY...*
Loud and insistent	bending his knees and kicking	be having colicky pain	1. flex legs at hips 2. Gripes water (an English preparation for colic available at pharmacy) 3. rub back in circles 4. burp baby
Fretful	passing gas and having green stool	have indigestion	call pediatric health professional
Fretful	putting fingers in mouth; flexing and tensing arms and legs	be hungry	1. feed 2. allow hand-to-mouth activity
Whining	hardly moving and listless	be ill or frail (cry of premie)	call pediatric health professional
Shrill and sharp	moving a lot or hardly at all	be injured[2]	call pediatric health professional

*The suggestions for what to try are not included in the original research.

Other pediatricians have observed additional kinds of cries. Dr. T. Berry Brazelton, the famous child developmentalist at Harvard University, makes a point of alerting parents to their infants' "fussy" time, which usually occurs in the late afternoon.[3] At that time baby releases tensions that have built up during the day, and his cry effectively blocks out any additional stimulation from his environment. Knowing that babies typically cry at this time may be helpful in scheduling family routines and in figuring out what, if anything, is wrong. Of course, the four to six P.M. period is also difficult for parents, because they are tired from the day's labors and are probably trying to prepare dinner while their baby is fussing.

Other researchers have isolated cries that indicate boredom and wetness.[4]

Whatever the reason for crying, some parents hesitate to respond to their infant's cry for fear of "spoiling their child." Let me say most emphatically: *It is* impossible *to spoil your child with love and attention during the first six months of life.*

Up to six months of age infants don't have the memory ability that would allow them to manipulate their environment. In fact, children learn to trust their environment and feel secure (obviating the need for them to be manipulative) when their cries are answered *quickly, consistently, and completely.*

Research by Dr. Eleanor Maccoby at Stanford University, Palo Alto, California, as well as studies by other social scientists have shown that children whose parents respond in this manner develop greater independence once they start to play and show less distress when temporarily separated from parents.[5]

To Show Love and Affection and Develop Trust, Answer Your Baby's Cry:

QUICKLY (within 1 minute)
CONSISTENTLY (every time)
COMPLETELY (he should hear, see, and feel you)

Your baby's cry is a very loud and unusually grating 84 decibels. It is so grating that it creates a rise in blood pressure for anyone eight years old or older who hears it.[6] No wonder parents become frantic when a baby can't seem to settle down! Ironically, crying may eventually *help* your baby become calm by effectively blocking out the environment.

When Samantha cried, she couldn't hear the musical mobile or the stereo. She might not even have heard her mother's attempts at shushing her. So, although your baby is most alert when in the crying state, you should remember: *The crying state is not the best time to use Infant Stimulation with your baby.* Unless, of course, you are gently consoling him. Love your baby when he's crying—don't show him a rattle. Once consoled, he'll move into the alert states and be more receptive to stimulation.

When Baby Is Overstimulated

Cari A. was holding her three-week-old son Eric on her lap during one of my Infant Stimulation Workshop classes with parents. The little boy seemed fascinated by the black-and-white bull's-eye that his mother held up in front of his eyes. I observed their interaction and moved on to the next family group. Two minutes later, however, Mrs. A. tapped me lightly on the shoulder.

"Dr. Ludington," she said, "I'm afraid something is terribly wrong. Eric seemed to love the bull's-eye. Then suddenly, he started kicking and he got all squirmy. Could it be that he doesn't like what I'm doing?"

I looked at her son. He was indeed squirming, with his arms and legs flailing about. "Eric is in the state of alert activity," I replied. "He's telling you that he has had enough stimulation for the moment. Why don't you both take a break?"

The state of alert activity means that your baby is awake and *moving*. This state is an indicator that your baby can no longer engage in play. He has attended to you and what you presented to him, but he can no longer pay attention. He is in a state of tension, and releases the tension by moving. His body movements are very distracting to him, so it becomes even more difficult for him to pay attention to any further stimulation.

Let me point out that this response is not limited to infants. Think of children of nursery school age. When their teacher tries to read them a story that's too long, we say that they get "antsy" or "squirmy." One youngster may jump up and run around the story circle, tacitly asking to be released from having to be attentive by moving. Adults are not much different! Although our attention spans are much longer, we still take coffee breaks at work and look forward to intermissions at long plays.

When your child shows signs of alert activity (that is, awake and moving) he is telling you that *he is not ready to be played with, or he has had enough play.*

He really needs to be released from concentration and allowed to recover his attentiveness. Any attempts at actively engaging him will probably be futile now. Rather, you might just hold him close and stop the talking, rocking, and picture-showing. Looking at a blank wall may even help him recover attentiveness and become alert and inactive.

Mrs. A., like most mothers, interpreted Eric's squirm as a sign of his disapproval. That's a common mistake. Remember, a newborn's attention span is very short, only 4 to 10 seconds. After he has taken in all of the information that he can process in a series of bursts of attention, he will feel tension. *The state of alert activity is a "time-out" signal.*

Dr. Heideleise Als, a fellow in Neonatology at Boston Children's Hospital, has developed a system for determining when a child has had enough stimulation:

- SALUTE: Baby thrusts his arms out in front of him.
- AIR-SITTING: He sticks his legs out into the air like a dancer practicing leg lifts when lying on his back.
- PRAYING: He rubs his hands together as if in pious devotion.
- EXTENSION: He splays his fingers and toes.
- TONGUE THRUSTS: He thrusts his tongue out.
- FATIGUE: His chin droops.[7]

Looking back on the six activity states—alert inactivity, drowsiness, light and deep sleep, crying, and alert activity—it is clear that during the period of alert inactivity, when your baby is awake and quiet, he is most available to learn from you and the Infant Stimulation Program that you present.

VI. HOW TO DRAW OTHERS INTO YOUR INFANT STIMULATION PROGRAM

20. Getting Everyone into the Act

Although historically our culture has ascribed the role of nurturer to mother, in the last decade father, older siblings, grandparents, and day-care centers have been playing an increasingly important role in the nurturing of infants.

So, in a very practical sense, from time to time responsibility for the care of your infant may fall into different hands.

But no matter who cares for your baby, *the key to quality care is consistency.* Simply stated, the same group of people—family, day-care center staff, baby-sitter—should deal with your child day-in and day-out.

Research has shown that over time, adults develop emotional attachments to the children under their regular care. It stands to reason that with these attachments comes concern about the growth and well-being of the infant. The more consistent the care—established routines, little or no turnover in care-givers—the greater the attention that baby receives. The greater the attention, the more sensory interactions provided. And those sensory interactions *are* what help your baby to learn.

Each person in your baby's life can make unique contributions to his development and ought to take advantage of the special opportunities afforded him or her to do so.

Mothers

I often advise mothers to stay at home, if at all possible, for six months to a year following their baby's birth. Why? The benefits are twofold. I firmly believe women need maternity leave for their physical and emotional recuperation. Secondly, a mother's psychological and physical accessibility to her infant during the earliest days of life has a definite correlation with her child's secure and firm attachments.[1]

When your infant's six-month birthday rolls around, you, like most women, may quite naturally find yourself ready to be out in your pre-pregnancy world again, needing relief from the *constancy* of child care. This is a good juncture at which to consider going back to work.

I do recognize, however, that the ideal of six months may be a practical impossibility for many women, given the economic and social realities of the eighties. If you are unable to spend at least three months at home, then make good use of other consistent resources that might be available to you, including your husband, parents and/or day-care facilities. If you go back into the work force during this period in your child's life, it is extremely important that you find ways of providing daily UNDIVIDED *quality* time with your baby—*at least* 15 minutes per day, but preferably more.

I say 15 minutes a day because that's a manageable amount of time, even for the busiest mother. Infant Stimulation is easily accomplished in three 5-minute intervals conveniently spaced over the day (before baby's morning feeding, when you return from work in the afternoon, and in the evening, before baby's last feeding). More frequent, short exposures to stimulation are better for your infant than a single 15-minute session. Your baby simply doesn't have the attention span to tolerate one long sitting. And in those 5-minute sessions, you *can* stimulate your baby's five senses enough to make a difference, if you are *consistent*. Book II is filled with stimulation games that take only 1 minute each to accomplish.

Remember, however, that 15 minutes is only the barest minimum. You will feel drawn to spending unstructured time with your child; talking and singing, laughing and playing in an ongoing way. In Book II we also suggest ways to make your ongoing interactions with baby fruitful. But above all else, follow the dictates of your heart and love your child as much as possible whenever you have the chance.

Fathers

Time was—and it wasn't that long ago—when men took pride in their absolute ignorance of feeding, changing, and caring for babies. Macho scorning of this "women's work" often masked deeper fears: a husband's fear that his special, exclusive relationship with his wife would now be disrupted by this little intruder; a wage-earner's fear of increased financial burden; a new father's fear that his baby was too fragile to handle and might break on contact.

Today, we view fathering in a bright new light. Beyond being just financial providers, more and more men are taking steps toward becoming emotional providers to their children. Sharing of household responsibilities and child care (which has come on the heels of the feminist movement) has helped move men comfortably into the nursery. Infant Stimulation can, and should, be as much a father's activity as it is a mother's.

Interestingly enough, current research shows that fathers' involvement in child-rearing has an important, positive effect on child development; a differing effect from that of mothers.

Fathers have a particularly marked impact on the growth and development of their male children. Boys need a nurturing, powerful, and available father as a role model. That is how they learn their eventual sex role.

In addition, studies have shown that fathers' presence is important in improving cognitive development and academic achievement in boys. Since boys have a natural desire to emulate their fathers, they copy and learn his problem-solving strategies and thinking patterns. According to Dr. Norma Radin, a University of Michigan scholar in the field of fathers' impact on child development, "The more contact boys have with fathers, the more their intellectual development flourishes."[2] She emphasizes that there is no point at which the good effects level off. The positive results are limitless.

A father's influence is equally important for female children. Paternal involvement significantly affects math ability in girls aged 1 through 9.[3] Strong father-daughter relationships have been correlated with women's success in later life. One study found that women who achieve a high level of success are likely to have had a strong relationship with a father who accepted his daughter's femininity but expected her to be persistent and competent.[4]

Men also have a great effect on their children's feelings of social competence. Positive fatherly qualities of "high warmth" coupled with "limit-setting" help both boys and girls form affectionate relationships and positive interactions with others. A study by M. A. Easterbrooks at the University of Michigan found that "in children under twenty months of age, high father involvement in childrearing is related to security of the child's attachment and optimal child behavior."[5] Clearly, the more daddies are involved, the better for all concerned.

Some dads who become involved in child-rearing report feeling increased tension about child care. Suddenly, they find themselves dealing with conflicts that they had never faced before.[6] It's quite natural for them to feel tension, when one considers that today's father often lacks experience from his own childhood and the role model of his own father to guide him. Conflicts and anxieties are bound to arise when he breaks new ground in creating relationships with his children. This kind of tension can be relieved by talking with other fathers who are dealing with similar issues.

It is a sad commentary on our society that fathers spend, on the average, only two hours per week with their children.[7] Sometimes, of course, this can't be helped. But if you find yourself on a tight work schedule, make sure to plan for at least 15 minutes a day of undivided attention with each child. If you travel during the week, use weekends to make up for your absence.

Dr. Mitch Golant, a clinical psychologist in Los Angeles who has created the Finding Time for Fathering program, suggests that you learn to use bits of time creatively, especially if your work requires that you spend a lot of time away from home. "If you must be out of town, leave behind tape recordings of yourself telling stories and singing songs so that your child will hear your voice in your absence.

"Find ways to involve your child in your daily work. Bring your baby to the office and keep his or her picture on your desk to remind you of your relationship and to give you the perspective that your 'work world' is not your *only* world."

Dr. Golant adds that "men have several jobs or careers during their lifetimes, but fathering is the only career that is constant. So consider your family goals as carefully as you do your career advancement goals. Look at family time as you would money. It is essential to spend, share, save and invest in time in order to reap the family dividends later."

Grandparents

As she watched him play with her infant daughter, Louise T. marveled at the change in her father. When she was a child, he had worked a twelve-hour shift, from seven A.M. to P.M. By the time he got home, it was all he could do to wolf down dinner, flop into his easy chair, and fall into a dead sleep in front of the TV. On weekends there were chores and errands. She had looked forward hungrily to those yearly two-week vacations and Sundays at the beach. Those were the only occasions when she and her father spent family time together.

And now look at him, she thought. Down on the floor, playing with his granddaughter, Lizzy. He's a different man. Has he changed that much or is it the lack of pressure after retirement that makes him so available to his grandchild? Being a grandfather certainly agrees with him!

Through the ages, grandparents have sung the praises of grandparenthood. Often they have all the joys, all the pleasures of nurturing babies without the concomitant drudgery, loss of sleep, or discipline issues to deal with. When they retire, they no longer experience work-related tension. No wonder they are often portrayed as nudging their adult children to get married and have children.

Ira Gordon, a developmental psychologist in Gainesville, Florida, began teaching stimulating techniques to grandparents when he found that the teenage mothers he had tried to instruct were reluctant students.

He discovered that grandparents:

- were eager to acquire skills and knowledge about development and stimulating possibilities
- had a great emotional investment in their grandchildren
- were enthusiastic about providing pleasing play opportunities
- had an uncanny ability to avoid overstimulating their grandchildren (which he attributed to their years of experience)

Grandparents are a marvelous resource for new parents. They offer wisdom honed from years of practical experience with their own children. Of course, much of the material in this book may be new to them, so share what you have learned. Then they, too, can participate in your Infant Stimulation Program. Hang an extra black-and-white mobile in the port-a-crib at their home. Instruct them on the uses of Tactile Tillie™. Teach them how to read the signs of interest and those of overstimulation and shut-out. They will be as delighted as you when they see the results of stimulating interactions with the new addition to your family.

If grandparents become directly involved in the daily care of their grandchildren, especially in the event of single parenthood or when baby's parents must work, they should be encouraged to read this book so that they will be well versed in Infant Stimulation techniques. As primary care-givers, grandparents have an unparalleled opportunity to participate in the growth and development of their grandchildren.

Siblings

If there are older children in the house, they, too—with careful training—can be wonderful helpers in your Infant Stimulation Program. Your three-year-old can draw a black-and-white face or color in a checkerboard that you have outlined, to hang in his newborn brother's crib. Imagine your older son's pleasure when he recognizes that this interloping new baby actually enjoys looking at something *he* has made. While I'm not suggesting that Infant Stimulation is the way to overcome sibling rivalry (a natural part of your family dynamics), you might smooth the transition by involving older children in a positive relationship with the new baby.

In reconstituted families, and especially families with much older children (for example, ten years and older), many of the Infant Stimulation techniques I suggest can be carried out by a responsible sibling. Such sharing in your baby's growth and development cannot help but enhance the feelings of closeness, love, and harmony in your family circle.

Others

Aunts, uncles, cousins, nephews, nieces, favorite friends, and neighbors can all get into the act. Remember, however, that babies like periods of extended interactions. If Auntie Laura comes over to chuck little Tommy in the chin with a fleeting "gootchy, gootchy, goo," encourage her to stay for 3 to 5 minutes to engage him in talk and play. Otherwise, he will be confused by the quick "hi" and "bye," especially if he is accustomed to the longer interactions he has with you.

21. Choosing a Day-Care Center

That's Good for Your Baby

Anne Marie B. has been at home, happily, with her son Charlie, since his birth four months ago. Knowing her plan is to return to work in two months, she dreads the thought of leaving him. Not only is she unprepared for the separation, but she is also anxious about entrusting her baby to strangers. How could they possibly love him as much as she and her husband Arnie? And yet, she must get back to her job. She is filled to overflowing with conflict and guilt.

Anne Marie, like many parents, has fears and negative beliefs about day-care centers. Some of the most common of these include:

- Day-care centers are a form of institutionalization.
- They aren't nurturing and parents have no control over what happens to their children.
- Children don't like day-care. They feel deprived.
- Babies will attach to day-care center staff members rather than to parents because they spend so many hours at the center.
- Children don't receive individualized attention. Because of insecurity, children in day-care will become shy and retiring.

Actually, many of these fears are unfounded. *Most well-qualified centers do an outstanding job of caring for children*. By the time your child reaches the age of 2 or 2½, he will thoroughly enjoy the social interchange at the center and look forward to going. So let's take a moment to understand why these parental fears are unfounded.

Babies attach to mommy and daddy despite hours of separation. Your child has a very keen sense of belonging. He knows that you are his primary care-giver. He sees you, smells you, and recognizes the sound of your voice and the feel of your touch. That's one of the reasons why early sensory stimulation is so important. If you're anxious about this particular point, you might bring an 8×10 black-and-white photo of yourselves to the center to hang in your baby's crib, or an article of your clothing that he might cuddle with. You might even provide a tape-recording of you singing a lullaby. It's important to remember that your baby won't be living in the center all the time. In the evenings and on weekends, there will still be many opportunities for intense interactions with his parents.

Most day-care centers are very nurturing places. Provided the staff doesn't undergo frequent changes, adults make genuine emotional attachments to the babies left in their charge. And licensed day-care centers in the United States are required to have one adult in attendance for every three infants under two years of age. In centers where caring is consistent, children are less likely to feel insecure or shy. Your child may cry when you bring him to the center, not because he dislikes it, but because you, the person whom he loves, is leaving.

Anne Marie was wise to start thinking about day-care two months before she actually needed it, despite her anxiety and ambivalence. It takes time to locate the right center for your child's needs and your own. Allow yourself enough investigative time so that you won't feel rushed into making a decision. Ask your friends, neighbors, and coworkers about their child-care arrangements, but keep in mind that everyone has different expectations and values. What seems excellent to one mother may make another feel very uncomfortable, so be sure to call and *visit* the centers that sound promising.

Choose your day-care situation wisely, not hurriedly. If you find that you are dissatisfied with your original choice, do not hesitate to look further and initiate a change. Even though continuity is most desirable, it should not be attained at the risk of your peace of mind.

There are some guidelines that can help you assess a center when you do go for an on-site visit. I call them the ABC's of day-care.

A. Appearance
B. Behavior
C. Consistency and Caring

Appearance

Do the children and the center appear clean and well cared for? If a mess occurs, does the staff take the time to straighten the facility and wash the babies? Check for these signs of an advantaged environment:

- Are there age-appropriate books, toys, visual objects, cuddly toys readily available?
- Does each child have his own toy or transitional object (like blanket, diaper, pacifier) from home near him and accessible?
- Does each child have his own specific place for his things, regardless of his age?
- Does the facility look baby-proof or are dangerous or inappropriate objects in evidence? Remember, even though your baby may be starting at this center at four months of age, he may remain until he's old enough to enter nursery school.

Behavior

Think about how you behave toward your baby (or would behave if your infant is not yet born). You are responsive to your child's needs. When he's upset, you check to see why and you do what you can to help. When he's awake and alert, you make sure to talk and interact with him. Not only do you comfort him, but you also play with him. You take pleasure in his interactions with you and you smile and laugh frequently.

Expect no less from your day-care center. You will want to find a care situation where the staff is responsive to babies and treats them like people with whom they carry on good relationships.

There are several specific behaviors you can observe that will help in your decision-making process:

1. Check the staff members' behavior when they speak to, feed, and diaper the infants in their care.

2. Make sure you notice how they respond when babies signal distress.

3. Speech is a very potent form of behavior. Listen carefully to how staff members speak to the babies in their charge. Speech patterns are relatively constant, so if you listen and watch for a while, you will get the flavor of what your baby will be exposed to over a long period of time.

4. What kind of language do the care-givers use? When babies are vocalizing, do the care-givers reinforce that by talking back? Do they sing or laugh?

5. Check to see if the staff speaks as a result of infants' activity. That speech would reinforce the activity and show your infant that his behavior has had an effect on his environment. This responsiveness diminishes his feeling of helplessness.

6. Many emotions are expressed through the eyes, making eye contact a very powerful form of communication. And face-to-face vocalization teaches communication through nonverbal behavior. Taken together, we say that *face-to-face talking* and *eye contact* are the ultimate recognition of your child as a worthwhile being.

With these two thoughts in mind, observe the care-giver. Is the care-giver making face-to-face contact while speaking?

Next, listen for the quality of the speech. Are the care-givers' comments *positive*? Do they ask a lot of questions? (For example, "This is a doggy. Do you see the doggy? Doggies are nice and soft and furry.") Research indicates that the more positive comments, the sooner language is acquired and the better the child's self-image.[1]

Commands, criticisms, teasing, and shouting are negative communications and undesirable speech patterns from which you'll want to protect your baby. Run like hell if you hear any of that going on!

Speech Interactions Checklist

DOES THE DAY-CARE STAFF:
- **Reinforce babies' vocalizations by speaking?**
- **Reinforce babies' activity by speaking?**
- **Make face-to-face contact?**

- Use *positive* rather than negative comments?
- Ask your baby questions?

FEEDING: Look to see how quickly staff members respond to a baby's hungry cry. Do they enforce arbitrary schedules for their own convenience or do they provide food as soon as babies indicate their needs? It is my philosophy that infants *should not* be left crying. Immediate attention to the expression of needs helps to give your child trust in his world and to make him feel secure in the fact that such needs will be taken care of. Staff members should feed infants "on demand" and not on schedule.

Now watch the feeding interaction itself. Do care-givers take the time to feed? Is it a special event or something that just has to be rushed through in a perfunctory manner in order to get to the next baby? Does the infant get all of the time he needs to feel satisfied?

Does the staff use feeding time as an opportunity for positive interactions? Do they hold and embrace the baby lovingly or just prop a bottle? Do they rock and caress as they nurse, or are they robotlike in their attention? Do they make eye contact with the baby in their arms?

Feeding Interactions Checklist

DOES THE DAY-CARE STAFF:
- **Respond quickly to hungry cries?**
- **Feed "on demand" rather than by the clock?**
- **Take the time to feed?**
- **Hold, rock, and caress babies?**
- **Make eye contact?**
- **Seem loving?**

DIAPERING: Believe it or not, diapering is an important indicator of a day-care center's responsiveness to infants' needs. After all, diaper changing occurs frequently for infants and can be viewed as a time for interaction and exercise. Check to see if staff members talk to the infants and play patty cake or bicycle while they're doing the task.

For your baby's ultimate safety and comfort, it is essential that rules of cleanliness be observed at the day-care center of your choice. Make sure that babies' bottoms are washed gently from front to back. Are ointments applied for diaper rash? Is the supply of disposable diapers sufficient? Are diapers checked and changed frequently? In your observations, you might want to touch a few diapers, just to see how many wet babies there are. The smell of urine or feces in a facility is a definite indication that the staff is not doing its job properly. And perhaps most important, do the care-givers wash their hands after handling dirty diapers?

Diapering Interactions Checklist

DOES THE DAY-CARE STAFF:
- **Talk and exercise during changing?**
- **Observe rules of cleanliness:**
  - **Wash gently front to back?**
  - **Apply rash ointment?**
  - **Keep an adequate supply of diapers?**
  - **Check and change diapers frequently?**
  - **Wash their hands after handling dirty diapers?**

In addition to the behavior of the day-care center's staff, you'll want to observe the children's behavior. Are they laughing and playing or do they look sad and bored?

You'll also want to find out if the center's routine is reflective of the children's schedules. By six months of age your baby should have a set pattern of eating, sleeping and waking periods. Does the staff ask you what your child's routine is to see if it can be worked with, or do the care-givers simply assume that you and your baby will conform to their routine? Obviously, I favor a flexible program. That is indicative of the staff's caring about the infants in their charge.

On the other hand, you'll not want a placement that seems chaotic and crisis ridden. Calmness, competence, and loving attention should be your primary concern.

Caring and Consistency

The level of caring attention that a day-care center provides can be apparent to you as you first set foot in the place. Again, you'll have to observe the staff's behavior with babies. How nurturing do the care-givers appear? Do they seem happy in their work, and especially, how content are they in the presence of babies? Do they have physical contact with the children? Do they carry them about and get down to their level to talk to them? Are they compassionate when a child is in distress? If there are older children present, note the level of empathy they display toward the distress of one of their peers. That is sure to be a reflection of the care they themselves have received, both from their own parents and from the day-care center.

Does the center express willingness to embrace current knowledge about child development? Does the staff display an understanding of developmental milestones (for example, do they know when most babies begin to control their head movements, roll over, crawl or sit up with and without support)? Are the care-givers well versed in the current information regarding infant capabilities, sensitivities, and preferences? Would they be open to hearing new ideas on child-rearing? Might your suggestions for black-and-white mobiles or checkerboard-patterned comforters be taken seriously?

How long has the center been in operation? Ask for references so that you can contact other parents who have experienced the center. Find out how recent staff changes have occurred. You'll want to place your child in a setting where staff turnover is minimal.

Remember, research has shown that the more consistent the care-givers, the better the bonds that develop. With strong attachments, adults feel closer to and more responsible for their charges and infants feel more secure. Consistency and caring should be high on your list of priorities.

Caring and Consistency Checklist

IS THE DAY-CARE STAFF:
- **Nurturing and compassionate?**
- **Happy around babies?**

- **Well versed in infant development, capabilities, sensitivities, and preferences?**
- Composed of long-standing employees?

In the last two chapters we have discussed how all those people who share your baby's daily life impact on his growth and development. The Infant Stimulation Program that follows is designed to enrich life for you, your baby, and all who know him.

BOOK II

THE INFANT STIMULATION PROGRAM: WHAT YOU CAN DO TO STIMULATE YOUR BABY'S DEVELOPMENT

I. THE PROGRAM FOR PARENTS TO USE BEFORE AND DIRECTLY AFTER BIRTH

22. Making the Most of the "Waiting Game"

Preparing for the birth of your child is a time of excitement, anticipation, joy, and planning for the future.

Assembling an Unusual Layette

Of course, one of the most traditional ways of preparing for the new arrival is assembling the layette. The following is a list of *stimulating* toys, linens, and items of nursery decor that you can make or buy while you wait. Since many grandmas-to-be love to knit and sew and crochet, why not invite their participation in the "make-ready" plan? These baby items will be described in the Resource Guide in Chapter 33. Instructions for making ten of the toys are provided in Appendix 4. The pattern for the Bright Baby™ Blanket can be found in Appendix 4.

Nursery Items

LOOK FOR AND COLLECT THE FOLLOWING:

- Cradle or springs for crib
- Crib Cap
- Flashcards with checkerboard patterns, stripes and bull's-eyes
- Music and nursery rhymes
- Paper: large sheets of fanfolded computer paper
- Paper plates
- Pens: broad felt-tipped pens
- Photos: 8 × 10 close-up black-and-white photos of Mom and Dad's smiling faces
- Popsicle face (face drawn on paper plate with popsicle stick for neck)
- Rocking chair
- Posters: vivid, high-contrast posters with black-and-white or shiny background, dots, checks, wavy lines
- Scarves: one black-and-white checkerboard, one red, one blue—all about 24 × 24 inches
- Smart Smock
- Snugli®
- Yarn: thick yarn in bright, primary colors (red, blue, orange, green)

Toys to Purchase
(See Chapter 33)

- Bright Baby Brainy Bear™ or soft stuffed panda
- Bright Baby Mr. Mouse™
- Johnson & Johnson Child Development Kit
- Bright Baby Mind Mobile™
- Bright Baby Mind Mitten™
- Bright Baby Tactile Tillie™
- Bright Baby Teaching Tube
- Fisher-Price Wrist Rattle

Toys to Make, Sew or Crochet
(See Appendix 4)

- Eye Cube™
- Expressly Yours Poster™
- Mind Mitten™
- Mrs. Eyeset™
- Tactile Tillie™
- Taffeta Rattle

It's easy to make a popsicle face. Draw simple features on a paper plate and glue on popsicle stick.

Linens to Purchase or Sew
(See Chapter 33 and Appendix 4)

- Bright Baby™ Blanket
- Bright Baby™ Bed Bumper
- Crib Checks™
- Pillow Pals™

When creating linens for use in the crib, you may leave half of the surfaces plain. Your baby will then be able to turn away from the stimulating pattern when he feels that he has had enough.

Some Prenatal Stimulators That Are Available

Here are some tapes and programs that you may find useful. You can find the details on how to obtain them in Appendix 2.

- *Heartsongs: Infants and Parents Sharing Music* by Dr. Leon Thurman and Anna Peter Langness. Audio tape and booklet for singing to unborn, newborn, and toddler child.

- *The Loving Touch:* Audio tape and illustrated instructions for gentle fingertip massage and stroking.
- *The Prenatal University* by Dr. F. Rene Van de Carr. Audio tape and booklet for prenatal stimulation through auditory, touch, visual, and movement activities.

You'll find having these items handy before you go off to the hospital a big help in the hectic days that follow.

Preparing You for the Hospital and Preparing the Hospital for *You*

Your trip to the hospital will be eased if you make a checklist of items to take with you long before your due date so you won't have to rush around for last-minute items or feel obligated to *remember* so many details. (We included a sample checklist later in this chapter to assist you.) It helps to prepare far in advance.

You'll also find that we've made many suggestions for activities that might be new to your maternity professional and the nursing staff of the hospital where you expect to deliver your baby.

If you wish to implement any of our suggestions, it will be helpful to discuss alternatives with your health professionals *before* you actually go into labor. In that way, you will be structuring the birth experience to maximize your contact with your newborn in a positive and pleasing way. You do have the right to request that your wishes be observed, so feel confident in asking for what you want. But the medical staff cannot accommodate you if you don't make your requests known!

When you come in for your regular prenatal visits:

- Ask if you'll be permitted a "birth embrace" (See Chapter 23).
- Ask if Daddy will be permitted to "scrub in" and participate in the delivery room.

When you take the orientation tour of your hospital's maternity unit:

- Ask if baby can stay with you for the first hour rather than being carted off to the nursery.
- Ask if the nurses will administer a warm water bath within your view.
- Listen for rock and roll music in the nursery and ask if it can be turned off while your baby is there.
- Notice if newborns are wearing crib caps. If not, prepare to bring one along when you go to the hospital after labor begins.

If you want to carry out many of the activities with your newborn that we suggest in the next chapters, find out what you can do to gain their acceptance by the staff. It's most important to do this now, before you get caught up in the confusion and excitement of your labor.

And remember, listing your needs and asking your questions *early* ensures a smooth, frustration-free hospital experience.

A Labor of Love

The contractions have started. You're timing them. You're pacing. You've already called your health professional to report your status.

Now, as you pack your bag and make ready to dash to the hospital, remember to include the following stimulating items, which you'll need during labor and once baby is born.

What to Take to the Hospital

CONTAINER FOR BREAST MILK: When your labor contractions become regular, gently compress the breast tissue between your fingers to allow *colostrum*—the milky substance produced by the breast during the last month of pregnancy—to pass through the milk duct into a small plastic container. Collect about 4 tablespoons (¼ cup) of colostrum from both breasts.

Cover the container securely, label it clearly with your name and the date written on a piece of masking tape, and place it in the freezer until you leave for the hospital. This milk should stay frozen until you deliver. When you arrive at the labor and delivery unit, ask the nurse to place it in a readily available freezer. Baby will be using this colostrum shortly after birth. We'll tell you just how in the next chapter.

MUSIC: Pack a tape recording of the music you've been playing to your fetus along with a small cassette player with earphones.

HEARTBEAT TAPE: If you've taped your heartbeat during pregnancy, don't forget the recording. Label it well.

VISUAL STIMULATORS: Bring those black-and-white toys you created during your pregnancy. Make sure to include the 4-square checkerboard with 3- by 3-inch squares, the 2-inch black dot on a white background, the popsicle face, and the close-up photos of smiling Mommy and Daddy.

A CRIB CAP: Knitted stockinette caps to keep your baby's head warm are available at some baby stores. (Ask the maternity personnel at your hospital to order you one if you can't find it at a retail store.) You can also crochet or knit your own. Take one along to help stabilize baby's temperature after birth.

A SCARF: Mother should wear a scarf around her neck for several days as the due date approaches. Ideally, it should have a black-and-white checkerboard design. Without washing it, fold it up and tuck it into your hospital suitcase with your nightgown and slippers.

DADDY'S AFTER-SHAVE: Bring a small bottle of daddy's favorite aftershave (make sure it's a scent you will enjoy smelling over the next few months). Since baby has less contact with daddy's body and body odor, this strong perfume will help him to identify his father in the coming weeks.

TWO LARGE POLYESTER SCARVES—ONE RED AND ONE BLUE—SEWN TOGETHER: Simply open and lay two 24 × 24 scarves flat on top of each other and sew them together around the perimeter. You'll find this piece of "equipment" useful in helping baby to sleep in the nursery shortly after birth. I saw them used extensively for just this purpose at hospital nurseries in Helsinki, Finland. There, the nursing staff draped the scarves over the top of newborns' cribs to filter out the harsh hospital lighting.

THIS BOOK!

During Labor

The following suggestions are designed to help mother relax during labor. When she is relaxed, the smooth muscles that form the blood vessels are more relaxed, too, filling up with more blood to carry to the baby, who needs all the blood he can get to sustain him through each uterine contraction. An increased flow of blood means an increased supply of oxygen, which feeds baby's brain as well as mother's uterine muscle—the organ that's doing all the work.

FATHER CAN HELP WITH RELAXATION: The most important need of any woman in labor is the comfort and support of her baby's father. *Ideally, father should be present throughout labor and delivery.* During labor he can calm the kicking fetus by playing taped music on a headset placed on mother's abdomen at the fetal ears. It should be the same music played for the last six weeks before birth; this reinforces baby's memory and the feeling of familiarity has a calming effect on both mother and baby.

Father should take a few moments out of labor to ask the maternity nurse how to "scrub in." Once scrubbed in, his arms and upper chest can be exposed, making possible the intimacy of skin-to-skin contact with baby.

THE SOUND OF MUSIC: Most of my patients enthusiastically sing the praises of calming music during labor. They find it helps them relax. Physicians report that women listening to music require less pain medication. And fathers have commented on the warmth that familiar music brings to the hospital environment.

CHANGING MOTHER'S POSITION: It is important for mother to reposition her torso at least once every half an hour. Why? Movement enhances labor's progress, helps the contractions to gain strength and perform their work in a shorter period of time, and ensures good blood flow to the placenta. It's better for all concerned if mother has powerful contractions that do their work in short bursts and over relatively few hours rather than prolonged contractions which continue for hours.

Upright positions, such as sitting in a rocking chair, leaning or standing up beside the bed, walking about or inclining (as if reading in bed), facilitate labor and provide movement stimulation for your fetus.

If you're hooked up to monitors to trace your fetus's heart

rate, you can still walk, rock, and change position. You may request portable monitors, which will permit you a certain amount of freedom to move about while still providing good readings of your fetus's condition as you change position.

In fact, lying flat on your back in bed for more than 5 minutes at a time is the *last* thing you should be doing. This position decreases blood flow to your uterus and ultimately to your baby. If you *must* stay in bed, lie way over on your side, so your abdomen falls onto the bed to relieve pressure on your back.

SOFT LIGHTING: You may not think of the labor room as the ideal setting for a softly lit tête-à-tête with lovely music playing in the background, but that's exactly what I suggest to my patients.

Bright light may be very irritating, so ask to have the wattage lowered when you're in labor. Dim lights should make you feel calm and sleepy. Many women gain their composure in such an environment and some claim that it takes the edge off the intense reaction they feel to the process of labor. It has even been suggested that a darkened environment may improve the blood flow to the uterus and fetus.

During Labor

- Have father in the labor room for comfort and support.
- Father should learn how to scrub in and should ask to be issued scrub clothes.
- Play music to your fetus.
- Play music for yourselves.
- Change position frequently.
- Lower the lights.

With father to help keep track of these environmental niceties, together you will experience a safe, supportive, and satisfying labor.

23. The Main Event: Delivery

At the moment of birth you will notice that your baby is born wide awake and calm. His eyes are open as he looks around inquisitively. He lies quietly in any position in which you place him. He's ready to pay attention to you and is extraordinarily receptive to anything that happens to him.

Nature has provided him with this period of quiet alertness as a special adaptation so that he can find out who he is, where he is, to whom he belongs, and how much you care for him—right then and there—at the moment of birth, while you're still on the delivery table!

The Birth Embrace

Just-hatched ducklings *imprint* on and think they belong to the first thing they see. They'll follow *that* object around as if it were mother. Some scientists suggest that human babies have an imprinting period too. That's why it's so important for newborns to be in the arms of family members at the moment of birth.

You *can* embrace your baby immediately after birth—even before the cord is cut (most are long enough to afford this reach), and before he is washed, weighed, measured, and otherwise cared for. Your health professionals will let you know as soon as your baby's breathing has stabilized enough for you to hold him and say hello. His color should be pink.

If the cord has been cut, that's all right too. Just ask that he be given to *you* rather than taken over to his warmer. If the process is delayed for a few minutes, don't worry. You're eager to put your arms around your baby and embrace him close to your heart. This closeness immediately after birth is very special, helping both you and baby start a lifelong attachment.

Getting to Know You

Ask your health professional to place your newborn on your chest, between your breasts.

HEARTBEAT: Positioned there, your newborn will hear the reassuring sound of your heartbeat again. It is very comforting in its familiarity and will help him associate the person holding him with the one he has known for the last nine months.

SMELL: The pulsations of your pounding heart and the warmth of your body resulting from the exertions of labor will cause your body scent to emanate from your chest. You may even notice your newborn's nose twitching as he takes in the reassuring aroma.

Body scent is one of the most important markers by which your baby identifies his parents—by the time he is two weeks old he'll known that he belongs to you, just from your scent. He'll use that marker to help recognize you throughout the next six months. That's why babies seem to have an uncanny ability to identify mommy, regardless of how many other women are around.

THE LOVE NEST: You will find that your baby turns his head to nuzzle. He may put the side of his head on one breast or the other, as if it were a pillow. That's when you'll really notice his alertness! He will look at your face. He wants to see your eyes and learn your features. He will enjoy the black-and-white-circle visual stimulation of your eyes. If you need to, lift him closer so that his face is not more than 6 inches from yours.

Be certain that your newborn is resting on his tummy. You'll find that he tucks his knees underneath him, in the fetal position. This keeps him warm and comforted. His back, however, will still be exposed. Engulf your child with your forearms and arms, covering his back as you hold him near. Support his head gently with your hands because it may flop backward as he starts to look around. His sense of touch is gently stimulated by your tender caress and the feel of your skin against his.

Your newborn feels secure as he cuddles into you. He is now ready to identify your voice!

TALKING TO YOUR NEWBORN: Once you recognize that your newborn is ready to listen to you, use a tone that doesn't compete with the harsh, metallic sounds of the delivery room. This is the time to shut off any music. At this moment it's more important for baby to hear mommy's voice than Mozart. Soft, melodic, calming words will catch your baby's attention and ease his transition to life outside the womb.

Call his name. Say "Hello." Ask how he is. You'll find that you mention his eyes frequently. Ask him to open them and look at you. Shade his brow with your hand so that the bright lights of the delivery room don't inhibit his natural visual curiosity. Repeat your phrases (especially his name), calling him and saying, "Michael, I'm over here. Can you see me? Here Michael. Look here. That's it!" Talk directly to him. He's a person who understands your tone of love and loves the social engagement.

Your newborn's quiet alertness is one of his fascinating mechanisms for keeping you entranced and enthralled so that you will continue talking to him! He is empowering you to relate to him.

Daddy's Special Role

Daddy, if you've had the opportunity to scrub in during labor, you will be able to participate in the marvelous experience of getting to know baby. Place your hand on baby's back or side as he lies at mother's breast.

Repeat (within 3 feet of your newborn's right ear) those phrases that you used on the prenatal tape. If he has had enough exposure to your voice, he will show recognition by cocking his head in your direction. If you move to the other side, and direct your voice toward his left ear, with sufficient coaxing, he may turn his head to follow your voice.

Daddy, you're entitled to hold your newborn too. He will learn your body scent, bask in your warmth, hear your voice and heartbeat, and look into your eyes as well. You may want to unbutton your shirt so you can hold your child against your skin.

Have a nurse show you how to hold baby securely. When

your newborn's head rests upon your shoulder, he will nuzzle into your neck and relax his body. That's baby's way of saying "I love you and I love being held like this."

Of course, body check, vital measurements, and inventory are in order, so your newborn will have to leave mother's side. But there's no reason for you, Daddy, to stay behind. Your soothing voice, masculine touch, body odor, and proximity will help ease baby through these strange events. Feel free to place your hand on baby's abdomen or back to quiet him if he becomes distressed or cries fitfully.

The First Two Hours after Birth

A Very Special Time

If your new baby is healthy, there is no reason why he can't stay with his parents for at least an hour, provided he is kept warm. Every institution has an overhead heater called a radiant warmer that can be placed over your bed as you hold your baby. Request one to prolong your time together. You deserve and need the time alone with each other to experience these never-to-be-repeated moments and to feel your utter joy. It also is a marvelous opportunity for you to check out baby's "working parts," to count those tiny fingers and toes and gently explore baby's face with your fingertips.

Rhythmic Stroking

Now is a great time to begin rhythmic, repetitive stroking. Stroke your baby's head six to eight times from his forehead to the nape of his neck. Then continue from head to toe and from the center of his body out to his extremities.

The ideal rate is 12 to 16 strokes per minute, which mimics the gentle waves baby experienced in the womb as the amniotic fluid responded to mother's breaths. This gentle stroking helps to ease your newborn's breathing into a regular, deep rate.

This touch stimulation also helps intestinal functioning. Stroke gently, so your baby doesn't lose too much of his birth weight. Don't be surprised if your newborn urinates or passes some very thick, blackish stool. It's not only normal—it's desirable.

Thumb Sucking

If your newborn is lying beside you, you'll notice that he starts to swipe at his face. He'll stretch his fingers out and relax them. He's trying to get his fingers in his mouth to suck on them, as he did in the womb—but now he's working against gravity.

If he has a difficult time, gently direct his hand and place his thumb in his mouth. He'll suck on it. You'll want him to start sucking soon after birth because this pleasing and comforting activity quiets him, deepens and regularizes his breathing, satisfies his strong sucking instinct, and helps his jaw and cheek muscles develop.

Breast-feeding

Your newborn should nurse on colostrum within the first two hours after birth. At this time the colostrum your breasts secrete is especially enriched for baby and very valuable. It offers more antibodies and nutrients than it has previously or will again. Your attempts at breast-feeding will be important for your newborn's health, nutrition, and, of course, bonding. The colostrum you brought to the hospital should not be used; it has a different function, as you will soon see.

A Warm Water Bath

French obstetrician Dr. Fredrick Leboyer, in his now famous book, *Birth Without Violence*, recommends placing newborns in a 99-degree water bath to help simulate the buoyance of life in the amniotic sac.

Babies do enjoy this immersion. However, I recommend the warm water bath only after your newborn has spent at least 5 minutes on your chest and in your arms. Make sure that the nurses bathe your newborn in the delivery room within your view so that you can watch for baby's smile! He will visibly relax in the warm water, his eyes will brighten, and his color will turn a rosy pink. Talk to him in a reassuring voice.

When baby comes out of the bath, wrap him snugly so that he feels as contained as he did in the womb. Make sure that his arms and legs are bent or flexed in the fetal position. He is comforted by the touch of his own skin.

THE CRIB CAP: After birth, your newborn loses much of his body heat through his head, so now's the time to place that knit stocking cap on him. He should wear his little cap for the first twenty-four hours, or until his temperature has stabilized. The head covering seems to have a calming effect on newborns. If you cover his ears slightly, the cap will cut out some of the obnoxiously loud metallic sounds of the delivery room.

When Baby Is Taken Off to the Nursery

If you are in the recovery room collecting some much-deserved rest after your labor, it is very possible that your newborn will be taken off to the nursery. But that doesn't mean you have to lose contact with him.

DADDY HAS SOME OTHER JOBS: The neonatal nurses have many responsibilities, so it would be a great help if daddy followed baby into the nursery (with the nurses' permission, of course) to place the black-and-white stimulators brought from home around the little crib.

It is important to give your newborn a visual focal point, so be sure to place these stick-up toys directly within baby's line of sight. Don't make him crane his neck or bend to see them. You may place the checkerboard on his left side and the black-and-white photo of your smiling faces on his right, since he'll turn more often to his right. He'd rather look at mommy and daddy's faces than anything else in the world. Make sure that all these items are securely attached so that they do not fall on baby.

Daddy, if you notice the nurses have their radio turned to rock and roll music, ask them to turn it off. That kind of sound stimulation will be agitating to your newborn. Substitute your tape recording of mother's heartbeat by simply laying the recorder in the crib and playing it at a low volume if baby becomes irritable. Play the heartbeat for no more than 5 to 10 minutes at a time, or until baby has fallen off to sleep.

THE BLACK AND WHITE SCARF: Firmly attach mommy's scarf (the one that was worn for several days without washing) to the crib, close to your baby's head, so that he can once again enjoy her body scent. This fragrant scent will help your newborn tolerate the noxious alcohol wipes and antiseptic solutions he'll confront in the nursery as he's bathed and his cord is treated.

MILK TIME: Open the container of frozen colostrum you brought from home and place near your newborn's nose. He'll have the pleasure of becoming accustomed to the smell of Mother's breast milk as it thaws over the next two or three hours. What a great way for him to prepare for breast-feeding!

THE RED AND BLUE SCARVES: Drape the scarves over the head of your newborn's crib, making sure they cannot fall on baby's face. They will help to block out harsh light and will lull him to sleep.

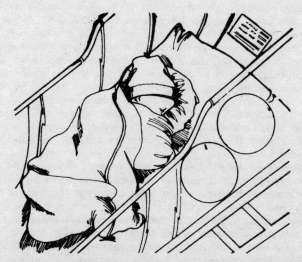

Place visual stimulators directly within baby's line of sight.

A SNUG NEST: Another way to promote baby's rest at this time is to create a "nest" in his crib by rolling up receiving blankets and tucking them around baby's sides, head, and feet. They should be relatively close to his body, so that when he extends his arms or legs, he'll feel the blankets. His sense of touch will tell his brain that he's in a nice, confined space—just as he was in the womb. The nest stimulates the intrauterine environment with its known and *tested* boundaries, and provides important, immediate sensory feedback to baby's brain.

In the Event You Have a Cesarean Section

In days gone by, women who delivered babies by C-sections felt deprived of the joys of the childbirth process. That no longer need be the case.

Today, mothers are usually alert during a C-section delivery. They can and should have daddy in the delivery room with them. And daddy is entitled to see the birth of his baby, whether mother is awake or not. Fathers who are permitted to watch the miracle of birth express more affectionate feelings toward their children.

Daddy also gives mother much support during the sometimes frightening events of a C-section. For her sense of security, he should follow her into the operating room—with permission, of course—*and stand by as she is placed on the operating table*. He can offer words of encouragement while the IV is started, her abdomen is scrubbed, and the drapes placed. Mother will benefit greatly from his reassuring presence during the *initial* phase of encountering the surgical room.

Father is mother's liaison to baby during a C-section delivery. Watching the birth while stationed at mother's head, he can explain to her how baby looks and what's happening to baby and to her. From this vantage point, he is away from the furious activity that follows the cesarean baby's arrival.

He can embrace his newborn several minutes after birth, stroking him, talking to him, calling his name softly. Baby can smell daddy's skin.

When baby goes off to the nursery, daddy should accompany him so that he can report the newborn's progress back to mother. He can continue to console him as the admission procedures are completed. If baby is able to stay with his parents during the recovery period, he should be in daddy's care.

It takes about 90 minutes for a C-section to be sewn up and for mother to be transferred to the recovery unit. Baby will be shown to mother as soon as possible after birth and she should be allowed to touch him, kiss him, and stroke his head several times.

Although I recommend room music for vaginal delivery, in the case of a C-section it can be very distracting because of the conversation necessary among hospital personnel. If possible, however, mother can listen to soothing music on her stereo headset.

"What's Going on Here?"

Baby is in a state of disorientation following the first hour or two of calm. He experiences a state of disorganization: asleep one minute, awake the next; arms flailing about, then quiet and calm; crying, then sucking; fussy, then content. During most of this time period he's in a state of semi-sleepiness/semi-wakefulness, waking and sleeping in short bursts.

In fact, baby's actions can be compared to those of an adult who experiences serious, dramatic, and abrupt life changes. But after about twenty-four hours, he calms down noticeably and behavior patterns begin to appear.

"The Pause That Refreshes"

"Breast-feeding instruction, post-partum exercise classes, baby-bath demonstrations, family planning counseling sessions, 'sore-bottom' soaking, newborn photo-taking and examinations, birth certificate signing, visitors, phone calls—and you, Dr. Ludington, want me to add Infant Stimulation

to all of this during the first two days after my baby's birth?"
you say.

Yes!

I *also* want you to get an absolutely, positively necessary
rest. With a determined effort, I *know* you can follow my
guidelines for the personal R & R structuring of your first two
post-partum days. Unfortunately, it is extremely difficult to
coordinate new mother needs with established hospital routine. Difficult, but by no means impossible.

Having labored for hours to bring your treasured child into
this world, you require (as do most women) six to eight hours
of uninterrupted sleep.

Without this recharging through sleep, you will be too
tired to give your child the quality loving time he deserves
when starting to know you. Have a nice long nap.

Daddy Takes Over

Rest assured that baby is in good, strong, loving hands, for
dad is on hand to help out now. He's thrilled to be able to
participate by calling family and friends to announce the
news. It's a perfect time for him to ask each one to hold
all visits and phone calls to you during your initial rest
period.

Daddy's second task is to check on baby to be certain he's
comfortable. He can see that the heartbeat tape is used
appropriately. When baby is irritable, daddy can play the
soothing sounds for 5 to 10 minutes. If he's alert and quiet,
the tape recording of mother or father singing a lullaby or
reading a nursery rhyme can play very softly within the crib.
A note of caution, however, about the earphones for baby.
The sound waves can bounce back and forth within his ears
and their continual high vibrations *can cause a hearing loss,
so don't use them*.

You'll notice that even though the nurses may lay your
newborn down with his arms and legs extended, he'll manage
to tuck them in under his body in the fetal position. This
position helps in the insulation of his nerve cells and prevents
the loss of some body heat. For the first two weeks of life (and
especially these first two days in the hospital) make sure that

baby is wrapped snugly in the fetal position on his tummy or side, with arms and legs flexed.

When you've all had a good rest, you'll feel up to participating in the Infant Stimulation task of the first two days: *focused love*.

24. The First Two Days:

Focused Love

The first *two days of life* are invaluable in establishing firm ties between you and your newborn. At this time you will be stimulating his senses merely with your own presence.

Let the nurse know that you want your newborn brought to you at least 15 minutes before feeding time. The period of alert inactivity—when baby is most relaxed and ready to learn—usually occurs 15 minutes before and 10 minutes after he is fed (unless he has fallen asleep during nursing).

It is important for you to assert your needs, because normal hospital routine consists of countless interruptions.

To Structure Your Interaction with Your Newborn

- Close the door of your hospital room.
- Post a note saying, "Quiet please, Infant Stimulation in progress. Do not disturb." If you share a room, draw the curtains around your bed.
- Have all phone calls held.

Readiness for Stimulation

Now that you've set the stage, you'll need to reassure yourself that your baby is *physically capable* of receiving stimulation—that it won't tax him, but rather will please him. In your eagerness to provide him with an advantaged environment, you don't want to create stress, anxiety, or irritation.

The following are some simple, concrete steps to help you determine if your newborn's physiological system can tolerate structured play and stimulation. This step-by-step approach will answer the question: *Does my baby have enough control over his physiological state (heart rate and breathing ability), motor coordination, and attentiveness to pay attention to and learn from the stimulation I'll be providing?*

STEP 1. Once your newborn has come out of his twenty-four-hour period of disorganization (See Chapter 23), he will settle into a regular pattern of sleep and wakefulness.

When he awakens and is quiet and alert, approach his crib and change his position—if he's on his back, turn him to his tummy. Or turn him from one side to the other. Be sure to watch his skin color closely as you do so.

If your newborn becomes very pink or bluish with this simple change of position, then you'll know he's not ready to tolerate environmental stimulation at this time—even though his eyes are open and he looks ready to play. Your newborn's autonomic nervous system—the one that controls heartbeat, breathing, and other involuntary functions—hasn't adapted *yet* to sensory stimulation. Anything you do now will be too much. Your newborn's color change should pass within 30 seconds but don't stroke, sing, or talk to him. Just leave him to be quiet and to look at the visual items you have hung in his crib.

STEP 2. If your newborn's color remains stable, place a hand on his belly or upper thigh. Just leave it there, without stroking. Again, watch for a change in color, a grimace, or flailing arm and leg movements. If you note any, go no further!

STEP 3. Without talking, lean down and present your face to baby in a face-to-face manner. Watch for a negative response.

STEP 4. Start stroking with the hand that's resting on his belly or leg. Watch his arms and legs. They may jerk abruptly. This normal startle reflex is not a response to agitation. It means baby recognizes something new has happened in his environment. Wait 30 seconds. If he relaxes, you may continue. If he continues to extend his arms and legs in an agitated fashion, go no further. Gradually withdraw your hand and face.

STEP 5. If steps 1 through 4 are tolerated well, start talking in a slow, deliberate manner, and softly call baby's name for

30 to 60 seconds. Again, watch for signs of overstimulation: skin color change, movements, a grimace, outstretched fingers and toes, unusual breathing—too heavy, shallow, or fast.

If your newborn can handle the stroking, the visual stimulation of your face, and the talking—*congratulations*—you're on! His neurological system *can* tolerate a structured Infant Stimulation session!

STEP 6. Gradually withdraw all exploratory stimulation in the same order that you presented it. Sit your baby upright in your lap and start with the stimuli suggested below.

If you are uncertain about your baby's responses, feel free to ask for help. An astute neonatal nurse will be able to verify and clarify your newborn's behavior. She has had a wealth of experience observing babies. And these nurses seldom underestimate a mother's vigilant observations. They offer you help and positive reinforcement.

Your Newborn Wants Desperately to Know Who You Are

At age one to two days, your newborn wants desperately to know who you are. In order to be able to attach to you and love you, he must be able to distinguish you from all the other people in his environment. He does this the best way he knows—through his *senses*.

Your *primary job*,1 then, in these first few days, *consists of stimulating your newborn's senses with little "bits" of yourself*. These mark you as being different from everyone else in the world and give your baby a sense of belonging to a family unit.

VISUAL CONTACT: You'll want to foster the very special closeness that eye-to-eye contact provides. Your love finds expression in your eyes and can be read by your child. Look into your baby's eyes to help him find yours.

Sometimes newborns get mesmerized by the dark shadows around your mouth and chin. In order to help your baby look beyond your nose and eventually up to your eyes, keep the lights dimmed. Make sure that you maintain face-to-face contact.

Use the visual stimulators you brought to the hospital to train your newborn to look at your eyes. Hold him upright and bring into his field of vision, from his right side, no more than 10 to 13 inches from his eyes, the 2-inch black dot you inked onto a white background, which stimulates the iris of your eyes and helps him to focus on circle stimulation.

Then use the popsicle face (a face drawn on a paper plate, with a popsicle stick glued where the neck should be) in the same way, to help your newborn learn the different components of a face so he'll be able to recognize yours more easily. It's great for eliciting smiles.

HEARING: Those first few days, your newborn wants very much to learn the sound of your voice.

It's most important that you maintain face-to-face contact when you talk to him. Don't attempt to carry on a conversation with him from across the room or speak to him way above his head.

When you're face-to-face, baby will learn non-verbal messages that accompany speech and you will be able to observe his cues. Only then will you respond appropriately to his smile, brightened eyes, or grimace. You can increase loudness, change intonation, add cooing, or even stop the conversation. When you talk directly to your baby, he learns that verbal and visual or non-verbal conversation is *important*. Otherwise, he may eventually tune you out.

While you talk, make sure that you:

- Repeat baby's name at least three times before you say anything else, so that he learns to recognize his name.
- Identify yourselves as "mommy" and "daddy" as you talk to him.
- Choose three nursery rhymes that you'll enjoy singing over and over again in his first year of life—songs with lots of repetition, like "Old MacDonald Had a Farm," "Row, Row, Row Your Boat," or "Mary Had a Little Lamb." Pick one of the three to sing during these first two days and be consistent in repeating it.

TOUCH: If he could, your newborn would ask, "What do you *feel* like, mom and dad?" To help him find the answer:

- Place your hand firmly on his abdomen for baby to accommodate to your body warmth and your encompassing touch.
- Each time you pick your child up, stroke his head (from

his forehead to the nape of his neck) ten times, and then stroke his body from head to toe. Your reassuring caress helps to relax his muscles and soon becomes a natural massage technique that tells baby, "Mommy or daddy is here and everything is just fine."

- Embrace your newborn warmly and develop a familiar holding pattern. Be consistent. Whether you've chosen to hold him on your right or left breast, repeat the same position whenever you embrace him. Remember, your newborn enjoys hearing your soothing heartbeat.
- Before birth, all that baby could feel was water. Now he has new areas to touch: air, cloth, skin. Let him enjoy his exploration by freeing his hands.
- Check your newborn's fingernails. If they're very long, ask to have them cut. In that way his hands won't have to be covered by the little flaps of his T-shirt (for fear of scratching his face).
- Give your newborn opportunities for skin-to-skin contact. Let him nuzzle into your neck. That way he'll have the double pleasure of feeling your skin and smelling your special scent.

SMELL: Very quickly your newborn's keen sense of smell helps him learn that you belong to each other.

- Place the scarf that you've worn for two days without washing near to him when he's sleeping. Alternate two scarves—wear one and leave one in the crib so you can exchange them every second day. Always make sure the scarf is securely placed so that it cannot smother or choke baby.
- When you get home, allow your newborn to sleep in the same room with you for the first month.
- Place a sachet of mommy's or daddy's perfume/after-shave in baby's room and clothing so when he's taken there, the familiar smell of one of his parents will comfort him.
- Let him smell your breast milk before nursing. If you're not saving it in bottles, just lightly compress your breast tissue on the top and sides to gently express several drops of milk on a cotton ball or breast pad. Pass the "delicious" odor under your newborn's nose, and you'll find he may begin to suck even before you put him to the

breast. (This may help eliminate nursing problems.) Some babies will even start to suck when a Q-tip dabbed with a drop of peppermint oil is passed under their noses. Others hold off sucking until they're on the *real* thing— the nipple! They're not easily fooled!

TASTE: Breast milk. Nothing matches it for nourishment, taste, and bonding! But don't expect your newborn to latch onto your breast immediately. It may take a little while to learn. Eating is a psychological event. You yourself see the food, smell it, think about enjoying it...and then salivate. You can help your baby learn to enjoy the breast-feeding experience by:

- Letting him look at your nipple before he gets the milk, and allowing him to smell the milk, as we've suggested above.
- Refraining from speaking during early nursing experiences. (Your newborn is so intent on learning to whom he belongs that he'll stop sucking just to look at and listen to you. His top priority is getting to know you.)

MOVEMENT: Never hesitate to pick up and hold your baby. Do it in the first two days, and ever after! *You cannot spoil him by picking him up too often and keeping him well embraced in a secure position close to your heart!*

- Your newborn needs horizontal holding in your arms, and vertical holding when you sit him up in your lap.
- Rock him in the nursery rocking chair for extra movement stimulation.
- Place him in the Snugli®—a sac-like carrier slung over your shoulders and resting on your chest, available at toy and baby stores—for the wheelchair ride down to your car as you go home from the hospital. That's a great way to offer movement stimulation while you add to his feelings of security. Always make sure that his head is well supported.

Mini-Milestones

We tend to think of infant growth and development in terms of major milestones—when baby sits unsupported, when he crawls, stands, walks, says "mama," holds a spoon in his own hand. But all of these "biggies" are built upon smaller, intermediate mini-milestones. After all, a *mile* is nothing more than a lot of *inches* strung together!

When you know what they are, each little step your baby makes is as exciting as the giant steps that we're accustomed to thinking about. When you're tuned into these "baby steps," you'll appreciate your baby's week-by-week growth and *your* contribution to these changes. You can easily see the effect of your loving attention and stimulation when you become aware of your baby's mini-milestones.

Of course, any list of developmental changes can be a terrible bore! So, I'm *not* going to bore you with *everything*. I will, however, share some experiences my patients enjoy. These are accomplishments that parents usually *see* without a real awareness of the importance of what they're looking at.

Mini-Milestones at 2 or 3 Days of Age

1. Your newborn adjusts his posture according to how he is held and by whom. When *daddy* holds him, for example, he'll snuggle differently into his shoulder and neck than when a stranger picks him up.

2. He smiles spontaneously, although briefly.

3. His hands remain tightly fisted. In the months ahead we'll watch as he learns how to relax and open up his hands.

4. He grasps when an object is placed in his hand; he does not grasp when an object is merely brushed against his hand. Put your finger in his hand to see how tightly he holds on. Though a reflex now, this kind of grasping experience eventually will teach him how to deliberately hold onto an object.

5. When you pick him up, your newborn will quiet down. He's saying, "The most important place for me is in your arms."

6. When you hold him up, you'll notice your newborn's head falls heavily on your shoulder. In the next few weeks he'll be lifting it up and bearing a good portion of the weight on his own shoulders with his neck muscles. Watch for this in the future.

7. When he's on his tummy, you'll notice that he turns his head from side to side but he can't lift it at all. This will change quite rapidly.

8. In that same position he pulls his legs up underneath him in such a way that his buttocks are higher than his head. That means that certain nerve cells haven't yet been insulated. When he can raise his head above his buttocks, you'll know that the insulation (myelination) and muscle tone development have occurred.

Now you'll be able to keep track of these little successes... to see that your newborn is growing *sensationally* and developing beautifully. But remember, these mini-milestones are *not* to be used as a yardstick against which to "measure" your child. Instead, they are merely small signs of development. And in the upcoming chapters, you will be able to follow further changes in these same areas to show you how well your baby is developing.

In the next six chapters we'll be giving you *specific instructions* on how to enhance your daily ongoing interactions with baby and what to do during your 15-minute-a-day Infant Stimulation play sessions once you're home.

Only satisfying results flow from seizing every opportunity to share yourself with your newborn. Love your baby and let it show!

II. THE FIRST
SIX MONTHS

25. Your Newborn:

Establishing Routines

As we set the stage in previous chapters for your baby's birth, we cited many exciting studies demonstrating the role you as a parent can play in enhancing your baby's mental, physical, and emotional development. Thus, we sometimes referred to material that we will be discussing in the following chapters on the Infant Stimulation Program. Now, however, we will be talking about it in greater depth and in a purposeful sequence designed to meet your new baby's increasing month-by-month developmental capacities.

Home Sweet Home

You are a family at home, together at last. Before the excitement and joy surrounding the event settle down, you'll notice in yourself some subtle signs of fatigue which you may want to ignore. *Don't!* They are real, understandable, inescapable, common, and *must* be dealt with. Let's see how some of these situations develop:

A newborn's stomach is quite small, therefore he may require frequent feedings. You, then, are on call at all hours of the day and night. While baby naps, there is laundry to do, meals to prepare, and countless personal chores. You will find yourself catching only sporadic sleep. Rest deprivation accumulates. Result? Fatigue!

Your body is changing. Your hormones are going through a period of readjustment which may cause unexpected, sudden mood shifts and more fatigue.

It's important for you to rest and it's okay once a day to do at least one thing you really love to do: garden, chat on the phone, bake a pie, read, enjoy a bath or nap.

All of this activity occurs at a time when you also start worrying about regaining your pre-pregnancy figure. And that raises conflicting thoughts regarding the Big Question— to Diet or Not to Diet, if you are nursing.

The best advice I can offer is to continue to eat well-balanced meals. You may continue to use the Smarter-Baby High-Protein Diet for Pregnant Women, if you wish (See Chapter 9), but after delivery make sure to *omit the protein shakes* and add *one extra cup of low fat milk or one extra serving of milk products* a day.

It takes about 750 calories of energy for your body to produce about 1 quart of milk a day. But the Recommended Daily Allowance for lactating mothers is only *500 additional calories a day*. If you've had a normal weight gain of 24 to 30 pounds during pregnancy, 4 to 9 of those pounds will be stored as fat. That extra fat will contribute 200 to 300 calories a day toward the production of milk. So, by following my recommendations for a well-balanced diet and breast-feeding your baby, you will lose weight naturally. And you will regain your shape as your organs decrease in size. A program of mild new-mother exercises will tone your muscles.

Establish Routine—Not a Rigid Schedule— in Order to Develop Trust

To help you cope with all of the unsettling changes and your own fatigue, it is most important that you begin to *establish a routine with your newborn this first month*.

In addition to giving *your* life some structure, routine gives some measure of predictability to your baby's day and helps to instill that all-important feeling of security. *Baby's task for the first month of life is to develop a sense of trust that his needs will be met by a consistent care-giver.*

When I talk about routine, I don't mean strict adherence to a rigid schedule. Basic routine should be based on your *newborn's emerging behavior patterns*. Babies don't tolerate changes in routine as easily as adults do, so willingly make adjustments to accommodate your baby's needs.

Routines You'll Want to Establish with Your Newborn

- Answer his cry quickly and completely.
- Feed him when he's hungry.
- Change his diaper regularly.
- Use the "setting event" (the same words of greeting) to begin each interaction.
- Stimulate baby for 5 minutes before and/or after his morning, midday, and evening feedings, because he is most alert at those times.
- Respect nap time.
- Always keep in mind: predictable pattern for the baby takes precedence over the care-giver's convenience.

Routine for Learning

With routine, your newborn also begins to gain an understanding of his environment. When you respond quickly and completely to baby's cry with your presence, your voice, your milk, and your attention to diaper change, he begins to learn *sequencing*. For example, he may think:

I cry.
Mommy comes.
She picks me up.
Then food follows.
My diaper gets changed.
We play and socialize.
Then she puts me back to bed again.

With repetition, this familiar pattern helps him understand a sequence of events. Such a consistent routine affects his cognitive development, and eventually baby can predict what will happen next.

Soon he begins to feel empowered. Routine has given your newborn a way to predict and structure his day so that he doesn't feel helpless. He realizes that when he cries, he can affect his environment. He develops a sense of trust in himself by learning that he *can* have some control over his life and he learns to trust you because he knows you'll be there when he needs you.

Fitting Others into Baby's Routine

During his first month of life your baby is still learning to identify his nuclear family unit—those to whom he belongs. It is important, therefore, that just a few people care for him consistently. Your newborn can only handle about three primary care-givers: mommy, daddy, and one other (perhaps nanny or grandma).

MOMMY: We have already covered what baby needs from you. You are a *sustaining human presence*.

DADDY: Dr. T. Berry Brazelton was among the earliest researchers to reveal newborns' interactions with fathers as being different from their interactions with mothers. Newborns are sensitive to interactions and know that play with daddy has a different quality from play with mommy.

Within the first two weeks of life newborns have been found to move differently when they hear a woman's voice as opposed to a man's voice. It is believed that babies can predict whether a man or woman is about to play with them from voice alone. This means that as early as two weeks of age, babies have developed a sense of *predictability* about the kinds of play they will experience.[1]

How right they are! Men are definitely very active, relating to children by picking them up and rocking them. They almost always couple movement with their stimulation. Women are quieter, calmer, and tend to stimulate by talking, singing, and showing their faces. These differing styles complement each other and offer baby all possibilities of interaction.

Daddy should establish a loving routine with his newborn as soon as possible. During those first two weeks at home he can make a habit of setting aside some special, undivided quality time with baby every day for a game that both enjoy. Daddy can take off his pajama top every morning before breakfast and let baby lie naked on his bare chest. Before bedtime, sit together in a rocking chair and read a favorite children's story to baby. Follow newspaper headlines, as we've suggested before. Play a facial game or peekaboo. Or just cuddle, kiss, and nuzzle. Be creative! You can do anything mommy can do and your play is a nice counterbalance to what she provides. Just be consistent in maintaining your loving routine.

A WORD ABOUT VISITORS: You can expect many visitors those first weeks that baby is home. Everyone wants to share in the miracle of life your new baby represents. Encourage friends and family to *telephone in advance* so that they arrive when your newborn is receptive to a visit.

Don't allow your visitors to interrupt baby's routine. It's unfair to wake a baby to see anyone! Your newborn needs his sleep and you would be doing him a grave disservice to arouse him just to socialize for the convenience of another person.

Using Bedtime Routine to Help Establish Security

You will want to establish a bedtime routine that fits your baby's sleep-wake patterns. By one month of age he'll be spending between 50 and 75 percent of his time asleep.

Help baby fall asleep by creating a routine that includes a secure, reassuring environment. During the day allow him to nap in the hustle-bustle of your household, not tucked away somewhere in a quiet, darkened room. Remember, this is the kind of environment he's accustomed to in the womb. At night, he can be near you.

To heighten your newborn's feeling of security and to continue with a well-known routine, recall familiar events from his "past" in ways we will show you. Play the heartbeat tape to remind him of the comfy, warm place he used to inhabit. If he had been exposed to classical music in the womb, continue to play the same music.

Establish a security toy. Choose one specific toy to keep your newborn company in his crib, cradle, or bassinet. A black-and-white panda bear is ideal. The toy should be small, soft, cuddly, and light weight. (You will see that within one to two months, your infant will scoot up against, put his arms around, and cuddle into it!) This toy is called a "transitional object"—an object to which he grows attached. It helps ease the transition from a familiar environment to an unfamiliar one.

Recognize and help baby practice his ability to console himself by encouraging him to suck his fingers, brush his hand across his face, and hold his hands together. Offer him a pacifier for additional sucking.

Choose a bedtime story, nursery rhyme, or lullaby that you'll enjoy repeating. (If you used one during pregnancy, continue with it now.)

Always wish your baby a good night with the same words— "Sweet dreams," "Night-night," "Sleep tight"—whatever you feel comfortable saying. The familiarity of the repeated phrase will help remind him that it's bedtime.

Sleep Routines: Helping Baby Fall Asleep

- **Put him down for daytime naps amid the hustle-bustle of your household.**
- **Hold, wrap, and nest him securely.**
- **Play familiar heartbeat and classical music tapes.**
- **Introduce a security toy.**
- **Help baby to console himself.**
- **Repeat same story, nursery rhyme, lullaby.**
- **Use the same "good night" words.**

---

26. The First Month:

Encouraging Alertness

In this and the following chapters we will be suggesting many ways for you to enhance your ongoing interactions with baby. These are meant to help you make fruitful use of the time spent together when not specifically playing Infant Stimulation games. *Please don't feel compelled to do all of the activities—these are simply suggestions for your mutual pleasure.* The second half of each chapter contains listings of toys, visual stimulators, and games from which to choose. That is your Infant Stimulation Program. Each chapter closes with a mini-milestones chart to help you follow your baby's growth and development.

Stimulation Sessions Build Alertness in the First Month

As you set up a daily routine with your newborn, your task as a parent is to stimulate and be sensitive to his senses in order to increase his alertness. All of your stimulation activities will center around this goal.

Ongoing Activities That Encourage Alertness

Here are some ongoing activities that you can easily integrate into your daily routine. Some take almost no effort at all!

TOUCH: Deliberately place objects in your newborn's hands. You'll be teaching him to turn his involuntary grasping reflex into a voluntary activity. Of course, at first he'll drop the objects, but eventually his muscle tone and control will develop to the point that he will hold onto toys himself and release the objects at will.

I recommend using a Taffeta Rattle like the one pictured. The taffeta makes a nice, soft rustling sound and is the perfect feather weight for baby's still weak muscles. You'll find simple instructions for making the rattle in Appendix 4. (Never leave baby alone with this toy or allow him to take the bells into his mouth, since he might try to swallow them.)

Try to keep up the skin-to-skin contact you began in the hospital. Stroke your newborn often. Caress him across the forehead and then over his head to the nape of his neck every time you pick him up to change or feed him. Your gentle touch will remind him that mommy or daddy is here and all is well. Keep up the body massage, as well, stroking from head to toe and from center to extremities. This helps baby to relax, especially during the fussy time between four and six P.M. Letting him rest on your bare chest is also ideal.

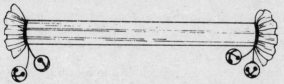

The feather-weight Taffeta Rattle makes a nice, soft rustling sound and is perfect for your one-month-old's weak muscles.

For your baby's emotional security continue the nesting within his crib when you put him down to sleep. Remember that the tucked-in, rolled-up blankets make him feel that he's safe and secure, back in the womb.

MOVEMENT: Just as baby enjoys nesting while he's sleeping, he loves the freedom to move around and engage in active self-regulated play while awake.

Ongoing Movement Stimulators

• Allow baby to play naked for 5 minutes in your bed in a 72-degree room.

- Provide 15 minutes of tummy time play daily during your stimulation sessions and/or when baby is left to sleep in his crib. Upon awakening, this position encourages him to lift his head to view visual stimulators which you have left in his crib for his enjoyment. (See our discussion of position in Chapter 10.)
- Place a mobile within kicking or batting range for 5 minutes a day and let baby kick and bat at it while on his back, after you've changed his diaper.
- Hold him over your shoulder in an upright position to let him view a stimulating black-and-white poster. This will help to build the muscle tone in your newborn's neck as he studies the poster longer and longer. (You'll find the address for the Infant Stimulation Facts Poster in the Resource Guide.)
- Use a Snugli®—a shoulder-harnessed pouchlike device worn across the chest—to transport your newborn, providing him with your heartbeat sounds, warmth, and body odor. Make sure his head is well supported.

VISUAL: Hold your blanketed baby closely and securely at your shoulder, so he can look at a black-and-white poster. He will try to look at it intently, and will seem very interested in the many designs he sees.

Continue using the popsicle face to help baby learn facial features, and securely hang the 8 × 10 black-and-white photos of your smiling faces in his crib. The 3-inch black dot on white background will reinforce his eye-to-eye contact with you.

When you talk to your baby, face him directly. This will help him learn the important non-verbal messages implicit in conversation, and will teach him to associate your voice with your face.

Move your baby's crib around the room once a week, as suggested in Chapter 10, to offer him a new perspective on his world. Alternate his position in bed so that he has new and different things to look at when he awakens.

The following is a list of visual stimulators that your newborn to one-month-old enjoys looking at. Choose from among these during playtime:

What Your Infant Likes to Look At in the First Month of Life

AGE	STIMULATOR—Held 10 to 13 inches from baby's face
Newborn to 2 weeks	• Your animated face, smiling and talking • Your eyes • The breast as he nurses • Simple black-and-white drawing of your smiling face on a paper plate • Black stripes (8 inches long by 2 inches high) pasted or drawn on white 8 × 11 cardboard background • A 4-square black-and-white checkerboard, each square 3 × 3 inches • One black dot, 3 inches in diameter, pasted on white 8 × 11 background
2 to 4 weeks	Add (held 10 to 13 inches from baby's face): • Simple bold drawing of two round faces, each at least 6 inches in diameter—one male and one female—done in heavy black ink on white 11 × 14 background • A 4-to 6-square checkerboard, each square 2½ by 2½ inches • Black or red stripes (3 inches long by 1½ inches high) pasted or drawn on white 8 × 11 cardboard background or crocheted • Two black dots, 3 inches in diameter, pasted or drawn on 8 × 11 white background • Simple black-and-white bull's-eye: one 3-inch black dot in the center, surrounded by a 2-inch white band and a 1-inch black outline at the edge drawn on a paper plate • Simple two-dimensional mobile made from 4 dessert-size paper plates with drawings of stripes, 4-square checkerboard, a black dot, and a simple bull's-eye, hung so that the plates face down 10 to 13 inches from baby's eyes • Simple drawing of face on paper plate glued onto popsicle stick (Popsicle face)

Simple black-and-white bull's eye: a 3-inch black dot in the center surrounded by a 2-inch white band and a 1-inch black outline at the edge.

SMELL AND TASTE: During this first month your baby is still learning to whom he belongs, so continue with the same smell and taste stimulation that you used in the hospital—the scent of your body odor and taste and smell of your breast milk.

You may notice that when Mother picks up baby, he gets fussy. Actually, that should be a sign that he knows Mommy from everyone else! The odor of her breast milk is so strong and appealing, he feels he should be nursing. When anyone else picks him up, he just doesn't respond in the same way!

We hope that these recommendations for ongoing activities will help you enjoy your family life while balancing love, learning, security, and trust. And here we risk being repetitive. Take care of yourself by taking control of the planning you *can* control. Carry on, mom and dad. . . .

The Burst-Pause Rhythm

In time you may notice that your newborn gets intensely involved in stimulators for brief periods of time, with pauses in between. He may hold a rattle and shake it for 2- to 3-seconds, then stop; shake it again for 2 to 3 seconds with increasing vigor, then stop again. His activity may build to a crescendo and then taper off in what we refer to as a "burst-pause rhythm." *Newborns enjoy up to seven to nine 2- to 3-second exposures of a single stimulating object in one sitting.*

Choosing Stimulation Games

In choosing games to play with baby, be selective. As you cannot utilize all of the games we've suggested in any one day, a good method of selection is to look through the listings in the second half of this chapter and choose one visual, one auditory, one smell, one movement, and one touch game per day. Each one takes a minute or so to accomplish. When you do all five in one sitting, you will have engaged in 5 minutes of stimulating play with your child. Simply repeat the same five games three times a day and you will have accomplished your Infant Stimulation goal. (Try to carry out your play sessions before morning, noon, and evening feedings, when baby is most alert.)

It's best to vary the fare from day to day to keep interest high. Use the suggested time as a guide to help you plan your fun. (But by no means should you sit, stopwatch in hand, to regulate your session.) My utmost concern is that you all *relax and enjoy.* So, before you begin, remember to determine if your newborn is physiologically ready for environmental stimulation.

You may play the music baby heard in the womb or classical suggestions in Chapter 13 as background to your sessions.

Toys You Will Need This Month:
(See Resource Guide in Chapter 33)

Never leave baby alone with toys in which he may become entangled or on which he may choke!

VISUAL TOYS
- Some items listed in this chapter
- Bright Baby™ Blanket (p. 308)

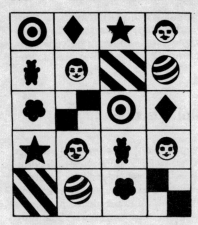

The Bright Baby™ Blanket provides hours of stimulating fun and play.

- Popsicle face
- Bright Baby Mind Mobile™

- Unbreakable mylar mirror
- Bright Baby Teaching Tube™ (p. 277 or firm pillows

MOVEMENT TOYS
- Snugli® (optional)

TOUCH TOYS
- 2 powder puffs
- 2 swatches of fabric with different textures like velvet and satin

- Mr. Mouse™ (p. 282)
- Tactile Tillie™ (p. 325)

HEARING TOYS
- Taffeta Rattle (you can make your own, Appendix 4)
- 2 small jingle bells
- Black and white yarn

- Rattle (like the one from Johnson & Johnson's Child Development Series or something similar)
- Daily newspaper
- Phonics reader

SMELL TOYS
- Mother's perfume
- Father's after-shave
- Oregano, cinnamon, vanilla extract

- *Sweet Smell of Strawberryland* (p. 287)

Building your baby's alertness must, of course, be accomplished gently, with a full and loving respect for your child's own rhythm. You never want to force a program on your baby or overstimulate him by ignoring his rhythm. But how do you identify that rhythm?

He's Got Rhythm

The best time to learn about your newborn's rhythm is when he's awake and quiet, 20 to 35 minutes before feeding time. After diapering him, you'll notice baby's legs naturally bend at the knee. Wrap your newborn in his receiving blanket with his legs gently flexed. You may leave his hands free so you can watch for their responsiveness. Begin by sitting baby up in your lap. Cradle him in your left arm on the left side of your chest.

When there are no other sound distractions, call your baby's name two to three times in a lilting, singsong voice. Identify yourself as mommy or daddy and say "I love you." Repeat this setting event again, two to three times.

Now watch his reaction:

- Do his fingers stretch out toward you?
- Does he turn his head to the sound of your voice?
- Do his eyes widen in order to take you in more fully?
- These signs mean that he's *attentive*.

Next, add touch and movement to the visual and auditory stimulation by stroking his leg and rocking. Again, watch him closely. But this time see if you can detect arm and leg movements like flailing or kicking.

When arm and leg movements begin:

- Stop rocking
- Gradually stop stroking
- Slow and soften speech

Then wait to see *how long* it takes for your newborn to come back into a quiet alert state.

If your baby continues the kicking movements, don't try to actively soothe him because that most probably would overstimulate him. Vigorous patting, shifting position, and rocking to and fro can be overwhelming and lead to agitation and distraction.

It will take time for you to recognize what is happening, so don't hesitate to call your baby's name again to get a sense of what his pattern of interaction is like. When you learn your baby's rhythm, you will know how to avoid overstimulating. You can then set the pace of your interactions to suit his individual patterns.

Once you have spent 5 to 10 minutes learning your newborn's rhythm, you may feed him. Since you don't want to distract him from eating, refrain from talking, stroking, or rocking during nursing—at least for the first week or two of life, or until he can attend to his sucking without distraction.

Understanding What Goes into Your Stimulation Sessions: Three Kinds of Stimulating Play

Before you begin your stimulation sessions, it's important to know that you'll be engaging in three different kinds of play:

- Contingency
- Interacting
- Observing

All of the games that we suggest at the end of this and the other how-to chapters include each of the above kinds of activities.

CONTINGENCY: Contingency play often involves movement. When baby moves, he gets "rewarded" as a result of his actions. Kicking or waving his arms in the air may produce the twirl of a mobile, the ringing of a bell attached to a bootie, or the banging of a rattle.

Contingency play encourages baby to learn to move his body with voluntary, coordinated motions rather than with the jerky actions that characterize his early reflexes. At the same time, it stimulates continued play because the results of baby's action—such as sound, wind, design changes—please him. Your baby needs that reinforcement. And this type of play is crucial to his sense of self—he learns he has some power over his environment.

Furthermore, baby learns the relationship between a stimulus and its response ("If I bat the mobile it will turn") and that different stimuli give different responses ("A mobile does something quite different than a rattle!").

Movement exercises are equally important. The human body is a unique machine. The more it is moved, the better it performs and the longer it lasts! Babies need to move their arms and legs and all of their body parts in order to gain control over them and make the movements deliberate.

All physical exercises teach your baby important lessons about:

- How to control his world
- What his body is all about
- Where he is located in space
- Where his body and actions stop and the world begins
- How he can move through his environment

Movement stimulation is necessary for motor and mental learning.

Move your baby to learn so he can learn to move. I consider this a very important concept, and therefore I have included movement games in each stimulation play session I recommend.

INTERACTIVE PLAY: When your newborn is placed in his infant seat (an angled traylike chair that supports baby in an upright position) at three weeks of age, and you coo or rub noses, you're engaging in an interaction game. It's never too early to start playing peekaboo. Diaper changing and bath time are excellent times for interactive play. Making friendly faces at each other, smiling, tongue thrusting—anything that engages your baby one-to-one with you is a form of interactive play.

You can also interact with your newborn when playing with toys. It's your responsibility to show your baby all the different ways he can manipulate his stimulation toys.

Take a simple rattle. You can rattle it, turn it upside down, bang it, or roll it gently over his skin. When you do these things, you change the use of the toy. When you read a book, hold baby securely in your lap, read slowly and with expression, talk about the pictures, involve your child in the game.

Try using your own face! Puff up your cheeks. Then blow the air out so baby can feel wind or hear a pop. There are countless imaginative acts you can perform that help him to learn!

Every toy your baby encounters leads to new learning lessons called Toy Teaching Tasks. He'll learn:

- What it is, how it feels, smells, tastes
- No matter which way he turns it, it's still the same toy
- How to make the toy look different
- How to make the toy disappear and then reappear
- How to use the toy alone and how to use it with other toys and objects (for example, what happens when you put the rattle into a glass of water)

Keep these five teaching tasks in mind. They will serve as reminders of how to use the toy in productive interactions with your newborn.

OBSERVATION PLAY: When baby looks at a checkerboard, listens to a lullaby, smells a whiff of your perfume, or tastes breast milk or formula, he is engaging in passive, or observation, play. This simple activity is important during the first month of life because your newborn's attention span is brief at first. Since baby is not as active in observation play, it should be interspersed with interaction and contingency play to keep his attention span growing and provide relief from the more challenging interactive and contingency games.

To ensure that the toys used for all three types of play remain appealing, it is important to keep Infant Stimulation items separate from other playthings. If baby sees them around everywhere, he's less likely to pay attention to them. (See our discussion of habituation in Chapter 10.) Put them in a special box and keep them hidden between stimulation sessions. It's also a good idea to rotate visual items—show checkerboards one day and bull's-eyes the next—again, to avoid habituation.

The 15-Minute Daily Play Plans

We've promised 15-minute-a-day stimulation programs and here they are! All of the games listed below and in each of the next five chapters take into account your baby's developmental tasks for the month. They appeal to each of his senses.

Why not think of the list as a smorgasboard? When presented with an array of delicious foods, you most likely will select one hors d'oeuvre, one salad, one entrée, one dessert, and one beverage for your meal—or, as we said earlier, one visual, one auditory, one smell, one touch, and one movement game. For example, for your very first 15-minute program with your alert newborn, you might want to try:

- *Visual Game 1*. Show baby a visual stimulator
- *Touch Game 1*. Two minutes of skin-to-skin stroking
- *Hearing Game 2*. Give baby a Taffeta Rattle
- *Smell Game 4*. Delicious kitchen spices and herbs
- *Movement Game 4*. Baby seesaw

After the listing of games, you'll find a mini-milestones chart to help you follow your newborn's growth and development.

Visual Games
(See Chapter 33 and Appendix 4 for where-to-buy and how-to-make instructions)

1. PURPOSE: Visual stimulation
   YOU'LL NEED: Any of the visual stimulators listed above (birth or two weeks and then two to four weeks, as appropriate)
   TIME: 1 minute
   BABY'S POSITION: Sitting upright in your lap, wrapped securely with arms and legs flexed
   WATCH FOR: Baby's head and eyes to follow stimulator

- Bring the patterned design into the center of baby's field of vision, not more than 10 to 13 inches from his eyes.
- Move it in a small circle three times, then stop for the count of 5.
- Slowly move it 6 inches out to baby's right to train baby's neck muscles, and stop for the count of 5.
- In that position, move the stimulator in a circle twice and stop for the count of 5.
- Return the stimulator to the center of baby's field of vision and repeat on the left side.
- If he appears to want to continue, you may repeat the entire sequence.

2. PURPOSE: Learning about faces and visual stimulation

YOU'LL NEED: Popsicle face, a visual stimulator from the above list, and Bright Baby Teaching Tube™ or firm pillow

TIME: 2 minutes

BABY'S POSITION: Sitting upright in your lap, wrapped securely with arms and legs flexed.

WATCH FOR: Baby's first smile and his head and eyes to follow stimulator

- Show your own animated face and make friendly, smiling "faces."
- Show the popsicle face, moving it to the left and right, as you did in Exercise 1, for 1 minute.
- Place baby on his tummy on tube or pillows in an inclined position so his head is raised.
- Hold a visual stimulator directly in his line of vision and slowly lift it 3 inches and then lower to its starting position.

3. PURPOSE: Visual stimulation

YOU'LL NEED: Bright Baby™ Blanket

TIME: 1 minute

BABY'S POSITION: Lying on his tummy on the blanket (you should lie down facing him)

WATCH FOR: Baby's alertness and intent gaze

- Point to the black-and-white face, naming its features.
- Point to stripes on the blanket. Say? "Do you see these stripes? Look at the stripes. Can you follow my finger? Watch. See where my finger is going? Come with your eyes, come with your head . . . follow my finger. Oh, you do that so well!"

4. PURPOSE: Visual stimulation, training neck muscles, and self-identification

YOU'LL NEED: Unbreakable mylar mirror

TIME: 30 seconds

BABY'S POSITION: Held snugly in your lap, wrapped with arms and legs flexed

WATCH FOR: Baby's alertness and head movements

- Place mylar mirror in front of baby's eyes, identifying his reflected facial features.
- Lift mirror 3 inches upward, so his eyes follow.

5. PURPOSE: Visual stimulation and teaching baby relationship between objects and movement

YOU'LL NEED: Bright Baby Mind Mobile™ strung between the legs of two chairs, within baby's arms' reach, directly in front of him

TIME: 1 minute, 30 seconds

BABY'S POSITION: On his tummy on the floor (you should lie facing baby on the other side of the mobile)

WATCH FOR: Baby to follow as the shape on the mobile comes forward and falls back

- Choose two shapes at random. Move each one toward baby's face and release so that the shape hangs vertically in its original position.
- Point out movements in the other shapes that result from the accented ones falling back in order.

6. PURPOSE: Visual stimulation, attention span lengthening, and baby following his finger with his eyes

YOU'LL NEED: 2-inch crocheted black dot on white background (if no crocheted toy is available, use a paper plate with desired design)

TIME: 1 minute

BABY'S POSITION: Sitting up, wrapped in receiving blanket with legs flexed but arms free

WATCH FOR: Black dot to be reflected in pupils of baby's eyes, and baby's finger activity.

- Bring the dot into baby's visual field (13 inches from baby's eyes) from his right-hand side.
- Leave the stimulator within his view for a count of 10, noting if he's still paying attention to it.
- When he closes his eyes, lower visual item. If baby reopens eyes, bring the design back within view. Watch his eyes carefully—the black dot will be reflected in his pupils if he's looking at it.
- Have baby touch the stimulator. Place his fingers so that they trace the perimeter of the black dot slowly four times. (If the dot is crocheted, he will get the added stimulation that comes from a ribbed surface.)

Touch Games

*(See Chapter 33 and Appendix 4 for where-to-buy and
how-to-make instructions)*

1. PURPOSE: Touch stimulation
    YOU'LL NEED: Just you and baby
    TIME: 2 minutes
    BABY'S POSITION: Lying naked in warm room, on your lap
or in bed
    WATCH FOR: Baby's relaxation

   • Stroke his skin slowly (about 12 strokes per minute) from
     head to toe and from center out to the extremities.
   • Name body parts as you go.

2. PURPOSE: Touch stimulation
    YOU'LL NEED: A clean powder puff
    TIME: 1 minute, 30 seconds
    BABY'S POSITION: Lying naked in warm room, on your
lap or in bed
    WATCH FOR: Baby's relaxation

   • Stroke baby down the front for three strokes with powder
     puff.
   • Stoke baby down the back three times with powder puff.
   • Name each body part as you stroke.

3. PURPOSE: Touch stimulation and grasp reflex
    YOU'LL NEED: 2 swatches of fabrics with differing tex-
tures, like velvet and satin
    TIME: 1 minute
    BABY'S POSITION: Held snugly on your lap, with hands
and feet exposed
    WATCH FOR: Baby's alertness, and grasping reflex for
fingers and toes

   • Tell your baby what texture it is—smooth, fuzzy, or
     whatever is appropriate—and place the cloth in his hands.
   • Let him grasp it tightly, and then unfold his fingers for him.
   • Stroke the palm of his hand with the texture.
   • Repeat three times.
   • Repeat with his feet. You'll see his little toes curl in to
     grab on!

4. PURPOSE: Touch and grasp training

YOU'LL NEED: Bright Baby Mind Mobile™ and Mr. Mouse™

TIME: 1 minute, 30 seconds

BABY'S POSITION: Sitting up in your arms, with his arms released from his blanket

WATCH FOR: Baby's alertness and grasp

- Place the cylinder of black-and-white mobile in baby's hand.
- Allow him to grasp and release the nubby surface for 30 seconds. (If the mobile is made of rubber, help him to squeeze the cylinder.)
- Place baby's hands over the eyes, ears, and nose of the black-and-white crocheted mouse.
- Let him stroke the crocheted surface for 30 seconds.
- Place the mouse's tail in baby's hands and allow him to grasp it.
- Pull it through when he releases his grasp.

5. PURPOSE: Touch stimulation and grasp reflex

YOU'LL NEED: Tactile Tillie™

TIME: 1 minute

BABY'S POSITION: Lying naked on your lap in a warm room

WATCH FOR: Baby's alertness and grasp

- Fold Tactile Tillie™ to stroke baby's body, palms, and soles of feet with a ribbed surface and a smooth surface.
- Stroke for 1 minute, naming body parts and identifying texture. Say, "This is ribbed. Ribbed is on your nose. . . ."

Hearing Games
(See Chapter 33 and Appendix 4 for where-to-buy and how-to-make instructions)

1. PURPOSE: Hearing stimulation

YOU'LL NEED: Just you and baby

TIME: 30 seconds

WATCH FOR: Baby's alertness

BABY'S POSITION: Held snugly in your arms

- Sing at least 2 verses of "Old MacDonald" or any other repetitive nursery rhyme.

2. PURPOSE: Hearing stimulation, sound localization and grasp

    YOU'LL NEED: Feather-weight Taffeta Rattle

    TIME: 30 seconds

    BABY'S POSITION: Sitting up in your lap, with arms released from blanket

    WATCH FOR: Baby's grasp reflex and turning to follow sound

- Shake rattle directly in front of baby.
- Watch his eyes brighten and fixate on the toy.
- If baby makes even a vague attempt to reach for rattle, put it in his hand so he feels the success of that reaching.
- Move his arm to make bells jingle.
- If he drops rattle, begin again, shaking it in front of him.
- Slowly move it to baby's right side. Move it up slightly and then down. Only your newborn's eyes will follow the movements at first. The more you practice this activity, the sooner he'll be able to turn his head and eyes to follow.

3. PURPOSE: Hearing stimulation and drawing baby's attention to his hands

    YOU'LL NEED: 2 small "jingle bells," one tied securely on a white piece of yarn and the other on a black piece of yarn

    TIME: 2 minutes

    BABY'S POSITION: Sitting up snugly in your lap with his arms released from blanket

    WATCH FOR: Baby's alertness in looking for sound

- Wrap the yarn and bells around each of baby's wrists.
- Lightly move each arm twice, so baby learns to associate his movement with the noise he's making.
- Allow baby's own movements to jingle the bells for 1 minute while lying on his back.
- Add your smiling face and words of encouragement. Each time he rattles the bell, encourage him with loving words and exclamations: "Oh, you are so clever, aren't you!"

4. PURPOSE: Hearing stimulation and training neck muscles

    YOU'LL NEED: A rattle. I like the one from the Johnson & Johnson Child Development Series

    TIME: 1 minute

    BABY'S POSITION: Lying on his back

WATCH FOR: Baby's head turning to the right and then to the left

- Put the rattle slightly behind baby's head on his right and shake it three times.
- Watch for baby's head turning to the right.
- Repeat two more times and then do the same thing to the left side of baby's head.

5. PURPOSE: Hearing stimulation and early reaching

YOU'LL NEED: Phonics reader and the daily newspaper (father choose one and mother the other)

TIME: 1 minute

BABY'S POSITION: Held upright, wrapped snugly with legs flexed and arms released

WATCH FOR: Baby's alertness and attempts to turn pages

- *Newspaper:* Sit down and read the big headlines for 1 minute (of at least one stimulation session), exaggerating words and turning pages frequently.
- Continue, even if baby falls asleep.
- *Phonics Reader:* Read 2 pages slowly and with great exaggeration, underlining the words with your finger as you progress to help baby watch sequencing of letters and words.

6. PURPOSE: Hearing stimulation, familiarity with your voice, language acquisition and comforting

YOU'LL NEED: Heartbeat and classical music tapes

TIME: 1 minute or more, as desired

BABY'S POSITION: In his crib or held lovingly in your arms

WATCH FOR: Baby's relaxation and pleasure

- Continue with the familiar heartbeat and classical music tapes as they soothe and comfort your baby.
- Talk to your baby in a warm, loving way.
- Tell him how much you care for him and what a wonderful child he is.
- Sing a lullaby.

Smell Games

1. PURPOSE: Smell stimulation

YOU'LL NEED: Mother's favorite perfume

TIME: 30 seconds
BABY'S POSITION: Held snugly on your lap
WATCH FOR: Baby's alertness

- Pass perfume quickly under baby's nose three times.

2. PURPOSE: Smell stimulation
   YOU'LL NEED: Daddy's after-shave
   TIME: 30 seconds
   BABY'S POSITION: Held snugly in your arms
   WATCH FOR: Baby's alertness

   - Pass daddy's after-shave quickly under baby's nose three times.

3. PURPOSE: Smell and touch stimulation
   YOU'LL NEED: 2 clean powder puffs lightly sprayed with Daddy's after-shave
   TIME: 1 minute
   BABY'S POSITION: Naked on your lap or in bed in a warm room
   WATCH FOR: Baby's alertness

   - Stroke from the right side of baby's forehead, down his cheeks and neck, and finally down the right side of his body to his thigh for a count of 10.
   - Repeat stroke on the left for a count of 10.
   - With both powder puffs, stroke baby from forehead to thighs on both sides simultaneously for a count of 10.
   - Finish activity by placing a powder puff in baby's hand, allowing him the opportunity to stroke himself at random for 30 seconds.
   - Help him by moving his hand so he strokes down his cheek and chest twice.

4. PURPOSE: Smell stimulation
   YOU'LL NEED: Oregano, cinnamon, and vanilla extract
   TIME: 1 minute
   BABY'S POSITION: Held upright in your arms
   WATCH FOR: Baby's alertness, twitching of his facial muscles, and possible smile

   - Pass each seasoning under baby's nose three times. Count to 10 between each seasoning.

5. PURPOSE: Smell stimulation

YOU'LL NEED: *Sweet Smell of Strawberryland,* or other scratch-and-sniff book (See Resource Guide, Chapter 33)

TIME: 30 seconds

BABY'S POSITION: Held upright in your arms, with arms and legs wrapped snugly

WATCH FOR: Baby's alertness

- Read the pages which identify 3 sweet or sour smells and let baby smell.

Movement Games

1. PURPOSE: Movement stimulation

YOU'LL NEED: Just you and baby

TIME: 1 minute

BABY'S POSITION: Begin with baby on his back in bed or crib

WATCH FOR: Baby's alertness

- Lay baby down and turn him from back to tummy and back again.
- Gently bend and straighten arms from side to side and over the head three times.
- Sing "Patty Cake" while performing second step.

2. PURPOSE: Movement stimulation

YOU'LL NEED: Just you and baby

TIME: 1 minute

BABY'S POSITION: Start with baby on his back on bed or in crib

WATCH FOR: Baby's alertness

- Hold baby's hands in midline up against his chest.
- Gently roll him from side to side three times.
- With baby lying on his right side, slide your hands under his body and lift him gently several inches.
- Roll him back to his left side and repeat.

3. PURPOSE: Movement stimulation

YOU'LL NEED: Just you and baby (and an optional Snugli®)

TIME: 1 minute

BABY'S POSITION: Begin with baby lying on his back

WATCH FOR: Baby's alertness

- Holding one foot in each hand, bicycle baby's legs at a moderate rate of speed for 30 seconds by flexing legs at the knee and thigh.
- Holding baby under arms, pulling him up to sitting position then slowly lower, making sure his head doesn't flop backward.
- Lift baby up into your arms (or place in Snugli®) and twist your body to the right and left saying, "Wheee, isn't this fun?" Repeat.

4. PURPOSE: Movement stimulation
     YOU'LL NEED: Just you and baby
     TIME: 1 minute
     WATCH FOR: Baby's alertness

- Cradle baby in your forearms on your lap with his head resting in your hands.
- Lift and lower baby slowly. Sing: "See, saw, Margery Daw..."
- Reverse baby's position so that he is lying with his head resting against your abdomen and his legs at your knees.
- Lift his legs up and repeat the song.

5. PURPOSE: Movement stimulation
     YOU'LL NEED: Just you and baby
     TIME: 1 minute
     BABY'S POSITION: Baby held in your arms up to your chest
     WATCH FOR: Baby's alertness

- Rock from side to side for 45 seconds.
- Stop and slowly turn 2 circles to right.
- Stop, and slowly turn 2 circles to the left.

Mini-Milestones in the First Month

1. You'll notice that when your baby is lying down, his buttocks are still higher than his head.

2. He can lift his head slightly but only ever so briefly, and he can't keep it up very high. You can confirm this easily when you hold him up at your shoulder. Even when he's sitting on your lap, he can hold his head up for a second.

In this position he turns his head toward sounds, especially those coming in on his right side.

3. When lying on his tummy, your newborn's legs are not so tightly coiled beneath him as they were during the first two days of life.

4. Baby's hands are still fisted and his grasp is still a reflex—not a voluntary act. He will grab objects, however, that are brushed by his hand.

5. Your newborn's communication skills are improving. His predominant sound is his cry, which heralds hunger, pain, or discomfort. But when he feels satisfied that his needs are met, he'll voice little grunts and squeaks of contentment.

6. Since he is beginning to identify his parents by their smell and the sound of their voices, he'll snuggle differently into *their* bodies than he will with anyone else.

27. Maximizing Your Infant's Interests at Two Months: Vision, Hands, and Dialogue

Your baby's visual abilities take a quantum leap during his second month and it seems appropriate that his visual preferences change as a reflection of his improved abilities. His range of vision expands enormously, from 15 inches at the end of the first month to 10 feet by the middle of the third month. Many of the suggestions for ongoing activities and visual stimulation games that follow take into account baby's new visual capabilities.

At about the sixth week, your infant begins to lose interest in stripes, becoming much more fascinated by circular objects and bull's-eyes. He starts to focus on his parents. in good eye-to-eye contact, usually by the end of the second month.

Instead of 4 squares to look at, your two-month-old should have 6 to 8 square checkerboards.

Though your infant still likes to look at the edge of an object, you'll notice that *by the end of the second month he is also interested in its center.* Faces, in particular, hold his attention. And he enjoys visual stimulators of increasing complexity. He is fascinated by a more complicated checkerboard—one that has 1-inch squares rather than the 2-inch squares he has been looking at. In order to be able to distinguish designs, he still needs the contrast of a white background.

Those *Handy* Hands

Baby's own hands hold the greatest fascination for your two-month-old. This is the time for hand exploration, and you'll often see him tugging and pulling at those wondrous objects. He will be making hand-to-hand contact as if he were actually engaged in hand-to-hand *combat* as he tries to get his fingers to open. And when he grabs his own hands, your infant is learning that they can be both the subject and object of touch—they touch and can *be touched*.

The tight little fists of the first month of life begin—like the rest of his body—to relax and unfurl. And as sight improves, baby starts to learn how to coordinate what he sees with what he touches. You can encourage the development of eye-hand coordination in an ongoing way by keeping visually appealing toys within baby's reach at all times. Dress a pair of bookends in Mind Mittens™ (see Chapter 33), for example, and station them on either side of baby on the changing table. Leave his black-and-white panda close by.

Your infant must touch the object he looks at in order to form an understanding of that object in his mind. He moves from experiencing with his senses alone to *perceiving*. With perception comes an understanding of what the object is and how it relates to the universe.

What Your Two-Month-Old's Hands Can and Can't Do

Only after his fists fully relax (at about the third month) will baby be able to grasp toys voluntarily.

For now, when an object brushes up against him, he still may not go for it himself. *But you can help him by placing a toy in his hands.* Then, he experiences both the object and the feeling against his skin of something touching his hand. If he randomly brings the toy into his line of vision, he even provides himself with a visual stimulator.

Draw Baby's Attention to His Hands

Draw your infant's attention to his hands by placing in them a plush black-and-white mouse (Bright Baby Mr. Mouse™), a black-and-white cylinder or square from the Bright Baby Mind Mobile™, or a Johnson & Johnson Development Kit rattle. (See the Resource Guide in Chapter 33 for where to buy these.) Objects of varying diameters put in his palms will also ease the tension of his fists. Here are some ongoing activities that will encourage your baby's understanding of his hands:

- Tie lots of colorful ribbons around his wrists. They will attract his attention to his hands. Just make sure they're short enough so that baby won't get entangled in them.
- Let baby wear black-and-white mittens adorned with well-secured bells. Be careful never to leave him alone with these. You wouldn't want him to pull the bells off and put them in his mouth!
- Try the Fisher-Price Toys Wrist Rattles available at baby and toy stores. (See Resource Guide for manufacturer's address.) They are rattling, plush animal faces that fasten to your baby's wrist with Velcro. The pandas are ideal, since they offer a black-and-white design in addition to the sound stimulation.
- When stroking baby's hands, press firmly but gently into his palm to stimulate firm grasp. Then stroke back of his hand to help him release his grasp.

To stimulate baby's understanding of his hands' function, move them over different parts of his body, stroking from head to toe and naming body parts for at least one of the "touch" minutes of your daily stimulation sessions. (You can say, "Now your hand is on your head. Now your hand is on your neck. Now your hand is on your shoulder.")

Or play finger games to encourage muscle tone and strength. Walk baby's fingers on his body with:

- "Here comes Mousie, here comes Mousie into housie."
- "Creepy-crawly, creepy-crawly, fingers!"

End the games with baby's fingers in his mouth.

For the greatest hand freedom during play, baby should be sitting, either in an infant seat or propped up in a box with pillows. In that way, he can reach out for the interesting objects that you show him.

A Loving Transition

Once your two-month-old learns to use his hands to touch himself, he'll transform that knowledge into using his hands to touch mommy, daddy, and others he really loves.

You probably will notice that he starts placing his hand on mother's breast as he nurses. He seems to curl his fingers around as if he's grabbing for the circle of the nipple that caught his attention in the visual phase of the first month of life. With this small but very significant gesture, your infant seems to say, "I really love this. I want to hold on so I can keep in touch with it as much as possible."

Once he has touched mommy in this way, he gains an understanding of mommy as a separate physical being. Babies touch only those things that interest them, an indication of how important people are to them. If your child is taking formula from a bottle, you'll notice that he'll start touching the bottle as he nurses.

Your Two-Month-Old Learns That He's a Human Being

Everything you have done to teach your newborn to recognize you—learn your face, identify your body scent, become accustomed to your presence and routine—helps him to begin his love affair with people in the second month. By looking at your face and realizing that visages can express many emotions, he suddenly dazzles you with his first full social SMILE. What a thrilling moment for his loving family.

From this, baby learns a very valuable lesson: when he moves his own face, he'll keep you interested in him! And so, he begins smiling for other people, too, not just for mommy and daddy. These smiles mean that mommy and daddy provide security and affection to the point that he has discovered people can be exciting, comforting elements of his world.

In appreciation of the human race, baby will maintain his alertness longer when playing with people than when left to play alone. That's the bait, you might say, that he lays for you. It's as if he's saying, "Mommy and daddy, in the past you've told me how important my eyes are. Now, I really want to look at you because I've grown so attached! And when I'm awake, you'll want to be with me!"

You can capitalize on baby's preference for being social in an ongoing way by bringing him out to play on his infant seat wherever you are in your home rather than leaving him alone in his crib to look at his mobiles. Some parents even move their infants from room to room in their strollers as they do their daily household chores. It's easy to come up face to face to him, every once in a while, talking and singing as you take little breaks in your work.

You might like to make an Expressly Yours™ poster—a red felt board with stick-on faces illustrating a variety of expressions—to help your baby begin to associate words, gestures, and feelings. At two months he is able to learn about expressions other than your smile. Just draw on small white paper plates simple faces showing a smile, a laugh, a frown, a cry, and a look of surprise. Bring your baby up to the board and stick on one plate-face at a time using tape or Velcro backing. Mimic the caricature on your own face, accompanying your gestures with appropriate words and sounds. (You'll find directions for making the Expressly Yours™ poster in Appendix 4.)

The Beginnings of a Lifetime Dialogue

In the second month, baby adds another bonding element to hold your fascination and keep you near. He "talks" to you in his own very special way! In the first month you may have noticed his little squeaks and grunts of contentment as he nursed. Now, he's going to hum along, especially when you sing.

It's vitally important for you to work on establishing ongoing dialogue with your two-month-old:

- When you talk to your two-month-old, pause during your monologue to permit his "response."
- Reinforce his sounds with further questions.
- Sing songs with hand or body motions like "Patty Cake," "This Little Piggy," and "Ring Around the Rosie" to help him learn the relationship between actions and words.

As you watch carefully, you'll notice baby's hand motions slow down as he shifts into a verbal mode of interaction.

Once your infant recognizes your voices during the first month of life, that knowledge stays with him forever. Now his efforts are directed toward understanding *what's* being said. Baby must become aware of the patterns, sounds, pitch, and tone of speech as well as the non-verbal messages that accompany your words. He wants to know whether you smile or frown with a particular tone; he wants to know whether *his sounds* cause you to approach or withdraw and if they bring on an affectionate pat or tension in your body.

Interestingly enough, rattles, bells, and toys that stimulate your baby's sense of hearing also help to contribute to his creating dialogue. To converse with you, your baby has to have gained exposure to and an understanding of the following sequence of events:

STAGE 1: An object can make a noise.

STAGE 2: Objects and noises occur simultaneously.

STAGE 3: When I hear a noise, there must be an object that made that noise. I'll seek it out.

STAGE 4: I am making noise.

STAGE 5: I, as an object, *can* make a noise.

STAGE 6: When I make a noise, mommy or daddy will respond to me—the object that made the noise.

Getting into the Swim of Things

In the first two months of life babies have a swimming reflex that enables them to dog paddle through water. If your child uses this skill, he'll retain it. Otherwise, he'll lose it by the end of the second month.

If you're interested in providing your baby with swim activity, seek out an experienced, licensed swimming instructor who has been trained in teaching infants to swim. I would not advise you to teach your baby to swim yourself. Often the YMCA has appropriate Baby-and-Me swim classes. However, wherever you seek instruction, *make sure that the technique does not include throwing your baby into the water or immersing his head. These practices are unsafe.*

If you do find the right program, try to get baby into a buoyant water environment at least once a week. Swimming is the only form of exercise in which every muscle of the body is used at the same time. And it's so easy for your baby to move and exercise in such a gravity-free environment. Babies who swim:

- Are more active sooner
- Roll over sooner
- Sit sooner
- Walk sooner, with phenomenal balance and muscle tone

Swimming helps immeasurably in the uncurling process.

Help Baby's Muscles Gain Tone and Strength

Other ongoing activities encourage your two-month-old's muscle development, as well.

- Stand him up for 10 seconds at a time, so his feet bear some weight.
- Allow baby to kick and splash freely as you hold him in the bath. Never ever leave him unattended in the tub.
- Hang a crib gym or rings across the crib so that baby can reach out for them.

Baby Begins to Emerge as an Individual

Your two-month-old is no longer a newborn. He has become a social little person who touches, reaches, "talks," and smiles. He is beginning to build confidence in the fact that he has some power to gain your attention and to be loved.

Stimulation Games for the Second Month

The suggestions we've made to this point (and will be making in the first half of the next four chapters) for ongoing interactions with baby are easily incorporated into your daily routine. We've knowingly presented a wealth of activities, so don't feel compelled to do them *all*. Just feel secure in choosing from among them, for they are all geared to your mutual pleasure.

Continue the pleasing structured 15-minute-a-day play program you began last month by gradually integrating a new set of games that appeal to your two-month-old's changing preferences and capabilities. If baby enjoys a particular game, don't give it up just for the sake of change. Be flexible and flow with your child's responses.

Toys You'll Be Using
(See Chapter 33 and Appendix 4 for where-to-buy and how-to-make instructions)

Never leave baby alone with toys in which he can become entangled or on which he can choke.

HEARING TOYS
- Bells, rattles
- Fisher-Price Toys Wrist Rattles
- Recording of nursery rhyme
- Recording of *Swan Lake* or *Nutcracker Suite*
- 10 paper plates with letters A,B,C,D,E and numbers 1,2,3,4,5 drawn one on each
- Johnson & Johnson Developmental Kit rattle or other rattle

SMELL TOYS
- Peppermint extract
- Cotton balls
- Father's after-shave
- Rose water
- 2 to 3 sweet-smelling flowers
- 3 different sweet-smelling sachets
- Cinnamon
- Coconut or almond extract
- Pineapple juice

VISUAL TOYS
- Mind Mitten™
- Bright Baby Mind Mobile™
- Crocheted black-and-white bull's-eye
- Bright Baby™ Blanket
- 3 to 4 white paper plates with drawings of designs described below
- Pillow Pals™
- Mrs. Eyeset™

Baby is fascinated by Mrs. Eyeset™.

TOUCH TOYS
- Full-length mirror
- Bright Baby Mind Mobile™
- Tactile Tillie™
- Mind Mitten™ or swatches of plush and nubbly fabrics

MOVEMENT TOYS
- Rocking chair
- Bright Baby Teaching Tube™ or cylinder made of rolled bath towel
- Mrs. Eyeset™

OTHER TOYS

- Short, brightly-colored ribbons
- Flat bookends
- Crib gym or rings
- Expressly Yours™ poster

- Black-and-white mittens with bells securely attached
- Brainy Bear™ or black-and-white panda

Designs That Your Two-Month-Old Likes to Look At

4 to 6 weeks—Designs held 13 to 20 inches from baby's face:

- A 3-inch-high black triangle pasted or drawn on white 8 × 11 paper or white paper plate
- 8 × 10 black-and-white glossy photos of Mom and Dad's smiling faces
- Black stripes 3 inches long by 1 inch wide, drawn or pasted on a white cardboard circle or paper plate
- Four black dots, 1 inch in diameter, drawn or pasted on an 8 × 11 white background or white paper plate

6 to 8 weeks—Add the following, held up to 24 inches from baby's face:

- Complex bull's-eye, at least 3 inches in diameter: black center, white band, black band, white band drawn on paper plate
- 6- to 8-square black-and-white checkerboard, each square 2 by 2 inches
- Crib sheet with 2- by 2-inch checkerboard squares
- Six black dots, 1 inch in diameter, arranged in a circle, side by side, or randomly on white 8 × 10 background or white paper plate

Complex bull's-eye at least 3 inches in diameter

Six 1-inch black dots arranged in rows

- 8 × 10 photos of mom and dad's faces with emotions portrayed dramatically (remember, only happy emotions!)
- Two 3-inch-tall black triangles drawn or pasted on a white background
- A line drawing or picture of a 4-inch-long by 2-inch-high cylinder decorated with checkerboard on white 8 × 11 background or white paper plate

Cylinder decorated with checkerboard

Remember to use the "smorgasboard" approach when choosing games for your two-month-old. Select one visual game, one touch game, one hearing game, one smell game, and one movement game, and repeat all five three times a day, preferably before morning, afternoon, and evening feedings. Here's a sample menu:

- *Visual Game 2.* Show baby the Bright Baby Mind Mobile™
- *Touch Game 1.* Teach baby about his hands by having him stroke himself
- *Hearing Game 3.* Read and repeat letters and numbers
- *Smell Game 1.* Let baby experience the scent of peppermint
- *Movement Game 5.* Gently lift and sway baby in different directions

Visual Games
(See Chapter 33 and Appendix 4 for where-by-buy and how-to-make instructions)

1. PURPOSE: Visual stimulation
YOU'LL NEED: A visual stimulator from the list of appealing designs above. Mind Mitten™ may be the most helpful for this activity
TIME: 1 minute
BABY'S POSITION: Sit baby up in your lap
WATCH FOR: Baby's eye and head tracking and looking in center of object

- Present the visual item in front of baby about 12 inches from his face. (As you progress through the month, move the visual stimulator farther to right and left, farther up and down—to develop muscle tone.)
- Tell baby what the design depicts.
- Move stimulator slowly to baby's right, three-quarters of the way to his ear.
- Bring it back in front of his eyes and then to his left.
- Raise the stimulator 6 inches above his eyes and repeat movement to right and left.
- Place the stimulator in front of baby's face and trace with his fingers the outline of outer design.
- Move his finger in toward center of the stimulator and highlight contrasting elements there.

2. PURPOSE: Visual stimulation
   YOU'LL NEED: Bright Baby Mind Mobile™
   TIME: 1 minute
   BABY'S POSITION: Sit baby up on your lap
   WATCH FOR: Baby's alertness, and reaching behaviors

- Turn the mobile to show all shapes, concentrating on cylinder and faces.
- Present mobile in middle of baby's field of vision.
- Follow steps listed above.

3. PURPOSE: Visual stimulation and training neck muscles
   YOU'LL NEED: Crocheted black-and-white bull's-eye (you may substitute another crocheted black-and-white stimulator in afternoon and evening sessions)
   TIME: 1 minute
   BABY'S POSITION: Sit baby up on lap
   WATCH FOR: Baby's alertness, head and eye movements, and reaching behaviors

- Bring bull's-eye in baby's visual field slowly, beginning 6 inches behind his right shoulder.
- When you reach the middle of baby's face, raise the stimulator 6 inches above his head and then bring it back to center.
- Say, "This is a bull's-eye."
- Stretch baby's arm to the bull's-eye and have his hand trace the inner and outer circles.

4. PURPOSE: Visual stimulation

YOU'LL NEED: Black-and-white patterned surface like the Bright Baby™ Blanket

TIME: 1 minute

BABY'S POSITION: Put baby down on comforter. Lie down on floor beside him.

WATCH FOR: Baby's alertness

- Place baby 10 inches from stripes.
- Say, "Today, we're going to look at some pretty shapes on your comforter. Let's look at some stripes."
- Gently push against the sole of baby's right foot. You'll find his reflex is to stretch out. If you keep your hand against his foot, you'll offer him enough resistance to scoot forward several inches. Repeat with other foot until he has reached the stripes.
- When baby gets to the stripes, reward him, saying, "What a wonderful baby!"
- Say, "Can you touch these stripes?" Help him to reach toward them and move his hand along the length of the stripes.

5. PURPOSE: Visual stimulation

YOU'LL NEED: 3 or 4 white paper plates with drawing of bull's-eye or cylinder, numbers, letters, faces—one drawing to a plate (for afternoon or evening sessions, substitute Pillow Pals™ or Mrs. Eyeset™)

TIME: 1 minute

BABY'S POSITION: Sit baby up in your lap

WATCH FOR: Baby's alertness

- Show salient features. (Use the same procedure recommended for Visual Game 1.)

Touch Games
(See Chapter 33 and Appendix 4 for where-to-buy and how-to-make instructions)

1. PURPOSE: Touch stimulation and baby identifying his hands

YOU'LL NEED: Just you and baby

TIME: 1 minute

BABY'S POSITION: Lying on his back in crib or sitting in infant seat

WATCH FOR: Baby's growing awareness of his hands

- Bring baby's hands together at center of his body.
- Clap them gently three times saying "Patty cake, Patty cake, Baker's Man."
- Rub hands together in 3 circles.
- Slide his right palm over his left inner arm, passing his elbow and moving on up to his shoulder, neck, and mouth.
- Make a kissing sound when his hand reaches his mouth.
- Repeat with left hand on right side.

2. PURPOSE: Touch stimulation, relaxation and baby learning body parts

YOU'LL NEED: Full-length wall mirror

TIME: 1 minute

YOUR AND BABY'S POSITION: Sit on the floor with your knees propped up 10 inches from mirror. Sit baby between your legs, facing mirror. Undress baby as much as you're comfortable with

- Stroke baby's body parts down one side of his body and then the other, naming parts as you go. (You may also use the "Loving Touch Stroking Procedure" or any other baby massage technique that goes head to toe, center to extremities.)

3. PURPOSE: Touch stimulation

YOU'LL NEED: Bright Baby Mind Mobile™ and Tactile Tillie™

TIME: 2 minutes

BABY'S POSITION: Lay baby on his back

WATCH FOR: Baby's alertness and awareness of body parts

- Brush the Mind Mobile™ against baby's feet so he begins to kick it. If he doesn't, move his legs so mobile is set into motion. Allow activity for 1 minute.
- Gently grab baby's foot with Tactile Tillie's™ mouth and lightly pull it up into the air 6 inches and lower it.
- Lift each foot twice and repeat with hands.

4. PURPOSE: Touch stimulation

YOU'LL NEED: Bright Baby Mind Mobile™

TIME: 1 to 2 minutes

BABY'S POSITION: Held upright in your arms with arms released

WATCH FOR: Baby's grasp reflex and release and batting activity

- Place each of the objects in the mobile in baby's hands, making sure he grabs on.
- Squeeze his hand with the object in it three times.
- Help him to release the object.
- Move baby's forearm so he bats the mobile.
- Allow at least 30 to 60 seconds of free play with mobile under your supervision.

5. PURPOSE: Touch stimulation

YOU'LL NEED: Furry surface and nubby surface like those found in Mind Mitten™, or swatches of plush and nubby cloth

TIME: 1 minute

BABY'S POSITION: Lying on his back, as undressed as you're comfortable with

WATCH FOR: Baby's alertness and relaxation

- Stroke baby in head-to-toe fashion, first on his right side then on his left, with fabric.
- Name body parts and texture that you're using.

Hearing Games
(See Chapter 33 and Appendix 4 for where-to-buy and how-to-make instructions)

1. PURPOSE: Hearing stimulation and baby's awareness of his hands

YOU'LL NEED: Bells or rattles attached to baby's wrists or ankles. The Fisher-Price Toys Wrist Rattles, and especially the black-and-white panda bears, are ideal. If you use bells and yarn, be sure *not* to leave baby alone with these, as the bells might come undone and end up in baby's mouth, causing him to choke.

TIME: 1 minute

BABY'S POSITION: Lying on his back

WATCH FOR: Baby's alertness and awareness of his hands and eventual own movements in anticipation of a special word

- Sing a repetitive nursery rhyme like "Mary Had a Little Lamb."
- Shake the bells or rattles each time you come to one special word (like *lamb*) to accentuate it consistently.

2. PURPOSE: Hearing stimulation

YOU'LL NEED: A recording of the nursery rhyme you've been singing unaccompanied for the past month

TIME: 1 to 2 minutes

BABY'S POSITION: Held in your arms as you rock in rocking chair

WATCH FOR: Baby's alertness and vocalization

- Rock while you sing along with recording.
- Repeat for 1 or 2 minutes as desired.

3. PURPOSE: Hearing stimulation, movement, and letter recognition

YOU'LL NEED: 6-inch-tall, heavy black A,B,C,D,E and numbers 1,2,3,4,5 drawn on individual paper plates with thick non-toxic marker

TIME: 1 to 2 minutes

BABY'S POSITION: Held upright in your lap with arms released from blanket while you rock in rocking chair

WATCH FOR: Baby's alertness and vocalization

- Say: "This is A. Do you see A? Can you say A? It's A, A, A. This is A. Say bye-bye to A. Good-bye A."
- Repeat with other characters.
- Have baby touch and trace the letters and numbers with his fingers.

4. PURPOSE: Hearing and movement stimulation

YOU'LL NEED: A recording of ballet music, like *Swan Lake* or *Nutcracker Suite* or the piece that you've been using

TIME: 1 to 2 minutes

BABY'S POSITION: Held upright in your arms at your chest

WATCH FOR: Baby's pleasure

- Dance for 20 seconds back and forth.
- Holding baby under his arms, lower him to the ground, letting his feet bear weight, and then lift him back up into your arms.

- Repeat three times.
- Finish dancing to the music for the remaining minute.

5. PURPOSE: Hearing stimulation and training for sound localization

    YOU'LL NEED: Johnson & Johnson Infant Development Kit Rattle or other rattle

    TIME: 1 minute

    BABY'S POSITION: Lying on bed or in crib

    WATCH FOR: Baby's head movement to follow sound

- Shake rattle in front of baby.
- Move rattle out toward his right and then left shoulder.
- Move rattle up and down 6 inches.

Smell Games

1. PURPOSE: Smell stimulation

    YOU'LL NEED: Peppermint extract

    TIME: 1 minute

    BABY'S POSITION: Held upright in your arms

    WATCH FOR: Baby's nose twitching and any changes in facial expression

- Pass scent quickly under baby's nose three times.
- Comment on any change in facial expression that you see. Say, "Oh! You look pleased! That's exciting, isn't it? Oh, you like it!"
- Pass the scent under your nose so baby can see your reactions. Say, "Mmm, that's exciting."
- Make a second pass under your own nose. Say, "Oh, that *smells* good."
- On your third pass exaggerate your sniffing gesture. Say, "That's peppermint!"

2. PURPOSE: Smell stimulation

    YOU'LL NEED: 2 cotton balls sprayed lightly with father's after-shave cologne

    TIME: 30 seconds

    BABY'S POSITION: Lying in crib or on bed

    WATCH FOR: Baby's facial expression to change

- Place cotton balls in baby's hands.

- Bring his hands up to his nose and extend his arms out again.
- Repeat three times.

3. PURPOSE: Smell stimulation
   YOU'LL NEED: Rosewater or up to 3 sweet-smelling flowers
   TIME: 30 seconds
   BABY'S POSITION: Held upright in your arms
   WATCH FOR: Baby's changing facial expression

- Pass pleasant scents three times under baby's nose. Repeat the type of conversation you carried on in Game 1.

4. PURPOSE: Smell stimulation
   YOU'LL NEED: Three different sweet-smelling sachets
   TIME: 30 seconds
   BABY'S POSITION: Held upright in your arms
   WATCH FOR: Baby's changing facial expression

- Pass each sachet under baby's nose three times.

5. PURPOSE: Smell stimulation
   YOU'LL NEED: Cinnamon, coconut, or almond extract and pineapple juice
   TIME: 30 seconds
   BABY'S POSITION: Held upright in your arms
   WATCH FOR: Baby's changing facial expression

- Pass each scent under baby's nose three times, identifying the flavor. Repeat conversation used in Game 1.

Movement Games
(See Chapter 33 and Appendix 4 for where-to-buy and how-to-make instructions)

1. PURPOSE: Movement stimulation
   YOU'LL NEED: Just you and baby
   TIME: 1 minute
   BABY'S POSITION: On floor on his back, enclosed within your forearms (held at his sides)
   WATCH FOR: Baby's alertness and smile

- Roll baby from side to side five times to each side.

- Bring his hands together, as if in prayer.
- Bring them back to his chin and then stretch them out in front of him four times.

2. PURPOSE: Movement stimulation and reaching behaviors
    YOU'LL NEED: Bright Baby Teaching Tube™ or a cylinder made of rolled-up bath towel and a visual toy like Mrs. Eyeset™ or Mr. Mouse™
    TIME: 1 minute
    BABY'S POSITION: Place baby's chest over cylinder
    WATCH FOR: Baby's reaching behavior

- Set a stimulation toy like Mr. Mouse™ or Mrs. Eyeset™ 6 inches in front of baby.
- Roll baby slightly forward so he reaches for the toy.
- Allow him to touch it, then lightly roll him back.

3. PURPOSE: Movement stimulation and strengthening of baby's back muscles
    YOU'LL NEED: Just you and baby
    TIME: 1 minute
    YOUR AND BABY'S POSITION: Sit in chair and put baby on his back on your lap so his head is nestled against your abdomen
    WATCH FOR: Baby's enjoyment

- Holding baby by the thighs, lift his legs up into air until his back is slightly bent. Say "Wheee, up and down..."
- Repeat five times saying "Up and down. Up and down."

4. PURPOSE: Movement stimulation and strengthening muscles
    YOU'LL NEED: Just you and baby
    TIME: 2 minutes
    BABY'S POSITION: Hold baby around his chest and stand him up on the floor
    WATCH FOR: Baby's strengthening muscles and reflex-scoot

- Stand baby up and bring him down, five times.
- Sit him down, still holding him around his chest, and lean him slowly from side to side—each side five times. Support his head if it's wobbly.
- With baby still sitting up, lean him forward so he almost touches the floor and then slightly back, five times each.
- Lower baby to the floor so he's lying on his back, and

push with your hand up against feet so he propels himself several inches across the floor.

5. PURPOSE: Movement stimulation
   YOU'LL NEED: Just you and baby
   TIME: 2 minutes
   YOUR AND BABY'S POSITION: Lie baby down on his side. Gently slide your arms under him so he rests in the crook of your elbows.
   WATCH FOR: Baby's pleasure

- Lift baby 1 inch off ground and slowly sway him forward, back, side to side, diagonally, up and down, and around in a circle.
- Name the directions he is taking.

Mini-Milestones in the Second Month

1. Your baby starts "cycling movements"—he moves both sides of his body at the same time. These movements are smoother and not so jerky as in the previous month. This indicates that both sides of his body are maturing. He is changing from having a right-sided sensitivity into being bilateral—a both-sided person.

It is important to continue stroking both sides of his body now and offering toys to both hands. Once he loses his inborn lateralization, baby will determine his own right- or left-handedness. You will see this develop near the end of the month.

2. When on his tummy, baby is very alert. He can be alert even though he's primarily horizontal. Before, he fell asleep in that position.

3. Your two-month-old likes exploring sounds deliberately. They really please him now. He tries to make many sounds himself. To let you know how much he likes these sounds, he develops two responses:

- His sounds of contentment are expressed in a pattern.

- He begins babbling in response either to your presence or to your conversation at about 6 weeks of age.

4. At 6 weeks your infant will delight you with a full social smile which engages all the adults in his community.

5. You'll notice that he swipes at objects.

6. Watch for his hand opening in anticipation of touch as you brush objects against his fist toward the end of the month.

7. Your two-month-old can lift his head off the bed without wavering now.

28. The Third Month:
Helping Baby Learn about
His Body

Action!

Your baby becomes quite active in the third month. He reaches and grabs for toys, bringing them into his mouth or cuddling them to his chest. He shows preferences for what he likes to play with. He is learning balance and how to support himself on one arm. During this month he'll begin moving up and down rather than just rolling about from side to side. When lying on his tummy, he'll push his chest to a 90-degree angle with his arms.

Why does all this activity occur now? At three months baby has the ability to coordinate his senses of hearing and sight with his head and hand movements. This means that he is able to create stimulation for himself rather than just passively receiving what you have to offer. And he puts his head, heart, and hands into it—devoting himself to active play with tremendous energy and pleasure.

Here's How Your Three-Month-Old
Stimulates Himself

Once your three-month-old touches an object, he learns that his uncurling fist may give him the power to grasp and move it. He shakes toys and pushes against them in his effort to make them move. And if the movement creates a noise or

215

other changes in his environment, he's all the more fortunate, because he is providing himself auditory, visual, and touch stimulation.

To encourage your baby's eye-hand coordination in an ongoing way, you may want to:

- Make a game of putting on and taking off his mittens and booties (help him push the booties off with his own feet).
- Help him put his fingers into objects like:
    jars, canisters, paper rolls, Tactile Tillie's™ mouth, tissue paper, etc.
- Help his hands encompass small toys like:
    washed Ping-Pong balls, rolled-up swatches of cloth, cloth or rubber donuts, rattles, 6-inch lengths of fuzzy yarn, quartered carrot sticks, clothespins, teething rings. *Never leave him alone with these objects*.
- Help him to release the objects by stroking the backs of his hands.
- Sing the song "Open Shut Them," using hand motions, and then repeat with your eyes, mouth, arms, and legs.

The Mouth—the Ultimate Chemical Factory

Where does your three-month-old put objects once he has grasped them? Why, in his mouth, naturally.

Baby's mouth has been called the ultimate chemical factory. It's ultrasensitive to touch and, of course, taste. As the toy approaches baby's mouth, his sense of smell is activated. He wants to know, does this new thing have an odor? What can I learn from how it smells and tastes? You'll find he tries to place everything in his mouth—including his own hands and feet!

Baby Learns His Body Is
Whole and Separate

In the third month your infant's vistas widen. No longer interested in merely looking at his hands, he is discovering his whole body and learning that all of his body parts are attached! That's why you'll see him with his toes in his mouth. He may be thinking, "I go all the way down to there? And look, I can bring these funny bumpy things all the way up to my mouth! They're all a part of *me*! How do I smell? How do I taste?"

This information is significant to your infant's development. Not only does he learn the extent of his own physical self—his wholeness—but he also realize that he is separate from those around him. To encourage baby's ongoing awareness of this separateness, you may wish to:

- Play "This Little Piggy" with his body parts.
- Refer to his whole body. Say, "Daddy is holding Steven."
- Encourage baby's talk so he hears own voice.
- Gesture to your own body parts.
- Stroke baby, naming his body parts in front of a mirror.
- Show Tactile Tillie™ in front of a mirror, saying, "See Tillie over Kim, see Tillie under Kim, see Tillie around Kim."

Baby gains an awareness of how he can get his body to move to grab a rattle or a black-and-white mouse if he so chooses. He learns how his body works. In fact, right- or left-handedness begins in the third month, so be sure to present toys to baby's lesser-used side, to make sure both hands are given a workout. (Never force baby's handedness. Allow him to develop his own preference.) Here are some ongoing activities to encourage baby's growing awareness of how his body works:

- Allow tummy time for free, supervised play.
- When he is on his tummy, push against the soles of baby's feet so he propels himself forward.
- Tilt baby gently from side to side.
- Help him to get his hands and feet into his mouth.
- Place a soft toy—like the panda or Mrs. Eyeset™ (see Chapter 33)—against baby's chest and encourage him to encompass it with his arms.
- When in bed, place a rolled towel or Pillow Pals™ (see Chapter 33) at baby's feet so he can push against it and move his body forward.

- Place the Mr. Mouse™ (see Chapter 33) or a rattle in baby's hand and help him to release by stroking the outside of his hand.
- When baby sits up in his infant seat, hold the Mr. Mouse™ (see Chapter 33) or a visual stimulator out to the right or left so he moves his head to follow it.

Reinforcement Builds Pride

When your three-month-old tries to reach, touch, and grasp, it's important that you reinforce his *attempts* as well as his successes. You can clap your hands, smile or laugh, and say, "How wonderful! You tried to touch the ball!" You'll be integrating all forms of verbal and non-verbal communication and your baby will know that he has accomplished something monumental.

To encourage mastery over a task—the consistent accomplishing of one of your baby's goals—praise him in the following progression:

- When he is *learning* a task, praise all the little steps and trials leading up to the task.
- Once he has *mastered* the task, praise only its successful completion.

If you're consistent in your praise, you'll find that around baby's eleventh month, he will clap at his own accomplishments. Your loving praise helps to instill a sense of pride in his personal achievements.

Baby Develops an Understanding of His Own Space

Your three-month-old needs a place for his toys (where, eventually, he will have the power to leave them the way he wants) and a spot for play which is separate from his sleeping quarters. You'll also want to provide him with a wide space for diaper changing so he can roll from side to side and reach

for appealing toys you've left within his arm's length.
Remember to change room decor at intervals:

- Rotate black-and-white posters and fabric swatches within his crib and on the walls.
- Reposition crib and changing table once a month.
- Alternate checked and plain sheets—this month, two days on, one day off (use sheets with 1-inch checkerboard or gingham squares).

Time to Begin Gymnastics

This is definitely the time for you to enroll your baby in a gymnastics program, if you're so inclined. It's important to capitalize on his new enjoyment of activity. You'll want to find a program that emphasizes teaching babies balance and support.

I highly recommend the "Gymboree" or "Playorena" baby gyms. They provide a well-rounded program of active, passive, and interactive play, and they enable parents and babies to get together with their peers for some social time. (You'll find the address of the main office in Appendix 2.)

If there's no Gymboree in your area, seek out private gyms or gym programs for infants at local churches and the YMCA. You can also create your own gym right in baby's crib by hanging a crib gym or bar across baby's crib rail. He will pull on the rings and bar and eventually pull himself up to a sitting position. The resistance that these devices offer help your baby's muscles develop strength.

Stimulation Games for the Third Month

The following are structured stimulation games for your 15-minute-a-day playtimes. They take into account your three-month-old's growing sense of his own body.

Remember, in selecting games, as in the previous months, choose five—one from each sense—to play before morning, afternoon, and evening feedings. Here's a sample menu for the third month:

- *Visual Game 3*. Baby studies his Bright Baby Blanket™
- *Touch Game 1*. Baby strokes his body with his own hand
- *Hearing Game 4*. Baby jingles bells in time to music
- *Smell Game 2*. Read a scratch-and-sniff book
- *Movement Game 2*. Baby's feet bear some weight as you lift and tilt him

Toys You'll Be Using
(See Chapter 33 and Appendix 4 for where-to-buy and how-to-make instructions)

VISUAL TOYS
- Mrs. Eyeset™
- Mind Mittens™
- Bookends

- Bright Baby™ Blanket
- Bright Baby Mind Mobile™
- Expressly Yours™ poster

SMELL TOYS
- Cotton balls
- Mother's perfume
- *Sweet Smell of Strawberryland* or other scratch and sniff books

- Banana, orange, and other sweet-smelling fruit
- Your dinner
- Honey, cinnamon, nutmeg

TOUCH TOYS
- Full-length mirror
- Crib rings or crib bar

- Tactile Tillie™
- Mr. Mouse™

MOVEMENT TOYS
- Bright Baby Teaching Tube™ or cylinder made of rolled bath towel

- Rings or crib bar
- Pillowcase

HEARING TOYS
- Mr. Mouse™
- Letters, numbers, baby's name written in 3-inch black letters on individual sheets of paper
- Book of nursery rhymes

- Jingle bells and 12 inches of brightly-colored yarn
- Grade 1 phonics book and newspaper

Visual Stimulators for the Third Month

Consider keeping some of the following items within baby's view and ready reach.

8 to 12 weeks—Hold up to 24 inches from baby's face:

- Two 2-inch triangles, set point to point, drawn on 8 x 11 white background
- 3-inch-tall heavy black numbers and letters, each on an individual card, paper plate, or fan-folded computer paper
- A 9- to 12-square black-and-white checkerboard, each square 1 inch by 1 inch
- Crib sheet with 1 inch by 1 inch checkerboard squares

Two 2-inch triangles set point to point

- More complex oval female face, about 8 inches long and 5 to 6 inches wide, with ears and eyebrows outlined, surrounded by wide black-band border on 11 × 14 white background
- 10 red 1-inch stripes drawn, pasted, or crocheted on white 8 × 11 background
- Drawing or crocheted black-and-white 4-inch-tall mouse with nose, eyes, and ears accented

Visual Games
(See Chapter 33 and Appendix 4 for where-to-buy and how-to-make instructions)

1. PURPOSE: Visual stimulation
   YOU'LL NEED: A visual toy like Mrs. Eyeset™ or Mr. Mouse™; it should be easy for your baby to hold onto
   TIME: 1 minute
   BABY'S POSITION: Sitting in his infant seat with arms free
   WATCH FOR: Baby's deliberate movements and visual tracking

   • Place toy in baby's hand.
   • Stretch out his hand, shaking object in front of him so he tracks his own movement.
   • Move his arm up, down, and from side to side.

2. PURPOSE: Visual stimulation
   YOU'LL NEED: Bookends dressed in Mind Mittens™
   TIME: 2 minutes
   BABY'S POSITION: On changing table with Mind Mittens™ on either side
   WATCH FOR: Baby's reaching attempts

   • Attach "daddy's face" and "mommy's face" to the Velcro part of the mitten.
   • Point to daddy and say, "Grab daddy's face. Come on, can you grab it? Take it off. When it comes off, it sounds like this."
   • Pull felt face off so baby hears Velcro sound.
   • Then replace it.
   • Move baby's hand to the design and help him rip it off. Use praise to encourage his attempts.

3. PURPOSE: Visual stimulation
   YOU'LL NEED: Bright Baby Blanket™
   TIME: 2 minutes
   YOUR AND BABY'S POSITION: Lie baby on tummy on comforter. Lie down eye to eye with him
   WATCH FOR: Visual tracking for designs

   • Point out 3 separate designs, naming them as you go.
   • Lift baby up, turn comforter over, and point out and trace 2 red-and-white checkerboards.

4. PURPOSE: Visual stimulation
   YOU'LL NEED: Bright Baby Mind Mobile™
   TIME: 2 minutes
   BABY'S POSITION: On his back in crib, seated in infant seat with arms free
   WATCH FOR: Reaching and batting behavior

- Suspend the mobile so that baby can reach forward to touch shapes with his hands.
- Allow him time for his own self-initiated play.

5. PURPOSE: Visual stimulation
   YOU'LL NEED: Expressly Yours™ poster
   TIME: 2 minutes
   BABY'S POSITION: Held upright in your arms
   WATCH FOR: Baby's alertness and vocalization

- Bring baby up to poster and let him touch the faces.
- Bring the illustrated expression alive with your own gestures, words, and expressions.

Touch Games
(See Chapter 33 and Appendix 4 for where-to-buy and how-to-make instructions)

1. PURPOSE: Touch stimulation and body part recognition
   YOU'LL NEED: Full-length mirror
   TIME: 1 minute
   BABY'S POSITION: Sitting up in infant seat, in front of mirror
   WATCH FOR: Baby's relaxation

- Stroke baby, naming all body parts.
- Taking his own right hand in yours, have him touch his head, arm, other hand, belly, leg and foot as you name the parts.
- Repeat with his left hand.

2. PURPOSE: Touch stimulation and muscle tone
   YOU'LL NEED: Resistance toys like crib bar or rings
   TIME: 2 minutes
   BABY'S POSITION: Lying on back in crib
   WATCH FOR: Baby's grasp and pull

- Present 2 rings to baby at baby's arm's reach.
- Move the toys closer until he grabs onto them.
- Once he holds the rings, push on them and say, "Push." Then pull and say, "Pull."
- Help baby open his hands and tell him to let go. You may pull on them to assist him.
- Encourage baby to grab onto the rings again and repeat his release.

3. PURPOSE: Touch stimulation and grasp training
   YOU'LL NEED: Tactile Tillie™
   TIME: 1 minute
   BABY'S POSITION: Held in upright position or seated in infant seat
   WATCH FOR: Baby's grasp

   - Choose any three textures on Tactile Tillie™, one from the black-and-white portion of the toy and two from the colored section.
   - Show the texture to baby first and then stroke his face and his palms.
   - Help him to grab, stroke, and let go.

4. PURPOSE: Touch stimulation
   YOU'LL NEED: Just you and baby
   TIME: 1 to 2 minutes
   BABY'S POSITION: Lying on his back or tummy in crib
   WATCH FOR: Baby's relaxation

   - Continue skin-to-skin stroking and massage in usual head-to-toe, center-to-sides pattern.

5. PURPOSE: Touch and hearing stimulation, grasping, and hand-mouth activity
   YOU'LL NEED: A noise-making toy like Mr. Mouse™
   TIME: 1 to 2 minutes
   BABY'S POSITION: Seated in infant seat
   WATCH FOR: Baby's developing grasp and eventual placement of toy in his mouth

   - Place mouse in baby's hands and shake his hands so he hears the noise.
   - Have baby release the toy and then help him grab it once more, but choose another part of it, like the mouse's ear.

(This is so he experiences different sizes.) Release again.
- Put the whole mouse in both of baby's hands in the center of his body and watch what he does with it.

Hearing Games
(See Chapter 33 and Appendix 4 for where-to-buy and how-to-make instructions)

1. PURPOSE: Hearing stimulation
   YOU'LL NEED: A noise-making toy like Mr. Mouse™
   TIME: 1 minute
   BABY'S POSITION: Held in your arms

- Put toy in baby's hand and shake it with pauses for 1 minute.
- Pick baby up and sing one nursery rhyme or lullaby while dancing about and shaking toy.

2. PURPOSE: Hearing stimulation, letter, number, name recognition
   YOU'LL NEED: Heavy black 3-inch letters A,B,C,D,E; numbers 1,2,3,4,5, and baby's name written with thick, non-toxic marker on individual sheets of fan-folded computer paper
   TIME: 2 minutes
   BABY'S POSITION: Sit baby up in infant seat
   WATCH FOR: Baby's vocalizations

- Slowly point each out and say, "This is A. This is A. Can you see A? Can you say A? A, A, A, A, can you see A?"
- Allow baby to touch alphabet and numbers as he sees fit.
- Read baby's name slowly and phonetically, pointing to the letters as you do.

3. PURPOSE: Hearing and movement stimulation
   YOU'LL NEED: Rocking chair and nursery rhyme book
   TIME: 1 minute
   BABY'S POSITION: Held in your arms while you rock in chair
   WATCH FOR: Baby's vocalizations

- While rocking, read one nursery rhyme like "Little Miss Muffet."

4. PURPOSE: Hearing stimulation and hand awareness

YOU'LL NEED: 2 jingle bells attached securely to baby's wrists with 6 inches of yarn. Make sure yarn is short enough that baby won't become entangled in it, and that bells can't come loose and be put in baby's mouth.

TIME: 1 minute

BABY'S POSITION: Seated on your lap

WATCH FOR: Baby's vocalizations

- Sing 2 songs to baby and move his hands in time to the music or when you repeat a particular word.

5. PURPOSE: Hearing stimulation

YOU'LL NEED: Grade 1 phonics book or 5 pages of newspaper

TIME: 1 minute

BABY'S POSITION: Held in your lap

WATCH FOR: Baby's vocalization and reaching

- Read slowly and in exaggerated voice.
- Be sure to repeat baby's name frequently to keep his attention.

Smell Games

1. PURPOSE: Smell stimulation and reaching behavior

YOU'LL NEED: 2 cotton balls sprayed with mother's perfume

TIME: 30 seconds

BABY'S POSITION: Held on your lap, next to a table

WATCH FOR: Baby's alertness and reaching

- Pass cotton balls under baby's nose.
- Place them in front of baby, on table, so he tries to reach for them.

2. PURPOSE: Smell and hearing stimulation

YOU'LL NEED: *Sweet Smell of Strawberryland* (see Chapter 33) or other scratch and sniff book

TIME: 1 minute

BABY'S POSITION: Held on your lap

WATCH FOR: Baby's alertness and vocalizations

- Read *Sweet Smell of Strawberryland* for 1 minute.
- Identify all scents by saying, "This is strawberry. Smell the strawberry. Isn't it good?

3. PURPOSE: Smell stimulation
     YOU'LL NEED: A banana, an orange, and one other sweet-smelling fruit in season
     TIME: 30 seconds
     BABY'S POSITION: Held on your lap
     WATCH FOR: Baby's alertness and changing facial expression

   • Pass each scent under baby's nose three times.

4. PURPOSE: Smell stimulation
     YOU'LL NEED: Your dinner
     TIME: 30 seconds
     BABY'S POSITION: Sitting in infant seat in the kitchen
     WATCH FOR: Baby's alertness and changing facial expression

   • Let baby smell the food you're cooking today.
   • Offer a whiff of pot roast or lasagne.

5. PURPOSE: Smell stimulation
     YOU'LL NEED: Honey, cinnamon, and nutmeg
     TIME: 30 seconds
     BABY'S POSITION: Seated on your lap
     WATCH FOR: Baby's alertness and changing facial expression

   • Pass each scent under baby's nose three times. Identify the scents.

Movement Games
(See Chapter 33 and Appendix 4 for where-to-buy and how-to-make instructions)

1. PURPOSE: Movement stimulation and balance
     YOU'LL NEED: Bright Baby Teaching Tube™ or a cylinder made by rolling up bath towel
     TIME: 1 or 2 minutes
     BABY'S POSITION: On the floor, place baby on his tummy across the cylinder
     WATCH FOR: Baby's balance and scrambling movements

   • Roll baby, holding his hips, forward and back two times.
   • Roll baby forward enough so his hands touch the ground in front of him.
   • Push lightly on the soles of his feet so he scrambles forward. His body will slide off the towel and down to the ground.

2. PURPOSE: Movement stimulation
   YOU'LL NEED: Just you and baby
   TIME: 1 to 2 minutes
   BABY'S POSITION: Holding baby around chest and under arms, stand him so his feet bear some weight

   - Gently tilt baby 45 degrees to the right and then to the left three times.
   - Tilt him forward and backward at the same 45-degree angle three times. His head should be in good control.
   - Raise him up off the ground and lower him so that his feet bear some weight.
   - Have baby take 3 steps forward and then 3 steps back, repeating three times.

3. PURPOSE: Movement stimulation
   YOU'LL NEED: Rings or crib bar
   TIME: 1 to 2 minutes
   BABY'S POSITION: Lay baby on his back
   WATCH FOR: Baby's strengthening muscles

   - Put rings or bar in baby's hands.
   - Holding his arms over his head, roll him to the right and then to the left three times while he grasps the rings or bar.
   - Pull baby halfway up to sitting position. If his head is wobbly at all or his grasp is poor, lift him only 2 inches off floor until his muscles are stronger. Hold for 5 seconds.
   - Lower baby to the floor. In lying position, slip your hands under his back and lift him 3 to 5 inches from the floor and lower him.
   - Repeat three times, saying, "Up and down, up and down."

4. PURPOSE: Movement stimulation
   YOU'LL NEED: Just you and baby
   TIME: 1 minute
   YOUR AND BABY'S POSITION: Slide your arms under baby's back so that he rests in the crook of your elbow
   WATCH FOR: Baby's alertness

   - Lift baby 1 inch from the ground and then go up, down, forward, backward, side to side, around in slow circles to right, around in circles to the left—three times in each position.

• Describe the direction of movements.

5. PURPOSE: Movement stimulation, reaching, and grasping

YOU'LL NEED: A pillowcase, folded in half lengthwise

TIME: 1 to 2 minutes

BABY'S POSITION: Place baby face down over pillowcase so that it supports him firmly across his chest and under his arms

WATCH FOR: Baby's reaching behavior

• Lift baby up at 45-degree angle and then lower. His arms will dangle in front of him. Repeat three times.

• Place a favorite toy like black-and-white bear in front of baby, just beyond his arms' reach as he is slightly inclined.

• Allow him to reach for the toy three times before lowering him to successfully grab it.

Mini-Milestones in the Third Month

1. Your baby smiles differently now for different people. For mommy and daddy he has a very special smile. This occurs once baby realizes people are different and separate from other people. He'll laugh out loud and coo when spoken to. He'll get excited when he hears the bath water running.

2. When he's sitting up, baby keeps his head up. Only occasionally will it bob forward. He gains good head control from the "rolling on the cylinder" activities and pull-ups done over the last month. When on the floor, he holds his head perpendicular to the floor, supported by arms stretched out before him.

3. Baby looks at objects within his 10-foot room. He'll follow an object 12 inches from his face with both his eyes and his head, turning them a full 180 degrees.

4. You'll notice that baby shows the beginnings of memory. If you bring him something he's seen before, his face will light up different-

ly than if you bring him something similar but not identical. This reaction shows he has recall of the previously experienced object.

5. Baby's preferences become well known now. He expresses himself with smiles and gurgles.

6. Baby's handling abilities take great leaps. He deliberately touches his hands and his feet. One hand becomes more frequently used than the other. He gazes at his hands and feet intently.

7. As baby uses his hands more often, his individual fingers make movements around a toy. When you see this, you'll know that baby has really learned from his previous touch experiences and is commanding his fingers to learn even more.

8. Baby can hold a rattle himself for about a minute and is very accomplished at getting both of his hands to come together. His hands are partially fisted and he'll swipe at objects with semi-open hand.

9. Baby has enough muscle control to kick his legs alternately. This indicates that he has learned from the different touch exercises and body-part isolations.

29. The Fourth Month:
Baby Learns the Special Relations
of *Spatial* Relations

Your four-month-old will be learning about the people and things in the space around him. Now that he knows he's a separate individual with definite boundaries, he needs to learn how other people and objects in his world relate to him and how they relate to each other. He learns to move himself through space.

Baby's Developing Eye-Hand Coordination Makes Learning Possible

You'll notice that your baby reaches for toys with outstretched fingers. However, he always seems to overshoot his mark. He has learned what his hands are for but he hasn't quite learned where they *end*. As far as he's concerned, his palm does the grasping. When you engage your infant in finger play, however, he gains more control over his individual fingers and he learns just how long they are. To help him along in an ongoing way, you may:

- Tie 6-inch lengths of brightly-colored yarn on his fingers.
- Trace the designs on his mobile, checkerboard, or stimulation poster with his outstretched finger.
- Fasten a helium balloon on a 6-inch string to his index finger for 5 minutes.
- Let him dig his fingers into deep-pile textures like those of his stuffed animals.

Baby's sense of sight is further refined in the fourth month. He now enjoys *binocular vision*, which means he can focus both eyes on one point in front of him. This will help in the many games you'll be playing with him this month that teach him about himself and objects in space.

Learning the Permanence of Objects

Since your four-month-old realizes he's a separate individual, he also recognizes that *other* objects and people that exist are not part of him. Much of your energy will be devoted to teaching your baby that "others" continue to exist, even if they're no longer in his sight. This important lesson will boost his sense of trust in his world.

Some of your infant's sense of permanence has already been established from your game of presenting toys from differing orientations. No matter what the angle, it's still the same rattle. And even though he sees mommy and daddy from the back or side, it's still the same wonderful mommy and daddy. The concept of permanence also simply comes from the loving routine you've established with baby.

A fun game of peekaboo teaches the concept of permanence first with objects and then with you—his favorite people. We'll show you how to play week by week in the structured stimulation games section of this chapter.

Baby's New Visual Ability Helps Him Learn Where Things Are in Space

Your four-month-old can see everything in his room. To help him understand space, approach him, toy in your outstretched hand, from the far end of his room. He will eventually receive the object with his own outstretched hand. He is learning how to command space by reaching for toys and bringing them in.

To help baby learn how to relate to objects in his world during your ongoing interactions, show him his clothes before you dress him, flowers before he smells them, jewelry before you put it on yourself. Talk to him about what you're doing.

Many of the visual stimulators you'll be using around baby this month incorporate familiar household items that are a part of his everyday world.

Baby Becomes a Space Traveler

Your four-month-old is gaining more vertical proficiency as he moves through space. He makes many movements with his trunk and legs. He rolls over, propels himself forward, and starts to push off with feet. You find him at the far end of his crib when he awakens from his nap. Crib springs, which can be purchased at J. C. Penney or Montgomery Ward, encourage baby's independent movements by allowing him to rock himself with ease.

Your infant also tries to pull himself up by grabbing onto his crib rails. He has become good at putting hands up to reach for the bar slung across his crib.

Baby Can Play on His Own— under Your Watchful Eye

Give your baby opportunities for free, unstructured sensory play and unstructured movement play. Your four-month-old has the capacity to play unassisted for 15 to 20 minutes at a time without your direct interaction or intervention. However, he should be under your visual supervision at all times. *When baby is at this young age, never walk out of the room or leave him* alone *with toys*.

You may wish to introduce three items of interest in the crib or play area. Of these items, two should be familiar objects and one, new. The novel toy can be as simple as a shoe box, a roll of toilet paper, balloons (stringless), spoons from kitchen, nested measuring cups and spoons, napkin rings, clean powder puffs, or fabric books like the *Touch Me* series (see the Resource Guide in Chapter 33 for details). Just *make sure everything is safe for baby's mouth and watch to make sure he plays safely*.

It's also important for your infant to have "sit and hit" opportunities. He'll sit up in his infant seat comfortably now as he is developing sitting balance. If you hang his three-dimensional mobile before him, he'll play at batting it. You no longer control the toy—he does. And he'll hit it, according to his own preference, in either direction. He's truly a bilateral being now, equally sensitive on both sides.

Start Stacking and Nesting

The fourth month is an excellent time to start stacking games. They teach baby how one object relates to another in space and especially that small things go on top of bigger things and not the reverse.

When offering stacking toys give baby several similar graduated objects like varying-size Tupperwares (all with the same shape) or stacking blocks available at toy stores (see the Resource Guide for manufacturers). Show him how to build towers.

Just as important as stacking is learning that the Tupperware tower collapses. Again, you are emphasizing permanence. The objects change places but are still there—if only in a new and exciting configuration. By your example and help, encourage baby's stacking, making "all fall down" and stacking again.

Stacking blocks often can be nested. That means smaller blocks fit inside larger ones. Nesting games also teach baby about how objects relate to shape. The stacking toys we recommend in the Resource Guide can all be used for nesting too.

What's That Mumbo-Jumbo?

Baby begins to mumble at this time. That's his attempt to initiate interaction with you—a wonderful sign to you that your sociable child wants to participate in your world. By all means, reinforce any speech sounds that resemble your native tongue. Repeat vowel sounds and sing songs often for language reinforcement.

Stimulation Games in the Fourth Month

Stimulation games this month take full advantage of your baby's heightened muscle control and coordination. They allow for supervised exploratory playtime. As in prior months, follow the smorgasbord approach. Choose five games—one from each sense—and repeat them before morning, afternoon, and evening feedings. Here's a sample menu for the fourth month:

- *Visual Game 1*. Play peekaboo
- *Touch Game 2*. Stroke baby with terry surface of Tactile Tillie™
- *Hearing Game 4*. Sing along with nursery rhyme or other tape
- *Smell Game*. Continue with pleasing scents
- *Movement Game 5*. Help baby propel himself on a Cookie Monster Crawl-Along™ Muppets, Inc.

Toys You'll Be Needing

Never leave baby alone with toys in which he can become entangled or on which he can choke.

VISUAL TOYS
- Panda bear or favorite stuffed animal
- 8 × 11 sheet of paper
- Baby's blanket
- 8-inch lengths of brightly-colored yarn
- Expressly Yours™ poster
- Bright Baby Mind Mobile™
- Crib gym
- 8 × 11 cards with 5-inch-tall heavy black outline drawings of familiar baby objects
- Red-and-white helium-filled balloons (on short strings)

HEARING TOYS
- Johnson & Johnson Rattle
- Wind chimes and string
- *Heartsongs* tape (see Appendix 2) or nursery rhymes recording
- Rocking chair
- 3-inch-tall thick black letters A,B,C,D,E and numbers 1,2,3,4,5 on 8 × 11 white background

TOUCH TOYS
- 4 differing fabric swatches or Mind Mitten™
- Terry-cloth towel or Tactile Tillie™
- Safe household items like: raisins, wooden spools, large popbeads (the size of wooden blocks), keys, Ping-Pong balls
- A plastic cup or paper bag
- Stacking toys like 3 Tupperware containers of graduated sizes with the same shape
- A feather, sticky tape, damp sponge, foil, and noisy cellophane wrap

MOVEMENT TOYS
- 2 familiar toys and 1 new
- Mr. Mouse™
- Recording of dance music
- Panda or favorite stuffed animal or Brainy Bear™
- Rattle
- Pillow
- Cookie Monster Crawl-Along™ Muppets, Inc.

Visual Stimulators in the Fourth Month

Leave the following designs within your four-month-old's view.

12 to 16 weeks—Hold toys up to 3 feet from baby's face

- 9-square black-and-white checkerboard, each square ¾ by ¾ inch
- Crib sheet with ¾- by ¾-inch checkerboard squares
- Picture of a 3- by 3-inch black (or navy blue), white, and red-striped ball drawn on 8 × 11 white background
- Your child's name on poster board in 6-inch-tall bold navy or black letters
- Black-and-white drawing of happy family pet with exaggerated ears, eyes, nose, and tail
- Simple black-and-white 5-inch drawings of a baby bottle, crib, pacifier, and other familiar objects in your baby's environment on separate 8 × 11 white cards
- 4-inch black-and-white pompoms attached securely to baby's booties (make sure they don't come loose and that they're too big for baby's mouth)

Visual Games
(See Chapter 33 and Appendix 4 for where-to-buy and how-to-make instructions)

1. PURPOSE: Visual stimulation and object permanence
   YOU'LL NEED: Baby's blanket, panda or other stuffed animal, and/or sheet of paper
   TIME: 1 minute
   BABY'S POSITION: See below
   WATCH FOR: Baby's recognition and giggle

Peekaboo Week by Week

WEEK 1:
   - Hide a corner of baby's favorite panda or other stuffed animal under baby's blanket.
   - Ask, "Where is your bear?" Reveal it and say, "Here he is!" Repeat two to three times a day.
   - Present your face, covering only your eyes with your hands. Say "Peekaboo!" as you reveal your features.
   - Cover baby's eyes with your hand and repeat "Peekaboo" as you release.

WEEK 2:
   - Cover all but bear's head and repeat as above.
   - Cover your mouth, nose, or ears and repeat as above.
   - Loosely cover baby's foot or leg with his blanket. Say, "Daniel's foot? It must be under the blanket." Uncover it.

WEEK 3:
   - Cover the entire bear but leave its contour evident. Repeat as above.
   - Loosely cover baby's face with his blanket.
   - Say, "I can't see Daniel's face but I can *feel* it. Here it is!"
   - Pass sheet of paper across bear to temporarily hide it. Say, "Here's the bear. Where did it go? Here it is again."

WEEK 4:
   - Talk to baby as you move away from him.
   - Begin talking out of sight and as you enter his room.

2. PURPOSE: Visual stimulation and initiation of own movements

YOU'LL NEED: 2 helium-filled balloons—1 red and 1 white—with 6-inch strings attached to baby's wrists

TIME: 1 minute

BABY'S POSITION: Sitting up in infant seat

WATCH FOR: Baby's visual tracking and deliberate arm movements

- Show baby how to bob balloons up and down in the air. Allow free exploratory playtime.

3. PURPOSE: Visual stimulation, vocalization, and facial expression

YOU'LL NEED: Expressly Yours™ poster with additional faces showing eating and yawning

TIME: 1 minute

BABY'S POSITION: Sitting up in infant seat

WATCH FOR: Baby's vocalizations and changing facial expressions

- Go through the whole realm of facial expressions on your Expressly Yours™ poster.
- Add to them exaggerated gesturing of your expressive hands and face.
- Make sure to show the hand movements associated with eating and yawning.

4. PURPOSE: Visual stimulation and self-initiated play

YOU'LL NEED: Bright Baby Mind Mobile,™ or crib gym suspended over crib within baby's arm reach

TIME: 1 minute or more, as baby desires

BABY'S POSITION: In crib, napping

WATCH FOR: Baby's interest, batting activity, or pulling on rings and clackers upon awakening

- Suspend mobile or crib gym across crib so when baby awakens, he may play with it at will.

5. PURPOSE: Visual stimulation, object recognition, and finger play

YOU'LL NEED: 8 × 11 white cards with 5-inch-tall heavy black outline drawings of common household or baby objects like bottle, rattle, pacifier, family pet

TIME: 1 minute

BABY'S POSITION: Held upright on your lap

WATCH FOR: Baby's visual alertness and vocalizations

- Show baby 1 card at a time. Say, "This is a bottle. Can you say 'bottle'? Bottle. Bottle. Bottle."
- Help baby trace outline of object with his outstretched finger.

Touch Games
(See Chapter 33 and Appendix 4 for where-to-buy and how-to-make instructions)

1. PURPOSE: Touch stimulation and self-initiated play
   YOU'LL NEED: 4 fabric swatches with contrasting textures, or the swatches from Mind Mitten™
   TIME: 1 minute
   BABY'S POSITION: Lying on floor with cloth swatches within reach
   WATCH FOR: Baby's finger activity and placement of cloth in his mouth

   - Allow baby free play with the different textures. Make sure that the fabric is clean, because it will inevitably go into baby's mouth.

2. PURPOSE: Touch stimulation
   YOU'LL NEED: Terry-cloth towel or Tactile Tillie™
   TIME: 1 minute
   BABY'S POSITION: Lying undressed on bed or in crib
   WATCH FOR: Baby's relaxation

   - Stroke baby with terry-cloth surface of Tactile Tillie™ or use a terry-cloth towel in usual head-to-toe, center-to-sides direction.

3. PURPOSE: Touch stimulation and self-initiated play
   YOU'LL NEED: A variety of safe household items like: raisins, empty wooden spools, large pop-beads, keys, Ping-Pong balls, and a plastic cup or paper bag
   TIME: 2 minutes
   YOUR AND BABY'S POSITION: Sit at a table with baby on your lap
   WATCH FOR: Baby's exploratory play

   - Arrange objects in front of baby with cup or bag next to them.
   - Pick up objects and drop in cup.

- Allow baby any free, safe activity he chooses with objects, but be careful that he not take any object into his mouth.

4. PURPOSE: Touch stimulation, stacking, and exploratory play
   YOU'LL NEED: 3 to 4 stacking toys like Tupperware containers of the same shape but graduated sizes
   TIME: 2 minutes
   YOUR AND BABY'S POSITION: Hold baby on your lap at table where you have arranged stacking and nesting toys
   WATCH FOR: Baby's exploratory play

- Allow baby to move forward to touch the items on the table.
- Show him how to stack one toy on the next and then knock over tower. Repeat three to five times.
- Let him reach and play with toys on his own.

5. PURPOSE: Touch stimulation
   YOU'LL NEED: A feather, sticky tape, damp sponge, foil, and noisy cellophane wrap
   TIME: 1 to 2 minutes
   YOUR AND BABY'S POSITION: Seated at table with baby on your lap
   WATCH FOR: Baby's finger explorations

- Set out objects in front of baby.
- Allow him free hand play for 1 minute.
- Stroke with the different textures, naming the textures for 1 minute.

Hearing Games
(See Chapter 33 and Appendix 4 for where-to-buy and how-to-make instructions)

1. PURPOSE: Hearing stimulation, sound localization, and muscle tone
   YOU'LL NEED: Johnson & Johnson rattle or other rattle
   TIME: 1 minute
   BABY'S POSITION: Lying on his tummy on the floor
   WATCH FOR: Baby's twisting movements as he tries to find the rattle

- Shake rattle behind baby's head. He should try to look back for it.
- Shake rattle behind baby on right side and he will try to twist his body, pushing with legs and arms.
- Repeat on his left side.

2. PURPOSE: Hearing stimulation and object permanence
   YOU'LL NEED: Just you and baby
   TIME: 1 minute
   BABY'S POSITION: Lying flat on his back in crib
   WATCH FOR: Baby's recognition and giggle

- Duck out of sight and then pop up saying "Peekaboo."
- Repeat from different positions around crib for 1 minute.

3. PURPOSE: Hearing stimulation and self-initiated play
   YOU'LL NEED: Wind chimes and a string long enough to attach dangling chimes to baby's arm or leg
   TIME: 1 minute
   BABY'S POSITION: Tie string to baby's arm or leg so that his movements activate chimes. Hold baby on your lap
   WATCH FOR: Baby's alertness and exploratory play

- Allow supervised exploratory play. Make sure baby doesn't break string, become entangled in it, or try to swallow it.

4. PURPOSE: Hearing stimulation
   YOU'LL NEED: *Heartsongs* tape (see Appendix 2) or nursery rhyme recording
   TIME: 1 or 2 minutes
   BABY'S POSITION: Held in your arms or engaged in appropriate activity
   WATCH FOR: Baby's attentiveness and vocalization

- Sing along with the bathing and bedtime songs on the *Heartsongs* tape, as appropriate, or sing along with nursery rhymes.

5. PURPOSE: Hearing stimulation, letter and number recognition, finger awareness, and vocalization
   YOU'LL NEED: 3-inch-tall letters A,B,C,D,E, and numbers 1,2,3,4,5 written in thick black lines on white 8 × 11 background, and rocking chair
   TIME: 1 to 2 minutes

BABY'S POSITION: Held in your arms while you are rocking in chair

WATCH FOR: Baby's vocalizations and outstretched fingers

- Read the letters A through E and the numbers 1 through 5 twice.
- Trace the letters with baby's fingers as you go.
- With the numbers, you can sing "One little, two little, three little Indians," and with the letters, the alphabet song.

Movement Games
(See Chapter 33 and Appendix 4 for where-to-buy and how-to-make instructions)

1. PURPOSE: Movement stimulation and free play activity

   YOU'LL NEED: Baby's blanket, 2 familiar toys, and 1 new one

   TIME: 1 to 2 minutes

   BABY'S POSITION: Lying on tummy on blanket, on the grass or indoors, as weather dictates

   WATCH FOR: Baby's self-initiated movements

   - Allow supervised free play, leaving toys within baby's reach.

2. PURPOSE: Movement stimulation and self-initiated movements

   YOU'LL NEED: Mr. Mouse™ or other favorite toy

   TIME: 1 minute

   BABY'S POSITION: Sit baby up on your lap in front of a table

   WATCH FOR: Baby's stretching and reaching

   - Show baby how to bang on table with hand. Let him bang for 30 seconds.
   - Put the toy on the table, slightly out of his reach so he leans forward and pushes off with his feet as he reaches for the toy.

3. PURPOSE: Movement stimulation and muscle tone

   YOU'LL NEED: A recording of dance music

   TIME: 2 minutes

   BABY'S POSITION: Held in your arms

   WATCH FOR: Baby's strengthening muscles

- Dance with baby with music playing for 1 minute.
- Put him down so his feet touch the ground, and take 5 quick movements forward and then 5 slow movements back.
- Pick him up in your arms and take 5 strong steps and 5 light, tiptoeing steps.

4. PURPOSE: Movement stimulation, balance, and muscle tone
    YOU'LL NEED: Panda or favorite stuffed animal, a rattle or Mr. Mouse™ and a pillow
    TIME: 1 minute
    BABY'S POSITION: Lay baby on his tummy on the floor and lie down beside him
    WATCH FOR: Baby's balance and reach

- Place panda in front of baby's right hand and help him reach forward with right hand. Allow him time to support himself with his left hand.
- Place the toy by his left arm and repeat.
- Roll baby onto his side, supporting him with a pillow.
- Place rattle or Mr. Mouse™ in front of him, slightly beyond his reach.
- Rattle it until he reaches forward, then give it to him.

5. PURPOSE: Movement stimulation and muscle tone
    YOU'LL NEED: Cookie Monster Crawl-Along™ Muppets, Inc. or infant skateboard
    TIME: 1 minute
    BABY'S POSITION: Place baby on an infant skateboard or Crawl-Along, securing him with the Velcro straps provided (or hold him on securely) and lie down beside him on the floor
    WATCH FOR: Baby's strengthening leg muscles

- Help baby propel himself forward by putting his feet on the ground and pushing him forward
- Never leave baby unattended on Crawl-Along.

Smell Games

Continue this month with a variety of pleasing scents as recommended in the previous months.

Mini-Milestones in Fourth Month

1. Baby is getting quite proficient as he lies on his back and tummy. When lying on his back, can lift his head and even lean it backward.

2. When he's on his tummy, can hold his head up and turn it to all sides and look in all positions.

3. You'll also notice that when he is on his tummy, baby will reach forward with one arm while supporting himself with the other. This means that the strength of his back is growing and only one arm is needed now to hold him up in addition to his back muscles.

4. Baby will roll from side to side—a sign of strength in his trunk muscles. He can turn from his back to his side and onto his tummy.

5. As his trunk strengthens, you'll notice that baby's arms and hands become more active. He bends his arms now and the *reflex* grasp has weakened to such an extent that his stronger *voluntary* grasp has come into fore. Now he can really hold onto objects.

6. Baby can lift himself up with his arms, holding onto a bar in front of him, and is almost able to pull himself up to a full sitting position. He'll want to pull down and bring in his mouth anything that's suspended above him.

7. Baby's movements no longer are abrupt and jerky. They have slowed down—a sure sign that he is gaining control.

8. Your four-month-old is a very social baby. He smiles, laughs out loud, expresses himself with happy gurgles. He gives particularly warm welcomes to mommy and daddy but begins to closely observe strangers and will size up people to adjust his responses to them based upon his experience.

9. Just as he has distinguished favorite people, baby now has his own favorite toy and is beginning to find ways to create play with his favorite toy or with people.

10. Baby starts using clicking noises in his mouth to initiate interaction and attention.

11. Fortunately for his parents, baby is usually sleeping through the night in 6- to 8-hour intervals. He usually sleeps for about 10 hours at night.

12. Baby is alert about 2 hours at a time during the day.

30. The Fifth Month:
Baby Takes Pride in His
Own Power

By baby's fifth month he will feel the security of having some power to affect his environment. Through the activities you have already provided, he gains control over his toys and can actively manipulate them. Now *he can actually use his body to get what he wants*. What's more, he knows his own mind and can exert his power with wails and squirms if someone tries to remove a favorite play thing!

This month your baby needs games that teach him that he has the power to keep the play going, to bring objects in, to influence the game's outcome. Stacking and nesting toys help him learn that he has the power to build and destroy—to change the configuration of his world. Games in which he pulls toys to himself teach him the value of pulling and the mental skill of cause and effect. "(If I do this, that will happen.") He sees that he has *direct power* as he uses his body to change his environment. This is all possible because of the growth of his memory ability, encouraged by your ongoing Stimulation Program.

Memory Grows, so Allow Unstructured Play

Your five-month-old has memory traces *which last from 7 to 9 seconds* and enable him to make guided movements. For example, if he sees a ball and turns away (for no more than 9 seconds), he'll remember its existence and turn back to get it.

Supervised but unstructured playtime enables your baby to

use his memory to explore objects. It also helps build his curiosity and persistence in discovering what happens next. His toys should be designed to give an *immediate* reward, since he is learning what sounds and/or movements they yield. He can handle up to 15 minutes of unstructured playtime during this month in an ongoing way. Allow him to play on the floor with such toys.

But remember, when I say "free unstructured play" I don't mean unsupervised play! Baby should be under your watchful eye constantly. Free play means that he has the freedom to explore a toy on his own without your direct intervention or interaction.

- Choose a mobile with elements that move *easily* in every direction: horizontally, vertically, diagonally, and in circles. (You may want to bring the mobile element to baby's hand. Bend his elbow so he draws the shape near, then help him to push it away.)
- Squeaky toys are great at this age. Ellen Duerr, a clinical nurse specialist at Children's Orthopedic Hospital in Seattle, Washington, has discovered that squeaky toys with just the right tension for all ages are available at pet stores. Some of the toys, like rubber porcupines, have great tactile value as well.
- Find simple items for baby to shake so he can learn the difference between his own gentle and vigorous movements. Provide different colored objects that are the same shape like black/white, red/white, and blue/white blocks. In this way baby learns there is a relationship between the blocks even though they are not identical.

Consistency

Give consistent, varying responses to baby's different activities. When he "talks"—making sounds that resemble your native tongue—answer those vocalizations consistently with the same feedback. (For example, every time he says "Baaa," answer, "Yes! Bottle!" and when he says "Maaa," answer, "Yes! Mama!") He'll learn, "If I make this sound, I get one result, but when I do something else, I get a different result." As baby practices these power games, he begins to learn there is a consistency between his behavior and the response from people and objects with which he is engaged. This consistency helps reinforce the sense of permanence learned last month.

From this your child derives a feeling of dependability, which is further enhanced when you provide him with an orderly, consistent, predictable world—in short, *routine*.

Reassess the ABC's of Your Routine

Now is a good time to reassess your routine. First, look at your own, personal routine. Are you taking good care of yourself?

Next, evaluate your baby's well-being through the following ABC's of assessment:

A: APPEARANCE: Is baby happy? If so, continue your activities. If not, review and repeat behaviors that promote security like the setting event and bedtime routine, discussed in the first month.

B: BEHAVIOR: Now that you've had time to adjust to your baby and he has had a chance to develop a pattern of behavior and sleep/wakefulness, make sure that you recognize his pattern and organize his day according to the 2 to 2½ hours of wakefulness he enjoys four times a day. At night he'll need 10 to 12 hours of sleep, which may be interrupted only by feeding.

C: CARE: Are you providing baby with:

- interaction play?
- solitary play?
- some structured play?
- free play?
- listening opportunities?
- vocalizing opportunities?

To add to baby's sense of dependability, talk about the sequence of your daily activities like bathing, bottle-feeding, and bedtime as you do them. For example, while bathing baby talk to him about what you're doing as you go through the routine of undressing, shampooing, washing, drying, diapering, feeding, and putting him to bed.

This month's activities are designed to instill a sense of pride in your baby. He'll feel good about the immediate rewards resulting from his power as his trials and successes change his environment and meet with approval.

Your baby's pride will be most evident when he plays with a toy without your assistance. You have given so much reinforcement that learning has become its own reward. Baby's own internal pleasure keeps him playing. And when that is coupled with your appropriate praise, you will be blessed with a very proud child who is secure enough in his control to be able to let go of it when appropriate and even be able to begin following simple directions.

Stimulation Games in the Fifth Month

As in previous months, you'll want to choose from among the suggested games when creating your structured Infant Stimulation play sessions. Review all the games and select five—one from each sense—which you'll repeat before morning, afternoon, and evening feedings. Vary the fare from day to day. Here's a sample menu for the fifth month:

- *Visual Game 3*. Teach baby the shapes of his Bright Baby Mind Mobile™
- *Touch Game 4*. Show baby how to pull his blanket to reach his favorite toy
- *Hearing Game 5*. Dance with baby in time to classical music
- *Smell Game*. Continue with pleasing scents from around your home
- *Movement Game 2*. Do baby sit-ups with baby holding a crib bar

Toys You'll Be Using

Never leave baby alone with toys in which he may become entangled or on which he may choke.

VISUAL TOYS
- Full-length mirror
- Baby's favorite toy
- Bright Baby Mind Mobile™

- ¼-inch checkerboard design drawn on paper plate
- Toys with highly contrasting colors (red-blue, black-white)
- Ball, half one color, half another

HEARING TOYS
- Baby's favorite toy
- Jingle bells
- Pencil
- 8 × 11 sheet of paper
- Recording of classical music

TOUCH TOYS
- Baby's favorite toy
- 4 squeeze toys
- Tactile Tillie™
- Blanket
- Plastic cap with handle

MOVEMENT TOYS
- Wooden dowel, crib bar, or smooth broomstick
- Blanket
- Baby's favorite toy
- Cookie Monster Crawl-Along™ Muppets, Inc.

SMELL TOYS
- Continue with pleasing scents

Visual Stimulators in the Fifth Month

Leave the following within baby's view:

- A 9- to 12-square black-and-white checkerboard, each square ½ by ½ inch
- Crib sheet with ½- by ½-inch checkerboard squares
- Red stripes on white background, ½ inch wide
- Let light from crystal prism dance on wall for baby
- Profiles or silhouettes of parents' faces pasted on 8 × 11 white background
- Outlines of common household objects on 8 × 11 white backgrounds—one per card
- Shiny three-dimensional objects and surfaces

Visual Games
(See Chapter 33 and Appendix 4 for where-to-buy and how-to-make instructions)

1. PURPOSE: Visual stimulation and teaching baby about body parts and cause and effect

    YOU'LL NEED: Full-length mirror, baby's favorite toys, and safe, unbreakable household items (plastic cups, blocks, etc.)

    TIME: 1 minute

    BABY'S POSITION: Sitting in supported position in infant seat or in box propped with pillows within arm's reach of mirror

    WATCH FOR: Baby's exploratory play and delight

    • Give baby supervised free time in front of mirror so he can touch his own body and the mirror image.
    • Place toys or objects in his hand one at a time.
    • Help him release the objects and show him how they fall to the ground as he watches in mirror.

2. PURPOSE: Visual stimulation

    YOU'LL NEED: Baby's favorite toy

    TIME: 1 minute

    BABY'S POSITION: Held on your lap while seated at table

    WATCH FOR: Baby's eyes staying on toy

    • Place a favorite toy on the table in front of baby.
    • Sway baby gently from side to side so that he learns to watch the toy even though he's moving.
    • Move baby up and down, encourage him to watch the toy.

3. PURPOSE: Visual stimulation and verbal understanding

    YOU'LL NEED: Bright Baby Mind Mobile™

    TIME: 1 to 2 minutes

    BABY'S POSITION: Lay baby on the floor on his tummy, with mobile lying loose on floor in front of him

    WATCH FOR: Baby's recognition of language

    • Verbally encourage baby to pick up square, cylinder, triangle, circle shapes.
    • Give the appropriate shape to him first two or three times so he begins to learn shapes.

4. PURPOSE: Visual stimulation and muscle control
   YOU'LL NEED: ¼-inch checkerboard design drawn on paper plate
   TIME: 1 minute
   BABY'S POSITION: Lying on the floor, on his tummy
   WATCH FOR: Baby's head and eyes to follow design as his body twists

- Hold design 5 inches above baby's head, facing him.
- Move it from side to side, getting baby to move and twist his body as he follows with his eyes.

5. PURPOSE: Visual stimulation and introduction to colors
   YOU'LL NEED: Several toys with highly contrasting colors (red-blue, black-white) and a ball that is half one color, half another (not necessarily black and white)
   TIME: 1 to 2 minutes
   BABY'S POSITION: Sitting on your lap at table
   WATCH FOR: Baby's visual interest

- Put several toys that have highly contrasting colors in front of baby.
- Allow baby to reach for them, one at a time.
- Encourage him to drop them.
- Pick them up and remove them from sight.
- Show baby ball. Slowly turn it in front of him, pointing out the colors as it turns. Allow him to hold ball.

Touch Games
(See Chapter 33 and Appendix 4 for where-to-buy and how-to-make instructions)

1. PURPOSE: Touch and self-initiated exploration
   YOU'LL NEED: Baby's favorite toy
   TIME: 1 minute
   BABY'S POSITION: Sitting on your lap at table with his favorite toy in front of him
   WATCH FOR: Baby's reaching behavior and self-generated play

- Let baby reach for toy and move it around.
- Allow supervised free play in his hands for the next minute.

2. PURPOSE: Touch stimulation and cause-and-effect training
   YOU'LL NEED: 4 easily activated squeeze toys
   TIME: 1 minute
   BABY'S POSITION: Sitting on your lap at table
   WATCH FOR: Baby's reactions and repetition of activity

   • Place squeeze toys in front of baby on the table.
   • Show him how to get reactions once or twice and then let
     him squeeze to activate the squeak himself.

3. PURPOSE: Touch stimulation, reaching, and positive rein-
   forcement
   YOU'LL NEED: Tactile Tillie™
   TIME: 1 minute
   BABY'S POSITION: Sitting supported in infant seat
   WATCH FOR: Baby's reaching and display of gratification

   • Hold Tactile Tillie™ 6 to 8 inches in the air above baby.
   • Encourage him to reach for the toy.
   • When he nearly touches it, give it to him and allow free
     exploratory play for one minute.
   • If he doesn't come near for 15 seconds, give him the toy
     and reinforce his future attempts.

4. PURPOSE: Touch stimulation and cause-and-effect training
   YOU'LL NEED: Baby's blanket and a favorite toy
   TIME: 1 minute
   BABY'S POSITION: On floor beside spread blanket
   WATCH FOR: baby's pulling activity

   • Place baby's favorite toy on blanket.
   • Give two or three demonstrations of how he can pull his
     blanket to get the toy.
   • Let him try.

5. PURPOSE: Touch stimulation and finger muscle control
   YOU'LL NEED: Plastic cup with handle
   TIME: 1 minute
   BABY'S POSITION: Sitting on your lap at table
   WATCH FOR: When baby starts this activity, he reaches
   with both hands open. After a week of experience, the hand
   nearest the handle curls in anticipation of grabbing the
   handle

- Place a plastic cup before baby so handle is by his right hand.
- Let him grab cup three times.
- Turn the cup around so the handle is by his left hand. Let him grasp handle with his left hand three times.

Hearing Games

1. PURPOSE: Hearing stimulation and learning that sounds can be signals

YOU'LL NEED: Baby's favorite toy, a jingle bell, and pencil

TIME: 1 minute

BABY'S POSITION: Sitting on your lap at a table

WATCH FOR: Baby will eventually learn that the bell sound is a signal for the toy's appearance and that all sounds can be used as signals

- As soon as baby looks away, make a sound, such as ringing the bell.
- Put toy out so he learns to associate that particular sound with appearance of toy.
- When he looks away again, make a different sound, such as tapping a pencil on the table, and remove toy.
- Baby will seek out sound and notice that toy is gone.

2. PURPOSE: Hearing and cause-and-effect training

YOU'LL NEED: 8 × 11 sheet of plain paper

TIME: 2 minutes

YOUR AND BABY'S POSITION: Prop baby in an infant seat and sit facing him

WATCH FOR: Baby's vocalizations

- Cover your face with a sheet of paper.
- Tell baby, "Talk to me, if you want to see me."
- Whenever he vocalizes anything, show him your face, give him a kiss, and start again.
- Continue for 2 minutes.

3. PURPOSE: Hearing and learning tone of voice

YOU'LL NEED: 2 plastic cups and a box large enough to cover 1 cup

TIME: 1 minute

BABY'S POSITION: Sitting on your lap at table

WATCH FOR: Baby's response to your changing tone

- Place both cups in front of baby on table but hide one under the box.
- Show baby the visual cup and say, "Here's a cup," in a matter-of-fact tone of voice.
- Reveal the hidden cup and using great expression and surprise say, "Look! Here's another cup!"
- Repeat three times, then let baby play with the objects.

4. PURPOSE: Hearing stimulation, rhythm, and routine
   YOU'LL NEED: Just you and baby
   TIME: 1 minute
   BABY'S POSITION: Held upright in your arms, in rocking chair, in bath or in bed
   WATCH FOR: Baby's vocalizations and pleasure

- Sing rhythmic verses as found in *Heartsongs* (see Appendix 2) or your favorite nursery rhymes.
- Establish one for bath, one sung before bed, and one during play session.
- Make sure you include lively music and slow music while moving baby rhytmically to the sounds.

5. PURPOSE: Hearing stimulation and vocalizations
   YOU'LL NEED: Recording of classical music
   TIME: 1 to 2 minutes
   BABY'S POSITION: Held in your arms
   WATCH FOR: Baby's vocalizations

- Let baby hear classical music and dance in time to it.
- As he mumbles with the music, reinforce his sounds with a kiss and a hug.

Movement Games

1. PURPOSE: Movement stimulation and strengthening of stomach muscles
   YOU'LL NEED: Just you and baby
   TIME: 1 minute
   BABY'S POSITION: On his back on the floor or bed
   WATCH FOR: Baby may put his toes in his mouth

- Gently bend both of baby's knees and place his hands on his knees.

- Release his grasp and stretch his legs up so that his toes touch his face.

2. PURPOSE: Movement stimulation and back muscle tone
  YOU'LL NEED: Wooden dowel, crib bar, or smooth broomstick
  TIME: 1 minute
  BABY'S POSITION: Lying on his back on floor or in crib
  WATCH FOR: Baby's strengthening back and neck muscles

- Place rod or wooden dowel in baby's hands.
- Protect his head and back with one hand, in case it should falter.
- Pull him up to standing position.
- Lower him gently.
- Repeat three times.

3. PURPOSE: Movement stimulation and muscle tone
  YOU'LL NEED: Baby's blanket and favorite toy
  TIME: 1 to 2 minutes
  BABY'S POSITION: On the floor
  WATCH FOR: Baby's strengthening muscles and free exploratory play

- Spread blanket on floor and place toy at far end.
- Hold baby's legs and encourage him to walk with his hands across blanket toward toy.
- Let him have the toy when he reaches it.
- Allow supervised free play on the floor with it for a minute.

4. PURPOSE: Movement stimulation and strengthening leg muscles
  YOU'LL NEED: Just you and baby
  TIME: 1 minute
  BABY'S POSITION: Sitting on your lap, facing you
  WATCH FOR: Baby's strengthening leg muscles

- Allow baby to push up into a standing position by letting him push his legs into your abdomen.
- Lower him to a sitting position.
- Lower him farther—gently between legs.
- Bring him back up to sitting.

- Repeat three times.
- Sing "See, saw, Margery Daw..."

5. PURPOSE: Movement stimulation and strengthening leg muscles

YOU'LL NEED: Cookie Monster Crawl-Along™ Muppets, Inc. (see Chapter 33) or baby skateboard

TIME: 2 minutes

BABY'S POSITION: Lying on his back on the floor

WATCH FOR: Baby's strengthening leg muscles

- Bend baby's legs alternately, bicycling for 1 minute.
- Roll him onto his tummy and place him on a baby skateboard or Crawl-Along™ Muppets, Inc., securing him with Velcro straps or holding him securely.
- Help him propel himself forward, using his legs, for 1 minute.
- Never leave baby alone on skateboard.

Smell Games

Continue with pleasing scents as in previous months.

Mini-Milestones

1. On his tummy he now can reach out with both of his arms because his back is strong enough to hold up his chest and head. When he's lying on ground, he can also play "airplane." Baby stretches his arms and legs straight out because his back can support his weight. This is important preparation for crawling and walking.

2. As he lies on his tummy, he will draw one leg underneath him. This is preparation for getting both legs under him for crawling. His leg doesn't support his weight yet, however, and baby falls back to the prone position.

3. You will see baby rocking and rolling this month. This exercise enables him to turn from his tummy to his back.

4. Once he is on his back, you'll notice that he cranes his head forward (so his chin rests on his chest) if you bring a toy into his view.

5. Just as he tries to get his head closer to objects in this way, his hand approach improves dramatically. He experiences his power in touch in the way he grabs toys. When he sees an object he likes, he begins by reaching for it with fingers outstretched. As he approaches the object, his fingers come together in a better position for a good grab. His hands accommodate to shape of toy as he grabs on with both of them.

6. Baby practices his hand power by turning an object over and over, dropping it and picking it up. With these exercises he is teaching himself object permanence. Congratulations! He has been stimulated enough so that now he's taking some responsibility for his own teaching and learning.

7. Baby's pride is reflected in squeals of delight, and burst-pause dialogue made with humming, mumbling, and some vowel sounds.

8. Baby gives mommy and daddy an especially warm welcome. He further modifies his responses to other people, based upon how well he knows them.

9. Baby sits upright, supported around the waist, for 30 minutes.

10. Baby leans over to look for a fallen object and will watch fast-moving objects.

11. Baby loves to watch himself in the mirror and reach out to his image.

31. The Sixth Month:
Baby Learns to Categorize

As your child learns how one object relates to another, he must also learn how to organize the things in his world according to their characteristics. He will find that objects may be similar or different according to how they look or what they're used for.

This month you will be providing a variety of examples of the same kind of object so that baby can learn to which category that object belongs. He will need many repetitions every day in order to master this complex cognitive task.

We suggest a wealth of ongoing "Category Games" for baby's learning pleasure later in this chapter.

Curiosity Reigns Freely

Allow your child to exhaust his curiosity and flow with his attention, wherever it may go. For example, when you are sitting with him to go over some cups, you may find that he gets distracted by the handle rather than sticking to the stacking task. Don't push him to continue stacking. His *unstructured* exploration is to be encouraged.

Gaining Indirect Power

As your six-month-old manipulates objects, he builds upon his power to control his environment. Last month he learned *direct power*—how to pull on a mobile or squeeze a squeaky toy. This month you will focus on *indirect power.* Baby will learn how to use one toy or object to reach or affect another. When he pulls the tail of his mouse to get the whole toy into reach, when he lifts his blanket to find his bear, when he pulls the placemat to get his bottle, baby is using indirect power. You may even see your bottle-fed infant try to use his bottle as an extension of his hands!

Baby learns how to control you indirectly through his vocalizations and sound-making ability. He'll gurgle and even pound cups on the table to get what he wants—whether it be attention, another bottle, or to be picked up.

And as your child gains direct and indirect power over objects, space, and you—his parents—you will find he exhibits tremendous delight! He is building one success upon another.

Abstract Games Build Abstract Thinking Ability

Abstract thinking games are ideal this month. Start by naming familiar objects in your home. Baby's blanket. His black-and-white bear. His high chair. When you meet them during your daily routine, you can address them with a friendly, "Hello, Blankie." Eventually, as you name objects, baby will reach for them when they are in sight. Later you will find that he can be sitting in the middle of the floor, paying attention to another toy, when you say "Dog!" He'll look around for the dog you've mentioned. Then you will know that he has attained a true understanding of object permanence and has learned that words represent objects.

Transition to the Transitional Object

You've given baby unlimited sucking opportunities. As he gains great manipulative skill, you may notice that he starts to play with his pacifier, as well. When he treats the pacifier like a toy, then you know he no longer needs it for a sense of security. You can safely remove it from his environment. (Some children may not relinquish their pacifiers until they're much older—two years old or more. In that case, of course, you should let baby keep it. However, when babies have had *unlimited* sucking opportunities, they often do without the pacifier at six months without much fuss.)

Though you may be able to discard baby's pacifier, you will know by now which toy has become his favorite—his transitional object. This is the time to reinforce that object—whether it's a stuffed animal, blanket, or fabric diaper. Give it a real name like Softie, Pinky, or Blankie. Make sure to keep it in bed with baby when he goes to sleep and make a habit of taking it with you wherever baby goes. He needs it.

Acknowledge your baby's right of ownership to his transitional object. If he wails in protest when you try to take it from him, give in and let him have it. You may have to slip it from his crib while he's napping in order to launder it. Baby deserves to own *one* item that is entirely his and over which he feels he has complete control.

When your child starts to control his environment, he feels secure that someone else is taking care of his life. He can devote his full energy to learning all the other tasks. Congratulations for the security that baby is exhibiting now. He's going to sit up this month and use his hands. Without your nurturing and a provision of sensory stimulation, he could not have come this far so soon!

Stimulation Games at Six Months

As in previous months, you will select five daily structured stimulation games—one from each sense—to play before morning, afternoon, and evening feedings. Remember to vary the fare from day to day. Here is a sample menu for the sixth month:

- *Visual Game 3*. Play a categorization game listed below.
- *Touch Game 4*. Teach baby how to fill and dump raisins from a cup.
- *Hearing Game 3*. Name and animate with their characteristic sounds household items and stuffed animals.
- *Smell Game*. Continue with pleasing scents from around your home.

• *Movement Game 1.* Push lightly on the soles of baby's feet to help him propel himself forward.

Toys You'll Be Using
(See Chapter 33 and Appendix 4 for where-to-buy and how-to-make instructions)

Never leave baby alone with toys in which he can become entangled or on which he can choke.

VISUAL TOYS
• Baby's favorite toy
• Collections of spoons, boxes, pots and lids, cotton balls, gauze
• Numbers 1 to 10, alphabet vowels, consonants written in 8-inch characters on fan-folded computer paper, 1 to a page

• 9- to 12-square checkerboard, each square ¼ inch
• 2 similar cubes, boxes, or cups (constrasting colors)
• Raisins

MOVEMENT TOYS
• Rings

TOUCH TOYS
• Block, apple, cup, ball
• Powder puff, cotton ball, bread, sponge
• Bright Baby™ Blanket
• Baby's favorite toy

• Raisins
• Mr. Mouse™
• Brainy Bear™ or panda
• About 5 feet of string

HEARING TOYS
• Rattle or squeeze toy
• 8 × 11 sheets of paper with A,B,C,D,E and 1, 2,3,4,5, mother's name, father's name, and baby's name

• Phonics book and/or newspaper
• Rocking chair

Visual Stimulators in the Sixth Month

20 to 24 weeks

- Black-and-white 9- to 12-square checkerboard, each square ¼ by ¼ inch
- Crib sheets with ¼- by ¼-inch checkerboard squares
- 3-colored face with hair, glasses (if you wear glasses), earrings, dimples, eyelashes boldly featured on white 8 × 11 background
- Polka-dot fabric, white dots ¼ to 1 inch in diameter on fluorescent green, fluorescent blue, black or red background, or reverse dots and background

Category Games

To help baby learn categorization by shape or size in an ongoing way, you can present him with:

- 3 teaspoons and a soup spoon
- 3 pot lids and 1 pot
- 3 cotton balls and 1 gauze square
- 3 shoe boxes and 1 empty cereal box

Place one item in front of baby and say, "Here is a spoon." He'll reach for it. Next place the second one and watch his astonishment and whether he compares the two. Does he drop the first spoon to reach for the second or does he hold both now? Look for his blink of recognition. Then put the third down and say, "It's the same. That's one, two, three spoons," and let him play freely with them.

When he loses interest and releases the spoons, line them up in his view but out of reach and present him with the soup spoon. Say, "Look! This spoon is different."

You can also teach your baby to categorize familiar household objects by what they do:

- Line up in front of baby a plastic butter tub, a cup, a washed yogurt container, and a block. Drop the block into one container, rattle it around, and spill it out.

Repeat with the other containers and then let baby try.
- Use a wooden spoon and a slotted spoon to show the difference when you try to pick up water or sand.
- Write the alphabet, numbers from 1 to 10, and all the vowels in sequence followed by the consonants in 8-inch characters on fan-folded computer paper. Flip through the pages, reading each character slowly and distinctly while showing the symbol to baby. Say, "These are letters . . . these are numbers . . . these are vowels . . . these are consonants."

As you teach baby to categorize the numbers and letters, you may want to sequence the characters by their order too. Say, "A comes before B, and B comes before C, and C comes before D."

The cups, boxes, spoons, pots, and containers can also be sequenced by size. Say, "This is the big cup. This is the bigger cup. And this is the biggest cup of all!"

When you give your baby collections of similar household objects to play with, make sure that they are all safe for his mouth because, most certainly, that's where they'll eventually be placed! And never leave him alone with the objects.

Visual Games

1. PURPOSE: Visual stimulation, object permanence, and abstract thinking
    YOU'LL NEED: Baby's favorite toy
    TIME: 1 minute
    BABY'S POSITION: In crib or on floor with toys
    WATCH FOR: Baby's recognition of words

- Name baby's toy twice while baby looks at it.
- When he's not paying attention to it, name it again.
- When he turns to it, give it to him.

2. PURPOSE: Visual stimulation and muscles strengthening
    YOU'LL NEED: Baby's favorite toy or a visual stimulator from this chapter
    TIME: 1 minute
    BABY'S POSITION: On his tummy, on the floor
    WATCH FOR: Baby's head to rotate as he follows toy

- Rotate the toy in 6-inch circles about 6 inches above baby's head.

3. PURPOSE: Visual stimulation and categorization

YOU'LL NEED: Collections of household items, as listed previously

TIME: 2 minutes

BABY'S POSITION: Sitting on your lap at a table

WATCH FOR: Baby's blink of recognition and interest in various toys

- Play a categorization game, as listed above.

4. PURPOSE: Visual stimulation, muscle strengthening, and object permanence

YOU'LL NEED: 9- to 12-square checkerboard drawn on 8 × 11 paper. Each square measure ¼ inch

TIME: 1 minute

BABY'S POSITION: Sitting up in infant seat or on your lap

WATCH FOR: Baby's whole body to twist and his reaching behavior

- Begin by showing checkerboard 12 inches from baby's eyes, directly in front of him.
- Move stimulator around to his right and behind him so he twists his body around to see it.
- Repeat on left side.
- Then place it in front of him on the floor and put a book in front of it.
- Encourage him to reach behind the book.

5. PURPOSE: Visual stimulation and categorization

YOU'LL NEED: 2 similar or nearly similar cubes, boxes or cups (preferably, of highly contrasting colors), and some raisins

TIME: 1 time

BABY'S POSITION: Sitting on your lap at a table

WATCH FOR: Baby's exploratory play and manual dexterity

- Put raisins in one container (to make it rattle) and leave other one empty.
- Show baby these objects and make one rattle while the other remains silent.
- Allow baby to grasp and visually explore these objects. *Do not allow him to eat the raisins.*

Touch Games
(See Chapter 33 and Appendix 4 for where-to-buy and how-to-make instructions)

1. PURPOSE: Touch stimulation and categorization by texture
    YOU'LL NEED: 4 hard objects (block, apple, plastic cup, and ball) and 4 soft objects (cotton ball, powder puff, bread, sponge)
    TIME: 1 minute
    BABY'S POSITION: Sitting up in infant seat or on your lap
    WATCH FOR: Baby's understanding of words and objects and the object's texture

- Hand hard objects to baby one at a time and say, for example, "This is a ball, it's hard."
- Remove hard objects from play area and give 4 soft objects.
- Describe soft objects similarly, making sure to name each item.
- Don't allow baby to put cotton balls in his mouth.

2. PURPOSE: Touch stimulation and indirect power
    YOU'LL NEED: Baby's favorite toy and his blanket
    TIME: 1 minute
    BABY'S POSITION: Sitting (supported, if necessary) on floor with blanket spread out before him
    WATCH FOR: Baby's pulling behavior and transferring of toy from one hand to the other

- Place toy on blanket.
- Show him how to pull blanket to reach toy.
- Give verbal encouragement and reward with toy if he tries to pull on blanket.

3. PURPOSE: Touch stimulation, push and pull, and toning of hand and arm muscles to enhance crawling
    YOU'LL NEED: Baby's favorite toy and blanket
    TIME: 2 minutes
    YOUR AND BABY'S POSITION: Sitting up, facing each other across spread blanket
    WATCH FOR: Baby's motivation and pulling activity

- Once baby has mastered Touch Game 2, put toy in middle of blanket and have baby pull blanket forward.

- When toy is halfway to baby, slowly pull the blanket back.
- Tell baby to pull again, but as he pulls you pull gently in opposite direction.
- After three tries, let him have toy and repeat. (Game won't be frustrating to baby if he is rewarded on his trials with your verbal praise, and eventually, the toy.)

4. PURPOSE: Touch stimulation and self-initiated play
   YOU'LL NEED: Plastic cup and several raisins
   TIME: 1 minute
   BABY'S POSITION: Sitting up in your lap at a table
   WATCH FOR: Baby's developing attention span and interest and finger play

- Give baby plastic cup containing raisins.
- Allow him to pick it up, shift it, spill raisins.
- Put raisins back in for him after he upsets cup.
- Encourage baby to pick up raisins himself

5. PURPOSE: Touch stimulation and cause and effect
   YOU'LL NEED: Mr. Mouse,™ Brainy Bear,™ or other light-weight high-contrast toy, and string 6 inches longer than your table
   TIME: 1 to 2 minutes
   BABY'S POSITION: Sitting up on your lap at a table
   WATCH FOR: Baby's excitement at his success

- Attach toy to one end of string.
- Hang toy over the opposite edge of table, out of baby's sight.
- Demonstrate how you can pull the string and bring the object back into sight two or three times.
- Let him try and repeat three times.

Hearing Games

1. PURPOSE: Hearing stimulation, sound localization, and muscle strengthening
   YOU'LL NEED: Rattle or squeeze toy
   TIME: 1 minute
   BABY'S POSITION: Sitting in infant seat
   WATCH FOR: Baby looking down for sound

- Shake or squeeze noise-making toy at ear level to baby's right or left.
- Continue making the noise as you move toy downward about 8 inches.

2. PURPOSE: Hearing stimulation and vocalization
   YOU'LL NEED: Phonics book and/or 10 pages of newspaper headlines and rocking chair
   TIME: 1 to 2 minutes
   BABY'S POSITION: Held on your lap while you rock
   WATCH FOR: Baby's alertness and vocalization

- Read slowly and phonetically to baby while rocking in rocking chair.

3. PURPOSE: Hearing stimulation and abstract thinking
   YOU'LL NEED: Just you and baby
   TIME: 1 to 2 minutes
   BABY'S POSITION: Held in your arms as you walk around the house
   WATCH FOR: Baby's vocalizations

- Name items all over the house, animating them with noises.
- Say, "The clock says 'tick tock,' the microwave goes 'beep, beep,' the dishwasher, 'whoosh, whoosh.'"
- Make the sounds of the animals in his bed.

4. PURPOSE: Hearing stimulation and vocalization
   YOU'LL NEED: Just you and baby
   TIME: 1 to 2 minutes
   BABY'S POSITION: Held in your arms in rocking chair
   WATCH FOR: Baby's vocalization

- Repeat the musical rhymes baby has come to enjoy
- Sing "Row, Row, Row Your Boat," and stop when you come to the word *boat*.
- Say, "Can you say 'boat'?"
- Let baby fill in or repeat the word.
- Lavish praise for his efforts.

5. PURPOSE: Hearing stimulation and baby's vocalization
   YOU'LL NEED: Flash cards with mommy's name, daddy's name, A,B,C,D,E, 1,2,3,4,5, and baby's name

TIME: 1 to 2 minutes
BABY'S POSITION: Held upright in your arms
WATCH FOR: Baby's vocalization

- Read each flash card slowly, three times.
- Encourage and praise baby's own speech sounds.

Movement Games

1. PURPOSE: Movement stimulation and preparation for crawling
   YOU'LL NEED: Just you and baby
   TIME: 1 minute
   BABY'S POSITION: Kneeling with his arms supporting him
   WATCH FOR: Baby's early crawl

   - Push lightly on soles of baby's feet to help him propel himself forward.

2. PURPOSE: Movement stimulation and strengthening of muscles
   YOU'LL NEED: Crib rings
   TIME: 1 minute
   BABY'S POSITION: Lying on his back
   WATCH FOR: Baby's strengthening muscles

   - Have baby grab onto rings you're holding in one hand while you support his legs from beneath his body with your other hand.
   - Lift him 1 inch from ground, moving up and down five times.

3. PURPOSE: Movement stimulation and muscle strengthening
   YOU'LL NEED: Just you and baby
   TIME: 1 minute
   BABY'S POSITION: On tummy in crib, near railing
   WATCH FOR: Baby's pulling himself up into sitting position

   - Encourage baby to pull himself up.
   - Help him to get into a sitting position.
   - Lavish praise.

4. PURPOSE: Movement stimulation
   YOU'LL NEED: Just you and baby
   TIME: 1 minute
   YOUR AND BABY'S POSITION: Sit up in chair. Seat baby on

your lap, his back against your chest. Clasp your arms under his legs, cradling him and making a little seat

WATCH FOR: Baby's pleasure

- Lift baby 1 inch from your lap.
- Gently swing him forward, back, up, down, side to side, and around in a circle, three times in each direction.
- Name the direction of movement.

5. PURPOSE: Movement stimulation and muscle strengthening
   YOU'LL NEED: Just you and baby
   TIME: 1 minute
   BABY'S POSITION: Held securely around his middle, facing you
   WATCH FOR: Baby's strengthening arm muscles

- Very gently and without shaking baby, reach him up above your head.
- When he extends his arms, lower him to your shoulders so that his hands are resting on your shoulders.
- Say "Push," and push him back up 3 times.

Mini-Milestones

1. Baby's free, unstructured play periods have led to contented playing alone for periods up to 15 minutes. As he plays, you may hear noise that reflects the inner delight and rewards coming from play.

2. Listen for baby's tone. He has learned tone variations from you. That tone is the first step in language acquisition.

3. You'll find that baby is able to sit with very little support, if any, for short periods of time. He can sit on the floor using his hands as support in front of him.

4. Baby's hands are no longer an object of gazing. He's using them. From the sitting position baby controls his toys with his hands.

5. Baby will reach out for objects at arms' length. His hand will adjust to the shape of the object as he is reaching and not just before he encounters it.

6. Baby's fingers are doing a lot of the work. At the beginning of the month he grasps objects with his little finger and ring finger. By end of month, he will use a thumb and little finger grasp.

7. Baby transfers toys from one hand to the other. He has control over speed with which he reaches for objects and picks them up. He reaches quickly for things he wants and picks them up deftly.

8. When baby is on his tummy, he holds his head way up high. His whole torso is supported by his arms and his legs are tucked under him in a crawling position. In this all-fours position, he can now reach out with one hand and maintain his balance.

9. When you hold baby, standing him up on your lap, he'll bounce up and down on his legs. He pulls on a table or crib rung to hoist himself up to a sitting position. He may even try to stand.

10. Baby's eyes now move in unison. They no longer are crossed. He inspects an item intently with a good ability to see clearly those objects within 10 feet. (If you notice that baby's eyes *don't* seem to move in unison at this time, you might want to consult with an eye doctor to correct any condition early that is correctable.)

11. Everything still comes into baby's mouth. He loves to start experimenting with foods.

12. Baby recognizes himself in the mirror. He'll smile and talk to his image.

13. Now when an object drops out of sight, baby will reach over and try to pick it up.

14. Baby reaches his hands forward to ask to be picked up. He loves to hold onto his own bottle.

15. Baby reaches accurately for a toy. He no longer overshoots his mark.

16. Baby starts performing for people to draw attention to himself. He makes unusual sounds,

different from those around him. He reaches out to touch people.

17. Baby mimics your expression and 2 to 4 vowel sounds in an attempt to keep you attending to him.

32. The Brighter Future

You've whetted your baby's appetite. He loves learning and has learned loving. Now he wants more!

And so do you. You will want to continue your Stimulation Program to sustain your child's gains as he grows beyond the first six months. Only positive rewards for your whole family will flow when you continue to be involved in his growth and development in a loving way. Baby's learning still depends on you.

We have provided the basic principles to guide your imagination. Now, feel free to create your own games that will both please and challenge baby.

Put the toys, tools, and techniques to use in new situations:

- Challenge baby by having a variety of people animate the toys differently than you do.
- Offer baby contrasts. If he's active, balance your stimulation by playing games that enhance his small motor movements. Play language games and abstract thinking games.
- Continue teaching baby active stimulation and manipulative play so that he can stimulate himself.

Your child's intelligence evolves as it is influenced by events in his environment. Continue to be a part of this all-important evolution. After all, the whole point of evolution is to make life better and fuller for the next generation. And isn't that what all parents want for their children?

III. THE TOOLS YOU NEED FOR YOUR INFANT STIMULATION PROGRAM

33. Toys and Tools You'll Use in Your Infant Stimulation Program: A Resource Guide

When you begin your Infant Stimulation Program, you may find many of these toys and tools useful during your play sessions with baby. Of course, you won't need every single one! Choose those that seem most appealing to you. Some you can make yourself. Instructions and patterns for creating your own Bright Baby™ Blanket, Bright Baby™ Bed Bumper, Crib Checks and Dots, Expressly Yours™ poster, Eye Cube™, Mind Mitten™, Mrs. Eyeset™, Pillow Pals™, Tactile Tillie™, and Taffeta Rattle can be found in Appendix 4. Other toys are easy to make, using a little imagination and readily available household items.

When constructing your own toys, remember these safety guidelines:

- No buttons for eyes. Baby can easily choke on them.

- No toxic or sawdust stuffing. Use only soft, polyester fiberfill.
- No beads. They, too, can be swallowed easily.
- Bells, when used, should be well encased in containers and buried in the center of the stuffed toys, or in the case of the Taffeta Rattle, should be very *firmly* secured.
- No long strings in which baby can become entangled and choke.

When purchasing toys, keep in mind that prices, where quoted, are subject to change.

Toys to Make or Buy

Prices given here are subject to change.

Baby's First Blocks
(12 colorful plastic blocks)

- 3 different shapes
- Drop through shape-sorting lid of bright plastic canister
- Provide visual and touch stimulation, stacking and sorting practice

AGE: 3 months and beyond
AVAILABLE: Fisher-Price Toys, East Aurora, NY 14052; in local toy and baby stores. $7.00.

Brainy Bear™
(Black-and-white panda)

- 6 to 8 inches tall
- Plush surface
- Light weight
- Arms and legs are small enough in circumference to be grabbed easily by baby
- Provides visual and touch stimulation
- Transitional or security toy: Helps baby move from familiar environment to unfamiliar when it accompanies him.

AGE: Birth to 6 months and beyond
AVAILABLE: Bright Baby Products, c/o Toymakers, Inc., 12301 Wilshire Blvd., Los Angeles, CA 90025. About $10.00

Bright Baby™ Bed Bumper
(Attachable, washable crib bumper)

- High-contrast two-dimensional designs
- One side black and white, the other side designs in color
- Bumper can be reversed when infant is 6 months old
- Version you purchase includes mylar mirror panels and squeakers for hearing stimulation
- Also provides visual stimulation

AGE: Birth to 2 years
AVAILABLE: Bright Baby Products, c/o Toymakers, Inc., 12301 Wilshire Blvd., Los Angeles, CA 90025. About $20.00. Or make your own.

Bright Baby™ Blanket
(Both sides covered with stimulating designs: faces, checker-boards, bull's-eye, spoons, cups, a dog, a duck, etc.)

- One side black-and-white geometric patterns and faces for birth to 6 months
- Reverse, red gingham (homemade version) or brightly colored objects for baby older than 6 months
- Provides visual stimulation and helps in teaching abstract thinking:
  - objects, even when covered with the blanket, reappear, and so are permanent
  - color training
  - similar objects can be categorized by size or shape
  - baby can use the blanket to move other toys closer (indirect power)

AGE: Birth to 2 years
AVAILABLE: Bright Baby Products, c/o Toymakers, Inc., 12301 Wilshire Blvd., Los Angeles, CA 90025. About $20.00. Or make your own.

Bright Baby Mind Mobile™

(A 5-element mobile composed of 4 geometric, three-dimensional shapes: a cylinder, cube, rectangle, pyramid, and a disc depicting a woman's face on one side and man's on the other)

- Made of soft, compressible, black-and-white rubber
- Each shape has different geometric patterns (homemade version is crocheted and has slightly different designs)
- Squeaker or bell making a differing high- to low-pitched sound is located in each shape
- Provides visual, touch, and hearing stimulation

AGE: Birth to 6 months and beyond
AVAILABLE: Bright Baby Products, c/o Toymakers, Inc., 12301 Wilshire Blvd., Los Angeles, CA 90025. About $20.00. Or make your own.

Bright Baby Teaching Tube™

(Inflatable vinyl cylinder)

- Elevates baby's body in movement games
- Provides visual stimulation with black-and-white and brightly-colored designs

AGE: Birth to 6 months and beyond
AVAILABLE: Bright Baby Products, c/o Toymakers, Inc., 12301 Wilshire Blvd., Los Angeles, CA 90025. About $10.00.

Bull's-eye and Stripes

(Crocheted black-and-white bull's-eye and stripes or designs drawn on paper plates and 8 × 11 white cardboard)

- Attached securely to crib or used during stimulation sessions
- Provides visual stimulation and a visual target point for newborn's eyes
- Crocheted version also provides touch stimulation

AGE: Birth to 6 months and beyond
Make your own.

B.W. Scarf

(A 24- × 24-inch polyester scarf with black-and-white check-erboard design)

- Worn next to mother's body for 2 to 3 days without washing, and tied securely to crib
- Provides smell and visual stimulation

AGE: Birth to 6 months and beyond
AVAILABLE: Local department or variety store, or make your own.

Cookie Monster Crawl-Along™ *Muppets, Inc.*

(A skateboard designed for infants to exercise arm and leg movements in preparation for crawling)

- Provides movement stimulation and muscle-strengthening activity

AGE: 4 months and beyond
AVAILABLE: Child Guidance® Toys, in local toy and baby stores. $23.00.

Coordination Shapes

(Collections of stars, triangles or cubes)

- 7 to 8 colorful plastic shapes of varying sizes (all the same shape) per box
- Provides visual and touch stimulation
- Teaches baby how to build towers (stacking), place toys one inside the other (nesting), and arrange by size or shape (categorization)

AGE: 4 months and beyond
AVAILABLE: C. Nordan Toys, Hong Kong, at local toy and baby stores. $4.99.

Crib Checks and Dots

(Black-and-white gingham, checkerboard, or polka-dot fabric with the largest design available for use as fitted crib sheets)

- Change designs to suit infant's preferences for each month (See Book II)

AGE: Birth to 6 months and beyond
Make your own.

Crib Cap

(Small, soft, pink, white, or blue knitted cap that fits over newborn's head)

- Helps preserve body heat after birth

AGE: Birth to 3 days
AVAILABLE: Hospital gift shops or baby stores. $2.00. Or make your own.

Deluxe Cradle Gym

(Activity center suspends across crib)

- Crib rings, multicolored balls
- Provides visual and touch stimulation, and muscle-strengthening activity

AGE: 2 months and beyond
AVAILABLE: Nursery Originals™, 280 Rand St., Central Falls, RI 02863; in local toy and baby stores. $5.00.

Donut

(Fabric donut, 6 inches in diameter with center hole 2 inches in diameter, stuffed with polyester fiberfill)

- Made of various swatches of black and/or white fabric: corduroy, satin, checks, polka dots, etc., sewn together and then cut to correct shape
- Provides visual and touch stimulation and helps train grasp

AGE: 2 months and beyond
Make your own.

Expressly Yours™ *Poster*
(Red felt fabric glued on a 2- × 2-foot board)

- Faces with expressions of: smile, frown, laugh, cry, boredom, surprise, sleepiness, drawn in black on small paper plates; stick on felt with Velcro glued on back
- Show, then mimic expressions with appropriate sounds
- Teaches non-verbal communication and provides visual stimulation

AGE: 2 months and beyond
Make your own.

Eye Cube™
(4 × 4 × 4 inches soft fabric cube stuffed with polyester fiberfill and bell—contained in a 35 millimeter plastic film canister and buried in the fiberfill)

- Each panel made of differing black and/or white fabric: black corduroy, white corduroy, black-and-white checkerboard, white background with black dots, black satin, and white satin
- Provides visual, touch, and hearing stimulation, and practice for grasp

AGE: Birth to 6 months and beyond
Make your own.

Fischerform® *Cot Toy Rod*
(Red plastic bar suspends across crib)

- Attachable stimulators: bull's-eye, simple face, mirror, jack-in-the-box, pecking bird
- Each sold separately
- Provides visual stimulation, cause-and-effect training, muscle strengthening

AGE: Varies according to attachments
AVAILABLE: Fischer America, Fairfield, NJ 07006. Bar alone, $16.00. Attachable toys vary in price.

Flash Cards

(6-inch-tall numbers and letters of the alphabet written with broad black felt·marker on fan-folded computer paper, 8 × 11, or paper plates)

- Provides visual stimulation and helps language acquisition

  AGE: 2 months
  Make your own.

Infant Stimulation Facts Poster

(A black-and-white poster with many stimulating designs— faces, bull's-eyes, stripes, etc.)

- Provides visual stimulation and trains neck muscles because you hold baby at your shoulder to study it and he moves his head as he searches the poster with his eyes

  AGE: Birth to 6 months and beyond
  AVAILABLE: Infant Stimulation Education Association, c/o Dr. Susan Ludington-Hoe, UCLA Center for Health Sciences, Factor Building, 5-942, Los Angeles, CA 90024. $4.00.

Johnson & Johnson Child Development Kit

- Series of 14 toys for first 2 years of life
- Arrive on a monthly basis with instructions for use

  AGE: Varies according to toys
  AVAILABLE: Through mail order: Johnson & Johnson Baby Products Company, Grandview Road, Skillman, NJ 08854. Prices vary from $5.00 to $25.00.

Mind Mitten™

(Black-and-white designs or fabric swatches are attached with Velcro to ovenlike hand mitt)

- Provides visual and touch stimulation

  AGE: Birth to 6 months and beyond

AVAILABLE: Bright Baby Products, c/o Toymakers, Inc., 12301 Wilshire Blvd., Los Angeles, CA 90025. About $10.00 Or make your own.

Mr. Mouse™

(A soft, light-weight, squeaky, rattling stuffed mouse with a 6-inch-long braided tail securely attached to body)

- Very prominent ears and nose, and large black fabric eyes (no buttons)
- Provides touch, hearing, and visual stimulation

AGE: Birth to 6 months and beyond
AVAILABLE: Bright Baby Products, c/o Toymakers, Inc., 12301 Wilshire Blvd., Los Angeles, CA 90025. About $5.00.

Mrs. Eyeset™

(A black-and-white crocheted flat pillow 6 inches in diameter, stuffed with light-weight polyester)

- White surface with raised black features
  ○ One side: female face with "hair"
  ○ Other side: male face
- Rattles when moved
- Provides touch, visual, and hearing stimulation, and grasp training

AGE: Birth to 6 months and beyond
Make your own.

Pillow Pals™

(12- × 12-inch black-and-white felt throw pillows stuffed with polyester fiberfill)

- One side: 6 1-inch-wide white stripes sewn on black background
- The other side: bull's-eye with a black middle circle of 3 inches and 2 concentric 1-inch black bands, spaced 1 inch apart
- Provides visual and touch stimulation

AGE: Birth to 6 months and beyond
Make your own.

Play Gym

(Crib gym secured across crib with adjustable straps)

- Roll-around rattle ball with colorful beads
- Gripper handles
- Provides touch, sound, and visual stimulation, cause-and-effect training, muscle strengthening

AGE: 2 months and beyond
AVAILABLE: Fisher-Price Toys, East Aurora, NY 14052; at local toy and baby stores. $12.00.

Popsicle Face

(Paper plate with simple facial features drawn in black, glued to popsicle stick)

- Provides visual stimulation

AGE: Birth to 6 weeks
Make your own.

Red and Blue Scarves

(Two 24- × 24-inch polyester scarves, one red and the other blue)

- Superimpose one on the other and sew together to make a single 24- × 24-inch square
- Provides soothing purplish light to help newborn fall asleep in hospital nursery
- Drape over baby's crib and safety-pin on rails to prevent them from falling on baby

AGE: Birth to 3 days
Make your own.

Smart Smock™

(Black-and-white striped apron or smock or white apron with Velcro attached swatches)

- Deep pockets, store rattles, bells, sweet smells, auditory tapes, flash cards, etc.
- Wear during Infant Stimulation sessions or when carrying baby around the house
- Provides visual stimulation

  AGE: Birth to 6 months and beyond
  Make your own.

Snap Lock Beads

(15 plastic pop-beads)

- Size of wooden blocks—too large for baby's mouth
- 3 different shapes—snap together, pop apart
- Washable, squeezable plastic
- Provide visual and touch stimulation, and categorization practice

  AGE: 4 months and beyond
  AVAILABLE: Fisher-Price Toys, East Aurora, NY 14052; at local toy and baby stores. $3.50.

Snugli®

(Baby carrier worn as a sack slung over parent's shoulders on chest)

- Provides warmth, heartbeat sounds, body odor, rotary movement while transporting baby

  AGE: Birth to 6 months and beyond
  AVAILABLE: Snugli®, Inc.; at local toy and baby stores. From $36.00.

Stacking Cubes™

(8 colorful plastic cubes)

- Build towers (stack) and place smaller cubes inside larger ones (nest)
- Provide visual and touch stimulation, stacking and nesting practice

AGE: 4 months and beyond
AVAILABLE: Playskool®, Milton Bradley Co., Chicago, Ill. 60651; at local toy and baby stores. $3.50.

Tactile Tillie™

(An approximately 3-foot-long, 4 inch-diameter polyester fiberfill-stuffed fabric cylinder resembling a friendly serpent)

- Serpent's head, 4 inches long, white cotton with circular black eyes (painted in non-toxic indelible ink—no buttons or swallowable objects used for eyes) and big red mouth
- Body: 9 3- to 4-inch segments of differing fabrics and textures, sewn together in horizontal stripes
- Top of body: black velvet, black-and-white plaid flannel and black satin
- Lower half: pink terry, blue plush, cotton calico, red burlap, velveteen print and orange wide-wale corduroy segments
- Bell (encased in film canister) buried in fiberfill of a central segment
- Provides different touch, visual, and hearing stimulation

AGE: Birth to 6 months and beyond
AVAILABLE: Bright Baby Products, c/o Toymakers, Inc., 12301 Wilshire Blvd., Los Angeles, CA 90025. About $15.00. Or make your own.

Taffeta Rattle

(Light-weight rattle 4 inches long and 1 inch in diameter)

- Made of 4- × 4-inch-square black-and-white plaid taffeta fabric gathered and tied at both ends with brightly-colored yarn to which are *firmly* attached small bells
- Allow play under *close* supervision. Do not allow baby to place bells in his mouth

- Provides touch, visual, and hearing stimulation, and practice for grasping

AGE: Birth to 3 months
Make your own.

Unbreakable Mylar Mirror
(Small—approximately 6 × 6 inches—unbreakable mirror)

- Provides visual stimulation and helps teach baby his own features and that he is separate individual

AGE: 4 weeks
AVAILABLE: Most bicycle shops

Wrist Rattles
(Small stuffed rattling panda bear on wrist strap with Velcro fasteners)
- Provides visual and auditory stimulation and helps baby locate his hands

AGE: 4 weeks and beyond
AVAILABLE: Fisher-Price Toys, East Aurora, NY 14052; at local toy and baby stores. $2.75.

Books for Baby

Prices given here are subject to change.

Hello Kitty's Book of Seasons (a scratch-and-sniff book), Random House, 1984. $3.95.
Pat the Bunny, Dorothy Kunhardt, Golden Books, 1942. $4.95.
Pat the Cat, Edith Kunhardt, Golden Books, 1984. $4.95.
Peter Rabbit's Sniffy Adventure, Jane E. Gerver, Random House, 1984. $3.95.
Richard Scarry's Lowly Worm Sniffy Book, Richard Scarry, Random House, 1978. $4.95.
Sniffy the Mouse, John P. Miller, Random House, 1980. $3.95.

Sweet Smell of Strawberryland, Michael G. Smollin, Random House, 1980. $3.95.

The Touch-Me Book, Pat and Eve Witte, Golden Books, 1961. $4.95.

APPENDIXES

Appendix 1

Chapter Notes

CHAPTER 2

1. Senn, Milton J., "Early Childhood Education: For What Goals?" *Children*, Vol. 16 (Jan.–Feb. 1969), pp. 8–13.

Pines, Maya, "A Head Start in the Nursery." *Psychology Today* (Sept. 1979), pp. 56–68.

Pines, Maya, "Baby, You're Incredible." *Psychology Today* (Feb. 1982), pp. 48–53.

2. Dennis, W., "Causes of Retardation Among Institutional Children: Iran." *Journal of Genetic Psychology*, Vol. 96 (1960).

Dennis, W., Sayegh, Y., "The Effect of Supplementary Experience Upon Behavioral Development of Infants in Institutions." *Child Development*, Vol. 36 (March 1965).

3. Ainsworth, M. D. S., *Infancy in Uganda: Infant Care and the Growth of Love*. Baltimore: Johns Hopkins Press (1967).

CHAPTER 3

1. Murooka, H., Koie, Y., Suda, N., "Analyse des sons intrauterins et leurs effets tranquillisants sur le nouveau-né," *Journal of Gynecological Obstetrics Biol. Reprod.*, Vol. 5 (1976), pp. 367–76.

Detterman, D.K., "The Effect of Heartbeat Sound on Neonatal Crying." *Infant Behavior and Development*, Vol. 1 (1978), pp. 36–48.

2. DeCasper, A.J., Sigafoos, A.D., "The Intrauterine Heartbeat: A Potent Reinforcer for Newborns." *Infant Behavior and Development*, Vol. 6 (1983), pp. 19–25.

Kolata, G., "Studying Learning in the Womb." *Science*, Vol. 225 (July 20, 1984), pp. 302–303.

3. Oehler, S., "Sensory Processing Abilities of Premature

Infants." *Journal of the California Perinatal Association*, Vol. 3 (June 1983), pp. 55–63.

4. Graves, P.L., "The Functioning Fetus." *The Course of Life: Psychoanalytic Contributions Toward Understanding Personality Development. Vol. 1, Infancy and Early Childhood*, ed. by S.I. Greenspan and G.H. Pollock. NIMH Publication, 1980, pp. 253–256.

5. Graves, P.L., p. 253.

6. Bradley, R.M., Mistretta, C.M., "Fetal Sensory Receptors." *Physiological Reviews*, Vol. 55 (1975), pp. 352–82.

7. Henshall, W.R., "Intrauterine Sound Levels." *American Journal of Obstetrics and Gynecology*, Vol. 122, No. 4 (Feb. 15, 1972), pp. 576–78.

Walker, D., Grimwade, J., Wood, C., "Intrauterine Noise: A Component of Fetal Environment." *American Journal of Obstetrics and Gynecology*, Vol. 109, No. 1 (Jan. 1, 1971), pp. 91–95.

Bench, R.J., Anderson, J.H., "Sound Transmission to the Human Fetus Through the Maternal Abdominal Wall." *Journal of Genetic Psychology*, Vol. 113 (1968), pp. 85–87.

Grimwade, J., Walker, D., Bartlett, M., Gordon, S., Wood, C., "Human Fetal Heartrate Change and Movement in Response to Sound and Vibration." *American Journal of Obstetrics and Gynecology*, Vol. 109, No. 1 (Jan. 1, 1971), pp. 86–90.

8. Sontag, L.W., Steele, W.G., Lewis, M., "The Fetal and Maternal Cardiac Response to Environmental Stress." *Human Development*, Vol. 12 (1969), pp. 1–9.

9. Forbes, H.S., Forbes, H.B., "Fetal Sense Reactions: Hearing." *Journal of Comparative Psychology*, Vol. 7 (1927), p. 353.

10. Querleu, D., Renard, X., Crepin, G., "Auditory Perception and Fetal Reaction to Sound Stimulation." *Journal of Gynecological Obstetrics Biological Reproduction*, Vol. 10 (1981), pp. 307–31.

11. Schell, L.M., "Environmental Noise and Human Prenatal Growth." *American Journal of Physical Anthropology*, Vol. 56 (1981), pp. 63–70.

Takahashi, I., Kyo, S., "Studies on Differences in Adaptabilities to the Noisy Environment in Sexes and in Growing Processes." *Journal of Anthropological Soc. Nippon*, Vol. 76 (1960), pp. 34–51.

Ando, Y., Hattori, H., "Statistical Studies on the Effects of

Intense Noise During Human Fetal Life." *Journal of Sound and Vibration*, Vol. 27 (1973), pp. 101–10.

12. Sakabe, N., Arayama, T., Suzuki, T., "Human Fetal Evoked Response to Acoustic Stimulation." *Acta Otolaryngologica Supplementum*, Vol. 252 (1969), pp. 29–36.

Scibetta, J.J., Rosen, M.G., Hochberg, C.J., Chik, L., "Human Fetal Brain Response to Sound During Labor." *American Journal of Obstetrics and Gynecology*, Vol. 109, No. 1 (1971), pp. 82–85.

Luz, N.P., Lima, C.P., Luz, S.H., Felders, V.L., "Auditory Evoked Response of the Human Fetus." *Acta Ob-Gyn. Scandavica*, Vol. 59 (1980), pp. 395–404.

Read, J.A., Miller, F.E., "Fetal Heartrate Acceleration in Response to Acoustic Stimulation as a Measure of Fetal Well-Being." *American Journal of Obstetrics and Gynecology*, Vol. 129 (1977), pp. 512–17.

13. Peleg, D., Goldman, J.A., "Heartrate Acceleration in Response to Light Stimulation," *Journal of Perinatal Medicine*, Vol. 8, No. 1 (1980), pp. 38–41.

CHAPTER 4

1. Trudinger, B. J., Boylan, P. "Antepartum Fetal Heart Rate Monitoring: Value of Sound Stimulation," *OB-GYN*, Vol. 55 (1969), pp. 29–36.

Read, et al., p. 512.

Grimwade, et al., pp. 86–90.

2. Gelman, S.R., Wood, S., Spellacy, W.N., Abrams, R.M., "Fetal Movements in Response to Sound Stimulation." *American Journal of Obstetrics and Gynecology*, Vol. 143, No. 4 (June 15, 1982), pp. 484–85.

Goodlin, R.C., Schmidt, B., "Human Fetal Arousal Levels as Indicated by Heartrate Recordings." *American Journal of Obstetrics and Gynecology*, Vol. 114, No. 5 (1972), pp. 613–17.

Sontag, L.W., Wallace, R.F., "The Movement Response of the Human Fetus to Sound Stimuli." *Child Development*, Vol. 6 (Dec. 1935), pp. 253–58.

3. Gelman, S.R., et al., p. 484.

4. Scibetta, J., et al., pp. 82–85.

Luz, N., et al., p. 484.

5. Rosen, M.G., Scibetta, J., "Documenting Human Fetal EEG During Birth." *Electroencephalography and Clinical Neurophysiology*, Vol. 27, No. 7 (Dec. 1969), p. 661.

Sakabe, N. et al., pp. 29–36.

Lind, J., "Music and the Small Human Being." *Acta Paediatrica Scandanavia*, Vol. 69 (1980), p. 133.

6. Patrick, J., Fetherston, W., Vick, H., Vogelin, R., "Human Fetal Breathing Movements and Gross Fetal Body Movements at 34–35 Weeks of Gestation." *American Journal of Obstetrics and Gynecology*, Vol. 130 (1978), pp. 693–99.

Coleman, C., "Fetal Movement Counts: An Assessment Tool." *J.N.M.W.* Vol. 26, No. 1 (Feb. 1981), pp. 15–30.

Timor-Tritsch, I., Zador, I., Hertz, R., Rosen, M.G., "Classification of Human Fetal Movements." *American Journal of Obstetrics and Gynecology*, Vol. 126, No. 1, pp. 70–77.

Adamson, J.D., Cousin, A.J., Gare, D.J., "Rhythmic Fetal Movements," *American Journal of Obstetrics and Gynecology*, Vol. 136 (1980), pp. 239–42.

CHAPTER 5

1. Ludington-Hoe, S.M., "Fetal Functioning." ISEA Publication, part of the Infant Stimulation Series (1985).

2. Ray, W.S., "A Preliminary Study of Fetal Conditioning." *Child Development*, Vol. 3 (1932), pp. 173–77.

3. Spelt, D.K., "The Conditioning of the Human Fetus in Utero." *Journal of Experimental Psychology*, Vol. 38, No. 3 (July 1948), pp. 338–46.

4. Personal communication from Dr. F. Rene Van de Carr, Nov. 1982.

Van de Carr, R., "Fetal Stimulation: Video-Taped Outcomes." Presented at Merritt Peralta Health Education Conference on Prenatal and Infant Stimulation, Oakland, California, June 14–15, 1985.

5. DeCasper, A.J., Fifer, W.P., "Of Human Bonding: Newborns Prefer Their Mother's Voices." *Science*, Vol. 208 (June 6, 1980), pp. 1174–76.

6. DeCasper, A.J., "The Cat in the Hat." Presented at the International Conference of Infant Studies, Austin, Texas (1982).

Kolata, G., "Studying Learning in the Womb." *Science*, Vol. 225 (July 20, 1984), pp. 302–3.

7. Querleu, D. (1981), p. 307.

CHAPTER 6

1. Graves, P., p. 236

Liley, A.W., "The Foetus as a Personality." *Australian and New Zealand Journal of Psychiatry*, (June 1972), pp. 99–105.

2. Richards, T.W., Nelson, V.L., "Studies in Mental Development: II. Analysis of Abilities Tested at the Age of 6 Months by the Gesell Schedule." *Journal of Genetic Psychology*, Vol. 52 (1938), pp. 327–31.

Richards, T.W., Newberry, H., "Studies in Fetal Behavior: III. Can Performance on Test Items at 6 Months Postnatally Be Predicted on the Basis of Fetal Activity." *Child Development*, Vol. 9 (1938), pp. 79–86.

3. Fries, M.E., Woolf, P.J., "Some Hypotheses on the Role of Congenital Activity Type in Personality Development." *The Psychoanalytic Study of the Child*, Vol. 8 (1953), pp. 48–62.

4. Olds, C., "Fetal Response to Music." *Pre and Peri-Natal Psychology Association of North America News* (April, 1984), p. 2.

5. Lewis, Peter H., "What's on Babies' Minds When They Come into the World." *New York Times*, Aug. 26, 1984.

CHAPTER 7

1. Dobbing, J., Sand, J., "The Quantitative Growth and Development of the Human Brain." *Archives of Diseases of Children*, Vol. 48 (1974), pp. 757–67.

Dobbing, J., "Human Brain Development and Its Vulnerability." *Biologic and Clinical Aspects of Brain Development*, Mead-Johnson Symposium on Perinatal and Developmental Medicine, No. 6 (1974), p. 11.

Reinis, S., Goldman, J., *The Development of the Brain and Functional Perspectives*. Springfield, Ill.: C.C. Thomas Co., 1980.

2. Dobbing, p. 9.

3. Dobbing (1974), p. 5.

4. Dobbing (1974), p. 8.

5. Dobbing (1974), p. 6.

6. Coursin, D.B., "Nutrition and Brain Development in Infants." *Merril-Palmer Quarterly*, Vol. 18, No. 2 (April 1972), p. 180.

7. Dobbing (1974), p. 6.

8. Dobbing (1974), p. 6.

9. Jensen, A., "I.Q. Linked to Firing of Brain Nerve Cells," paper presented at American Psychological Association (Sept. 1978), Toronto, Canada.

10. Sidman, R.L., Rakic, P., "Neuronal Migration with Special Reference to Developing Human Brain: A Review." *Brain Research*, Vol. 62 (1972), pp. 1–35.

Purpura, D.P., "Neuronal Migration and Dendritic Differentiation: Normal and Aberrant Development of Human Cerebral Cortex." *Biologic and Clinical Aspects of Brain Development*, Mead-Johnson Symposium on Perinatal and Developmental Medicine, No. 6 (1974).

11. Wigglesworth, J.S., "Brain Development and the Structural Basis of Perinatal Brain Damage." *Perinatal Brain Insult*, Mead-Johnson Symposium on Perinatal and Developmental Medicine, No. 7, Marco Island (1980), p. 5.

12. Wigglesworth (1980), p. 5.

CHAPTER 8

1. Sidman (1972), pp. 1–35.
Purpura (1974).

2. Wigglesworth (1980), p. 5.

3. Gottlieb, G., "Conceptions of Prenatal Development: Behavioral Embryology." *Psychological Review*, Vol. 83, No. 3 (1976), pp. 215–34.

4. Fisch, R.O., Bilek, M.K., Horrobin, J.M., Change, P.N., "Children with Superior Intelligence at 7 Years of Age: A Prospective Study of the Influence of Perinatal, Medical and Socioeconomic Factors." *American Journal of Diseases of Children*, Vol. 1130, No. 5 (May 1976), pp. 481–87.

CHAPTER 9

1. Crinic, L.S., "Effects of Nutrition and Environment on Brain Biochemistry and Behavior." *Developmental Psychology*, Vol. 16, No. 2 (March 1983), pp. 129–45.

Katz, H.B., Davies, C.A., "The Separate and Combined Effects of Early Undernutrition and Environmental Complexity and Different Ages on Cerebral Measures in Rats." *Developmental Psychology*, Vol. 16, No. 1 (Feb. 1983), pp. 47–58.

Brandt, I., "Brain Growth, Fetal Malnutrition and Clinical Consequences." *Journal of Perinatal Medicine*, Vol. 9 (1981), pp. 3–26.

2. Stein, Z., Susser, M., Saenger, G., et al., *Famine and*

Human Development: The Dutch Hunger Winter of 1944/1945. New York: American Library Books, 1974, p. 23.

3. Rush, D., Stein, Z., Susser, M., *Diet in Pregnancy: A Randomized Controlled Trial of Nutritional Supplements.* New York: Alan R. Liss—for March of Dimes (1980).

Wynn M., Wynn, A., "The Importance of Maternal Nutrition in the Weeks before and After Conception." *Birth*, Vol. 9, No. 1 (Spring 1982), pp. 39–43.

4. Crinic, L.S. (March, 1983), pp. 129-45.

Coursin, D.B., "Nutrition and Brain Development in Infants," *Merril-Palmer Quarterly*, Vol. 18, No. 2 (April 1972), pp. 177–202.

Katz, H.B., Davies, C.A. (1983) pp. 47–58.

5. Levitsky, D.A., ed., *Malnutrition, Environment, Behavior: New Perspectives.* New York: Cornell University Press, 1979, pp. 1–295.

Dwyer, J., "Impact of Maternal Nutrition on Infant Health." *Medical Times*, Vol. 3, No. 7 (July 1983), pp. 30–38.

6. Brandt, I. (1981), pp. 3–26.

7. Martinson, A., et al., "Neonatal Outcomes of Antepartal Alcohol Consumption." *Pediatric Research*, Vol. 18 (April 1984), p. 442.

8. Stephens, C.J., "The Fetal Alcohol Syndrome: Cause for Concern." *Maternal-Child Nursing*, Vol. 6 (August 1981), pp. 251–256.

9. Brewer, T., *The Brewer Medical Diet for Normal and Abnormal Pregnancy.* New York: Simon and Schuster, 1983.

CHAPTER 10

1. Wigglesworth (1980), p. 5.

2. Bower, T.G.R., *The Primer of Infant Development.* San Francisco: Freeman, 1977, pp. 10-11.

3. Bower, 1977, p. 11.

4. Kopp, C.B., Vaughn, B.E., "Sustained Attention During Exploratory Manipulation as a Predictor of Cognitive Competence in Preterm Infants." *Child Development*, Vol. 53 (1982), pp. 174–82.

5. Pope, K.S., "How Gender, Solitude and Posture Influence the Stream of Consciousness," in *The Stream of Consciousness: Scientific Investigations into the Flow of Human Experience*, K.S. Pope and J.L. Singer, eds. New York: Plenum Press, 1976.

6. Weeks, Z.R., "Effects of Vestibular System on Human Development: Overview of Functions and Effects of Stimulation." *American Journal of Occupational Therapy*, Vol. 33 (June 1979), pp. 376–81.

Porter, L., "The Role of Activity in Growth and Development," *Philippine Journal of Nursing*, Vol. 40 (1971), pp. 91–94.

7. Miranda, S.B., "Visual Abilities and Pattern Preferences of Premature Infants and Full Term Neonates." *Child Development*, Vol. 43 (1972), pp. 1289–90.

8. Turkewitz, G., "The Development of Lateral Differentiation in the Human Infant," in S.J. Dimond and D.A. Blizard, eds., *Evolution and Lateralization of the Brain*. New York: New York Academy of Sciences, 1977.

Turkewitz, G., "The Development of Lateral Differences in the Human Infant," in S.R. Harnad, R.W. Doty, L. Goldstein, J. Jaynes, and G. Krauthamer, eds., *Lateralization in the Nervous System*. New York: Academic Press, 1977.

9. Brazelton, T.B., "Early Parent–Infant Reciprocity." *The Family: Can It Be Saved?*, Vaughn and Brazelton, eds. Chicago: Yearbook Medical Publishers, 1976, pp. 133–141.

CHAPTER 11

1. Fantz, R., "Maturation of Pattern Vision in Young Infants." *Journal of Comparative and Physiological Psychology*, Vol. 55 (1962), pp. 907–17.

2. Fantz, R. (1962), p. 907.

3. Bower, T.G.R., *A Primer of Infant Development*. San Francisco: W.H. Freeman and Co., 1977, p. 9.

4. Salapatek, P., Kessen, W., "Prolonged Investigation of a Plane Geometric Triangle by the Human Newborn." *Journal of Experimental Child Psychology*. Vol. 15 (1973), pp. 22–29.

Salapatek, P.H., Kessen, W., "Visual Scanning of Triangles by the Human Newborn." *Journal of Experimental Child Psychology*, Vol. 3 (1966), pp. 155–67.

5. Ludington, S.M., *Sensory Stimulation in Vaginally and Cesarean Born Infants and Learning in the First Week of Life*. Unpublished Masters Thesis, University of California, San Francisco Medical Center, San Francisco, 1973.

——. "Tests Show Day-Old Infants Can Learn." *Modern Medicine*, Vol. 34 (January 17, 1966).

6. Ludington, S.M., Chaze, B.A., "Infant Stimulation in

the Intensive Care Nursery." *American Journal of Nursing*, Vol. 84, No. 1 (Jan. 1984), pp. 68–71.

CHAPTER 12

1. Lipsitt, L.P., "Taste in the Human Neonate: Its Effect on Sucking and Heart Rate," in J.M. Weiffenbach, ed., *Taste and Development*. Washington D.C.: U.S. Department of Health, Education and Welfare, 1977.

Lamb, M.E., Campos, J.J., *Development in Infancy*. New York: Random House, 1982, p. 86.

2. Rodgers, Bryan, "Feeding in Infancy and Later Ability and Attainment: A Longitudinal Study." *Developmental Medicine and Child Neurology*, Vol. 20 (1980), pp. 421–26.

CHAPTER 13

1. Bundy, R.S., Colombo, J., Singer, J., "Pitch Perception in Young Infants." *Developmental Psychology*, Vol. 18, No. 4 (1982), pp. 10–14.

Trehub, S., "Infants' Sensitivity to Vowel and Tonal Contrasts." *Developmental Psychology*, Vol. 9.

2. Swift, E.W., et al., "Predictive Value of Early Testing of Auditory Localization for Language Development." *Developmental Medicine and Child Neurology*, Vol. 23, No. 3 (July 1981).

Eimas, P.D., "Speech Perception in Early Infancy," in L.B. Cohen and P. Salapatek, eds., *Infant Perception: From Sensation to Cognition, Vol. II, Perception of Space, Speech and Sound*. New York: Academic Press, 1975, pp. 193–231.

3. Austin, P., "Synchronous Movements to Human Speech." *Perceptual and Motor Skills* (1983), pp. 455–59.

Bower, T.G.R., *A Primer of Infant Development*. San Francisco: W.H. Freeman and Co., 1977.

4. Roe, K.V., McClure, A., Roe, A., "Vocal Interactions at Three Months and Cognitive Skills at Twelve Years." *Developmental Psychology*, Vol. 18 No. 1 (1982), pp. 15–16.

5. Eimas, P.D., "Perception of Speech in Early Infancy." *Scientific American*, Vol. 252, No. 1 (Jan. 1985), pp. 46–52.

6. Taylor, H.G., Heilman, K.M., "Monaural Recall and the Right Ear Advantage." *Brain and Language*, Vol. 15 (1982), pp. 334–39.

7. Bower, T.G.R. (1977).

8. Leventhal, S.A., Lipsitt, L.P., "Adaptation, Pitch Dis-

crimination, and Sound Localization in the Neonate." *Child Development*, Vol. 35 (1954), pp. 759–67.

Rosenthal, M.K., "Vocal Dialogues in Neonatal Period." *Developmental Psychology*, Vol. 18 No. 1 (1982), pp. 17–21.

Oviatt, S.L., "Inferring What Words Mean: Early Development in Infants' Comprehension of Common Objects and Names." *Child Development*, Vol. 53 (1982), pp. 247–77.

9. Thurman, L., Langness, A., *Heartsongs: Infants and Parents Sharing Music*. Music Study Services, Denver, Colorado, 1984.

10. Salk, L., "The Role of the Heartbeat in the Relations Between Mother and Infant." *Scientific American*, Vol. 220 (1973), pp. 24–29.

CHAPTER 14

1. Ludington, S.M. "Effects of Extra Tactile Stimulation on Growth and Development of Vaginally and Cesarean Born Infants." *Communicating Nursing Research* (Spring, 1977), pp. 50–58.

2. Rausch, C.B., "Effects of Tactile Kinesthetic Stimulation on Premature Infants." *Journal of Gynecological Nursing*, Vol. 10, No. 10 (Feb. 1981), pp. 34–40.

CHAPTER 15

1. McFarlane, A., "Olfaction in the Development of Social Preferences in the Human Neonate," in *Parent and Infant Interaction*. Ciba Fnd. Symposium, 33 (New Series), Amsterdam: Elsevier Holland, pp. 103–13.

Porter, R.H., et al., "The Importance of Odors in Mother-Infant Interactions." *Maternal Child Nursing Journal* Vol. 12, No. 3 (Fall 1983), pp. 147–200.

2. Schwartz, R.K., "Olfaction and Muscle Activity: An EMG Pilot Study," *American Journal of Occupational Therapy*, Vol. 33, No. 3 (March 1979), pp. 185–92.

CHAPTER 16

1. Dunkeld, J., Bower, T.G.R., "Intersensory Differentiation in Infancy." Unpublished Manuscript, University of Edinburgh.

Bower, T.G.R., *The Primer of Infant Development*. San Francisco: W.H. Freeman and Co., 1977.

2. Condon, W.S., Sander, L., "Neonate Movement Is Synchronized with Adult Speech: Interactional Participation and Language Acquisition." *Science*, Vol. 183 (1974), pp. 99–101.

3. Bower (1977), p. 28.

4. Bower, T.G.R., Broughton, J.M., Moore, M.K., "Infants' Responses to Approaching Objects: An Indicator of Response to Distal Variables." *Perception and Psychophysics*, Vol. 9 (1970), pp. 193–96.

5. Porter, L., "The Role of Activity in Growth and Development." *Philippine Journal of Nursing*, Vol. 40 (1971), pp. 91–94.

Weeks, Z.R., "Effects of Vestibular System on Human Development: Overview of Functions and Effects of Stimulation." *American Journal of Occupational Therapy*, Vol. 33 (June 1979), pp. 376–81.

CHAPTER 17

1. Wolff, Peter, "Observations on Newborn Infants." *Psychosomatic Medicine*, Vol. 21 (1959), pp. 110–18.

CHAPTER 19

1. Anders, T., Emde, R., Parmelee, A., eds., "A Manual of Standardized Terminology, Techniques and Criteria for Scoring of States of Sleep and Wakefulness in Newborn Infants." UCLA Brain Information Service, BRI Publ., Los Angeles, 1971.

Barnard, K., "The Effect of Stimulation on the Sleep Behavior of the Premature Infant." *Communicating Nursing Research*, Vol. 6 (1973), pp. 34–40.

2. Turner, Jeffrey S., Helms, Donald B., *Exploring Child Behavior*. Philadelphia: W.B., Saunders Co., 1976.

3. Brazelton, T.B., *Infants and Mothers*. New York: Dell Publishing Co., 1979.

4. Turner, J.S., Helms, D.B., 1976.

5. Sears, R.R., Maccoby, E.E., Levin, H., *Patterns of Child Rearing*. Evanston, Ill.: Row, Peterson, 1957.

Bell, S.M., Ainsworth, M.D.S., "Infant Crying and Maternal Responsiveness." *Child Development*, Vol. 43 (1972), pp. 1171–90.

6. Sobel, D., "Baby's Cry, It Turns Out, Can Speak Volumes." *New York Times*, Nov. 3, 1981.

7. Als, H., Lester, B., et. al., "Toward a Research Instrument for the Assessment of Preterm Infants' Behavior (APIB)"

in *Theory and Reseach in Behavioral Pediatrics Vol. 1,* Fitzgerald, H.E.T., Lester, B.M., Yogman, M.W., eds. New York: Plenum Press, 1982, pp. 35–58.

CHAPTER 20

1. Sears, R.R., Maccoby, E.E., Levin, H., 1957.

2. Radin, Norma, "The Role of Fathers in Cognitive, Academic, and Intellectual Development," in *The Role of the Father in Child Development* (2nd ed.), M.E. Lamb, ed. New York: John Wiley and Sons, 1981, pp. 379–427.

3. Radin, pp. 402–403.

4. Biller, H.B., "The Father and Sex Role Development," in *The Role of the Father in Child Development* (2nd ed.), M. Lamb, ed. New York: John Wiley and Sons, 1976.

5. Russell, G., Radin, N., "Increased Paternal Participation: The Father's Perspective," in *Fatherhood and Social Policy,* Lamb and Sagi, eds. Hillsdale, N.J.: Lawrence Erlbaum Assoc., 1983, pp. 139–165.

6. Radin, Norma, "Fathers' Role in Child Development and Policy Implications." Paper presented at the 35th anniversary celebration of the Child Development Labs, Wayne State University, Detroit, Michigan (Oct. 21, 1982).

7. Russell, G., Radin, N., 1984.

CHAPTER 21

1. Ling, D., Ling, A., "Communication Development in the First Three Years of Life." *Journal of Speech and Hearing Research,* Vol 17 (1974), pp. 146–59.

CHAPTER 25

1. Brazelton, T.B., *The Family.* Paper presented at The Family conference, Philadelphia, Nov. 1974.

Appendix 2

A Guide to Programs and Materials

for Smarter Babies and

Their Parents

Prenatal, Newborn, and Infant Learning Programs

Heartsongs: Infants and Parents Sharing Music by Dr. Leon Thurman and Anna Peter Langness.
- Audio tape and booklet teaches techniques for singing to the unborn, newly born, and toddler child
- Facilitates language acquisition and provides music and singing pleasure and hearing stimulation

Music Study Services, P.O. Box 4665, Englewood, CO 80155. $14.95 plus postage and handling.

The Loving Touch.
- Audio tape and illustrated instructions
- A medically researched technique for gentle fingertip massage and stroking
- Promotes reflex maturation in newborns and provides touch stimulation

Cradle Care, Inc., P.O. Box 401548, Dallas, TX 75240. $20.00

The Prenatal University by Dr. F. Rene Van de Carr.
- Audio tape and booklet
- Prenatal stimulation through auditory, touch, visual, and movement activities

The Prenatal University, 27225 Calaroga Ave., Hayward, CA 94545.

Programs, Organizations, and Materials for Parents and Babies

American Baby Magazine: 575 Lexington Ave., New York, NY 10022.

American Baby Show: Weekly, 30-minute cable TV program filled with helpful advice on pregnancy, parenting, developmental milestones, nutrition, and emergency care of babies.

- Monthly program guide listed in *American Baby Magazine*

Finding Time for Fathering: An educational program for fathers by clinical psychologist Dr. Mitch Golant teaches:

- The role of fathers in child development
- How to really play with your children
- Setting limits with love
- Normal child development.

Finding Time for Fathering, Mitch Golant, Ph.D., 11973 San Vicente Blvd. Suite 205, Los Angeles, CA 90049.

Gymboree: An exercise program for infants and toddlers.

- Over 250 locations in 24 states and Canada.
- For information about a local Gymboree write:

Gymboree Corporation, 872 Hinkley Road, Burlingame, CA 94010.

Infant Stimulation Education Association: Provides lists of certified Infant Stimulation instructors around the United States and other educational materials.

Send self-addressed, legal-size envelope with $.44 postage to ISEA, c/o Dr. Susan Ludington-Hoe, UCLA School of Nursing, Factor Building 5-942, Los Angeles, CA 90024.

Mommy/Daddy and Me: Exercise and parenting classes at local YMCA.

National Association of Gifted Children: Provides information about special programs for gifted children. Enquire about local chapters and their activities.

Send self-addressed legal-size envelope with $.44 postage to: National Association for Gifted Children, 15 Gramercy Park, New York, NY 10003.

Playorena: Activities on equipment designed to help children develop balance, coordination, sensory-motor skills, and peer interaction starting at 3 months of age. Seventeen locations in New York area.

For information call (800)-645-PLAY, or write Playorena, Inc., 125 Mineola Ave., Roslyn Heights, NY 11577.

Appendix 3

Books for Parents

Prices given here are subject to change.

Baby Learning Through Baby Play by Ira Gordon. A parent's guide for the first two years. New York: St. Martin's, 1970. $4.95.

Birth Without Violence by Frederick Leboyer. New York: Knopf, 1975. $9.95.

The Brewer Medical Diet for Normal and Abnormal Pregnancy by Gail Sforza Brewer with Thomas Brewer, M.D. New York: Simon and Schuster, 1983. $8.95.

The Growing Child: Monthly newsletter about child development. 22 North Second Street, P.O. Box 620, Lafayette, IN 47902. $11.95.

Infants and Mothers: Differences in Development by T. Berry Brazelton. Revised Edition. New York: Dell, 1983. $10.95.

Nutrition for Pregnancy and Breastfeeding: A series of pamphlets prepared by the California Department of Health Services, Carol G. Corruccini, M.S., Nutrition Consultant. Titles of the pamphlets include: "Eating Right for Your baby," "Your Weight and Weight Gain," "Using Vitamin/Mineral Pills and Salt," "Relief from Common Problems: Nausea, Constipation, Heartburn." Write: Chief, Maternal and Child Health Branch, 714 P Street, Sacramento, CA 95814. Free.

The Secret Life of the Unborn Child by Thomas Verny, M.D. with John Kelly. How you can prepare your unborn baby for a happy, healthy life. New York: Delta Books, 1981. $6.95.

Smart Toys for Babies from Birth to Two by Kent Garland Burtt and Karen Kalkstein. Seventy-seven easy-to-make toys to stimulate your baby's mind. New York: Harper Colophon Books, 1981. $8.95.

Your Baby's First 30 Months by Lucie W. Barber and Herman Williams. Parents' guide to positive child-rearing. Charts and diaries help you follow your child's development. H.P. Books, P.O. Box 5367, Tucson, AZ 85703. $5.95.

Appendix 4

Patterns and Directions for

Making Selected Toys

All of the BRIGHT BABY™ products may be reproduced solely for the reader's private use, and any resale by anyone is strictly prohibited.

NOTE: All printed pattern pieces have been reduced by 50 percent. To make designs proper size, redraw to scale or have designs doubled in size by a copy machine. All pattern pieces may be found on pages 312–319.

The Bright Baby™ Blanket
(Developed by Priscilla Morse)

FINISHED SIZE: 40 × 50

MATERIALS:
- 1⅔ yards of 45-inch white polyester-cotton blend fabric
- 1 yard of 45-inch black polyester-cotton blend fabric
- 1⅔ yards of 45-inch red-and-white checkerboard quilted fabric (checks 1- to 3-inch squares)
- 1 package quilt stuffing, crib size (or cut to fit)
- Ruffling for outside edge: 5 yards of ½-inch-wide ruffling (or if making your own ruffle, 1 yard of 36-inch white fabric cut into 3-inch strips)
- Black and white sewing thread, embroidery yarn, and 4-ply knitting yarn or quilting thread
- Tracing paper
- Templates made of cardboard or plastic:
    One 11-inch square

One 10-inch square
One 5-inch square
One circle, 6½ inches in diameter

To Make 20 Squares:
1. Lay 11-inch square template on wrong side of white fabric. Draw 20 squares, 4 across and 5 down, with pencil directly onto white cloth, forming cutting line.

The Bright Baby™ Blanket

2. Lay 10-inch square template within each drawn 11-inch square (still on wrong side). Trace around 10-inch template, forming sewing line.
3. Cut squares on cutting line.
To Make Faces:
1. Place or pin circle template in center of square.
2. On *right* side of fabric, trace around circle. Make 4.

3. Trace blown-up designs for facial features on tracing paper. Trim and pin to folded black fabric. Cut:

2 mustaches
2 father's hair
2 mother's hair

4. Place hair and mustache pieces on appropriate circles. Sew in place with embroidery stitches (overcast) or by zigzag on machine.

5. Trace blown-up mom's and dad's faces onto appropriate circles.

6. Embroider faces and around lower edge of circle in black yarn or with zigzag stitch.

To Make Balls:

1. Place circle template in center of 2 white squares and trace on right side of fabric.

2. Trace enlarged circle stripes onto tracing paper. Trim. Pin on folded black fabric and cut 2 each of circle stripes. Pin to circles.

3. Sew in place by embroidery (overcast) or zigzag machine stitches.

4. Complete outline of circle with embroidery or zigzag.

To Make Checkerboards:

1. Cut 4 squares using 5-inch template from black fabric.

2. Pin 2 each on the sewing line of white squares (as shown in diagram of quilt), leaving 1-inch seam allowance.

3. Embroider or zigzag into place.

To Make Bull's-eye:

1. Tracing blown-up pattern, cut 2 large outer circles and 2 smaller inner circles from black fabric.

2. Pin and sew into place.

To Make Diagonal Stripes:

1. Trace blown-up pattern pieces. Trim and place on black fabric with center stripe placed on fold as directed on pattern piece.

2. Cut 2 center-stripe pieces.

3. Cut 4 outer-stripe pieces.

4. Assemble using diagram of quilt provided. Pin and sew into place.

To Make Star, Teddy Bear, Flower, Diamond:

1. Trace blown-up patterns. Trim and cut 2 of each design from black fabric.

2. Assemble using diagram of quilt provided. Pin and sew into place.

3. You may embroider a 1-inch white circle in the center of the flower.

To Assemble Squares and Stuffing:

1. Following diagram of quilt layout or your own layout design, lay out squares right side down on large flat surface.

2. Pin and stitch one square to the next, right sides together, using the 10-inch square seam line as guide.

3. Stitch quilt stuffing to wrong side of finished squares around outer edge of comforter.

4. Tack stuffing to quilt at various corners, if desired.

To Make Ruffle:

1. Sew 3-inch strips together to make a continuous strip 10 yards long.

2. Sew ends together.

3. Narrow hem one edge.

4. Gather unhemmed edge strip either by hand or with sewing machine ruffle attachment.

To Assemble Quilt:

1. Pin and baste ruffled edge of ruffle to outer seam line along perimeter of *right* side of quilt. (Hint: hemmed edge should face middle of the quilt, not edge.)

2. Pin right side of red-and-white checked fabric to right side of assembled quilt.

3. Stitch together, leaving last 6 inches open. Turn finished quilt right side out and hand stitch remaining 6 inches.

4. Tack quilt together where corners of squares converge with 4-ply knitting yarn or quilt by hand using quilting thread to sew quilting stitches throughout.

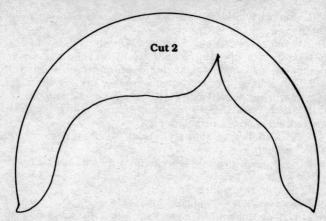

Cut 2

Father's hair

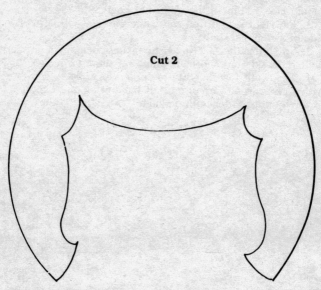

Cut 2

Mother's hair

Mother's face. Trace onto cloth in circle outline.

Mustache is optional.

Father's face. Trace onto cloth in circle outline.

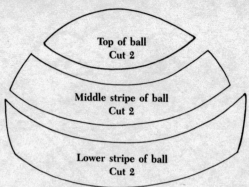

Top of ball
Cut 2

Middle stripe of ball
Cut 2

Lower stripe of ball
Cut 2

Ball shape

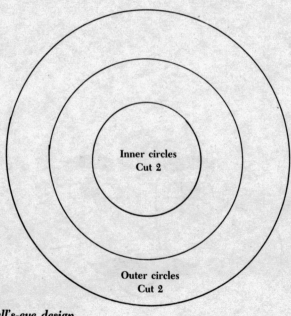

Inner circles
Cut 2

Outer circles
Cut 2

Bull's-eye design

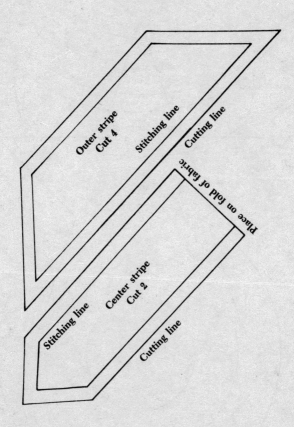

Outer stripe
Cut 4

Stitching line

Cutting line

Place on fold of fabric

Center stripe
Cut 2

Stitching line

Cutting line

Diagonal stripes

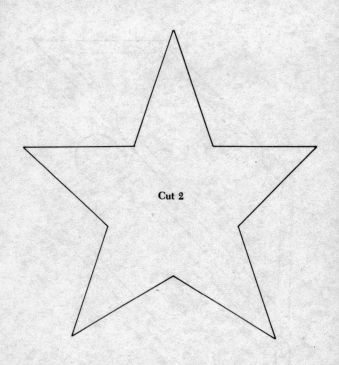

Cut 2

Star shape

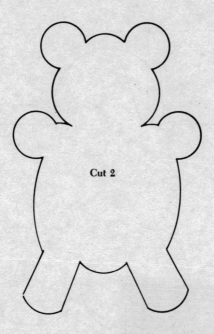

Cut 2

Bear shape

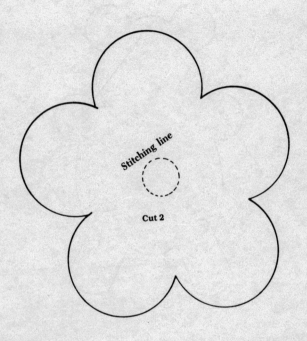

Flower shape

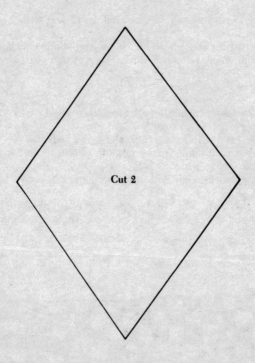

Cut 2

Diamond shape

Bright Baby™ Bed Bumper
(Developed by Dorothy Ludington)

FINISHED SIZE: Approximately 12 feet 8 inches by 8 inches

MATERIALS:

- Vinyl crib bumper (approximately 12 feet 8 inches by 8 inches)
- 2½ yards, 45-inch width, black-and-white checkerboard or gingham fabric in design appropriate to baby's age (See Book II)
- Thread for sewing

1. Cut fabric in half lengthwise down center fold.
2. Lay right sides together.
3. Pin and stitch together along one narrow raw edge, creating a continuous piece of cloth about 13 feet long and about 22 inches wide.
4. Lay fabric, right side up, on floor. Place crib bumper over it.
5. Fold fabric over crib bumper. Pin edges of fabric together, creating a sleeve for vinyl bumper. (Right sides should be in.)

Baby is fascinated by his "crib checks."

6. Slip bumper out and stitch along pinned edge.
7. Trim and turn right side out.
8. Finish open edges.
9. Slip over vinyl bumper every other day.

Crib Checks and Dots

FINISHED SIZE: Approximately 70 inches by 45 inches
MATERIALS:
- 1 yard of 45-inch width black-and-white gingham, checkerboard, or polka-dot cotton or cotton and polyester blend sheeting fabric (the size of design should correspond to your baby's capabilities. See Book II)
- 1 yard of 45-inch width white cotton and polyester blend sheeting fabric
- Thread for sewing

1. Pin the two lengths of fabric together, right sides in.
2. Seam along raw edges of one side, creating a sheet approximately 2 yards long.
3. Turn and hem remaining raw edges of fabric.
4. Use as sheet on baby's crib every other day. (Make sure to lay baby on sheet so that he can turn away from design to white side when he needs a rest.)

Expressly Yours™ Poster
(Developed by Melissa Saleh)

MATERIALS:
- 2 feet by 2 feet plywood or particle board
- 1 square yard red felt
- White glue
- 10 cake-size paper plates
- 10 inches Velcro
- Black marker

1. Glue red felt to board, being such to cover rough edges and corners.
2. Glue 1 inch Velcro to back of each paper plate.
3. Draw expressions of: laugh, frown, boredom, cry, yawn, surprise, smile, sadness, sleep, eating.
4. Stick, expression on board and mimic with your own exaggerated sounds, facial gestures, and words.

Eye Cube™

FINISHED SIZE: Cube, approximately 10 × 10 × 10 inches
MATERIALS:

- 1 square black fabric 6 × 6 inches
- 3 squares white fabric 6 × 6 inches
- 1 square black-and-white plaid or checkerboard fabric 6 × 6 inches
- 1 square polka-dot fabric (dots at least 1 inch in diameter) 6 × 6 inches
- Polyester fiberfill
- Non-toxic black marker (indelible)
- Thread for sewing
- Jingle bell encased in 35 millimeter film can

1. Draw simple, happy face on 1 white square.
2. Draw simple bull's-eye at least 3 inches in diameter on 1 white square.
3. Turn all squares inside out. Pin and stitch together seams, creating cube. Make sure to leave one seam partially open.
4. Turn cube right side out. Stuff half full with fiberfill.
5. Bury bell in middle of cube.
6. Finish stuffing and hand finish open seam.

Mind Mittens™

MATERIALS:
- 2 white oven-mitt potholders
- 2 inches Velcro and 12 inches fastening tape
- 2 circles of white fabric, 4 inches in diameter
- 2 squares of white fabric, 4 × 4 inches
- 4 squares of fabrics of differing textures (Wide-wale corduroy, velveteen, plush, burlap, etc.)
- Enough interfacing to back all fabric swatches
- Indelible non-toxic black marker
- Thread for sewing

1. Cut interfacing to fit each fabric swatch.
2. Sew 1 inch fastening tape to center of each piece of interfacing.

3. Using zigzag or overcast stitch, sew interfacing to fabric swatches, making sure that fastening tape faces out.

4. Sew 1 inch of Velcro to middle of finger section of each oven mitt.

5. On 1 circle, draw simple bull's-eye with 3 to 5 concentric black-and-white circles.

6. On 1 circle, draw simple face with hair, smiling mouth, nose, eyes, eyelashes and eyebrows.

7. On 1 white square, draw a 9-inch checkerboard, each check approximately 1¼ inches.

8. On 1 white square, draw an isosceles triangle with base of 4 inches and height of 4 inches. (Equal sides will be approximately 4½ inches.)

Mrs. Eyeset™
(Developed by Jean Calhoun)

If you are not an experienced crocheter, we suggest that you ask your local yarn shop to assist you in working with these instructions.

Baby is fascinated by Mrs. Eyeset™

MATERIALS:
- Crochet hook size G, H or I
- 1 white and 1 black skein 4-ply yarn
- Polyester fiberfill

To Make Nose: With black ch 2, 1 sc in 2nd ch from hook, ch 1, turn.

Row 2: 2 sc in sc on prev row (inc made) ch 1, turn.

Row 3: Inc in first sc, sc in next sc, ch 1, turn.

Row 4: Work around entire piece, inc in 1st sc, sc in next sc, inc in next sc. Turn piece to work down side, sc in side of piece, 2 sc in unused loop of beg ch, sc in next side of piece, join with sl st in beg sc. (9sc)

To Make Face: Change to white (change colors by pulling loop of white thru loop on hook). Tie off black.

Rnd 5: 2 sc in each sc around (18).

Rnd 6: 1 sc in next sc, 2 sc in next sc. Repeat around (27).

Rnd 7: 1 sc in next 2 sc, 2 sc in next sc. Repeat around (36).

Rnd 8: 1 sc in next 3 sc, 2 sc in next sc. Repeat around (45).

Rnd 9: 1 sc in next 4 sc, 2 sc in next sc. Repeat around (54).

Continue for 12 more rounds, increasing 1 sc each row.

Rnd 21: 1 sc in next 16 sc, 2 sc in next sc. Repeat around (162).

Tie off.

To Make Eyes: Make 2

With black ch 2, work 6 sc in 2nd ch from hook.

Rnd 2: 2 sc in each sc (12).

Rnd 3: 1 sc in next sc, 2 sc in next sc. Repeat around (18).
Tie off.

With white ch 2, work sc in 2nd st from hook.

Rnd 2: 2 sc in each sc (12).

Tie off. Make 2.

To Assemble:

1. Sew white small circles onto black larger circles to make eyes. (You may make black stitch within small white circles to indicate pupils of eyes.)

2. Sew black circles onto large white circle, using center black spot as nose.

3. With double strand of black, chain stitch mouth (2 rows wide) on white circle.

4. Make another face, reversing black and white.

5. Sew 2 faces together and stuff with polyester fiberfill.

6. Stitch several 8-inch-long strange of yarn securely to top of head for "hair."

Pillow Pals™

FINISHED SIZE: Approximately 12 inches by 12 inches

MATERIALS:

- 2 squares black felt 15 × 15 inches (1 for pillow, 1 for design)
- 2 squares white felt 15 × 15 inches (1 for pillow, 1 for design)
- Fiberfill for stuffing
- Thread for sewing

1. Use 1 square of black felt and 1 square of white felt to create your own design. For example:

- Cut white felt into 2-inch strips and stitch to black 15- × 15-inch square at 2-inch intervals, creating stripes. (Make sure to leave a 1-inch seam allowance at top and bottom.)
- Cut black felt into concentric circles, making a bull's-eye. (Center circle can be 2 to 3 inches in diameter.) Stitch onto white 15- × 15-inch square. (Make sure to leave 1-inch seam allowance. Outer circle should be no more than 12 inches in diameter.)
- Cut white felt into diagonal strips and stitch onto black 15- × 15-inch square, creating diagonal stripes.
- Create a checkerboard design, with 2- or 3-inch squares.

2. After you have appliqued design to large squares, turn squares right side in and stitch around edges, leaving one seam partially open.

3. Turn right side out and stuff with fiberfill. Finish sewing by hand.

Tactile Tillie™

FINISHED SIZE: Approximately 3 feet long

MATERIALS:

- 9 10- × 6-inch swatches of differing fabrics and textures (velvet, flannel, satin, terry, plush, cotton calico, burlap, velveteen, wide wale corduroy) some black and white, some in bright colors
- A large white sweatsock
- 8- × 6-inch swatch red cotton and polyester fabric for mouth

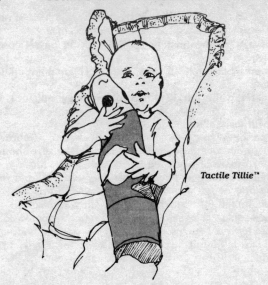

Tactile Tillie™

- Jingle bell encased in 35 millimeter film canister
- Polyester fiberfill
- Thread for sewing
- Black non-toxic indelible ink

To Make Head:
   1. Cut off heel and cuff of sock, leaving as much of toe and foot as possible.
   2. Slit reinforced portion of toe to make opening for Tillie's mouth and lips.
   3. Turn sock inside out and pin and stitch red fabric around edges of opening, creating a red mouth. Trim excess fabric.

To Make Body:
   1. Wrong sides together, pin swatches across 10-inch edges. (Hint: When laying pieces out, use black-and-white fabrics closest to Tillie's head.)
   2. Stitch swatches of fabric across 10-inch edges, creating a continuous multicolored length approximately 36 by 10 inches.
   3. Create a long tube by folding fabric in half lengthwise, right sides together, and stitching down length of toy.

4. Pin head (still inside out) to black-and-white end of tube and stitch together, easing gathers where necessary.

5. Turn Tillie right side out and stuff half the length loosely with fiberfill (the more you use, the harder the toy will be).

6. Bury bell encased in film canister in one of middle segments.

7. Stuff fiberfill carefully around bell to ensure softness for baby.

8. Finish stuffing and stitch tail closed by hand.

9. Draw large black circular eyes, eyelashes, eyebrows, and a suggestion of a nose on Tillie's face. Make sure she has a happy expression.

Do not use buttons or objects that may come off and find their way into baby's mouth when constructing this toy.

Taffeta Rattle
(Developed by Ellyn Cavanaugh-Duerr)

MATERIALS:
- 4-inch square of black-and-white plaid taffeta fabric (usually available around Christmas time)
- 12 inches brightly-colored yarn cut in half
- 2 jingle bells

1. Gather fabric at both ends and tie with yarn.

2. Thread yarn through bell tops and tie *very securely*.

3. Do not use after baby reaches 3 months of age.

Do not leave baby alone with this toy or allow him to put bells into his mouth.

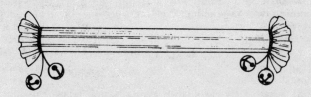

The feather-weight Taffeta Rattle

INDEX

Congratulations— But...

What about all those questions and problems that arrive with a new addition to the family? Here are several invaluable books for any new or expectant mother. They are filled with helpful hints for raising healthy children in a happy home. Best of luck and may all your problems be little ones!

BANTAM
SHOP·AT·HOME
C·A·T·A·L·O·G

Special Offer
Buy a Bantam Book
for only 50¢.

Now you can have Bantam's catalog filled with hundreds of titles plus take advantage of our unique and exciting bonus book offer. A special offer which gives you the opportunity to purchase a Bantam book for only 50¢. Here's how!

By ordering any five books at the regular price per order, you can also choose any other single book listed (up to a $5.95 value) for just 50¢. Some restrictions do apply, but for further details why not send for Bantam's catalog of titles today!

Just send us your name and address and we will send you a catalog!

By the year 2000, 2 out of 3 Americans could be illiterate.

It's true.

Today, 75 million adults... about one American in three, can't read adequately. And by the year 2000, U.S. News & World Report envisions an America with a literacy rate of only 30%.

Before that America comes to be, you can stop it... by joining the fight against illiteracy today.

Call the Coalition for Literacy at toll-free **1-800-228-8813** and volunteer.

Volunteer Against Illiteracy. The only degree you need is a degree of caring.

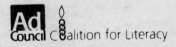

Ad Council Coalition for Literacy

LWA